TRAPS

THE DRUM WONDER

TRAPS

The Life of
Buddy Rich

THE DRUM WONDER

Mel Tormé

New York   Oxford   • OXFORD UNIVERSITY PRESS

Oxford University Press

Oxford   New York   Toronto
Delhi   Bombay   Calcutta   Madras   Karachi
Kuala Lumpur   Singapore   Hong Kong   Toyko
Nairobi   Dar es Salaam   Cape Town
Melbourne   Auckland

and associated companies in
Berlin   Ibadan

Library of Congress Cataloging-in-Publication Data
Tormé, Mel.
Traps, the drum wonder : the life of Buddy Rich / Mel Tormé.
p.   cm.   Includes index.
ISBN 0-19-507038-0
ISBN 0-19-507915-9 (PBK.)
1. Rich, Buddy, 1917–   . 2. Drummers (Musicians)
—United States—Biography. I. Title.
ML419.R52T7 1991
786.9'165'092— dc20
[B]   90–22594

10 9 8 7 6 5 4 3 2 1

Printed in the United States of America

for the entire Rich family

◙ *April 2, 1987*

MY FRIEND DIED today.

I want to put this down before I forget.

I was in my car on the way to see him when I heard the news. I pulled over to the curb and cried like a baby for ten minutes or so. Then I got hold of myself and sped to the house where he had been staying. I did my best to comfort his wife. His daughter arrived, numb, in shock.

The house had that strange, hushed feeling a house gets when one of its inhabitants has passed away. The phone rang incessantly. My friend had lots of friends. He was world famous.

It had happened so quickly, so unexpectedly. Yesterday we had sat, my friend and I, for more than two and a half hours while he reminisced about his early life. He had spoken with humor, self-deprecation, and pride. He was alert, articulate, stimulated, enjoying the recounting of a career that began in 1919, when he was a mere eighteen months old. Occasionally he grimaced in pain, and the male nurse in attendance had to lift him from behind to a more comfortable position.

Frequently he wept, dabbing at his wet cheek with a tissue held in his right hand, the hand that wasn't paralyzed. He dozed twice, awakened, and continued to talk, almost eagerly, about his life. Maybe he sensed the urgency, the need to get the facts down, to set the record straight as quickly as possible. Perhaps he had some sixth sense, some presage of what would happen today.

Weeks before he had seemed healthy and vigorous. Now he had to be waited on hand and foot, and it was tearing him apart. Suddenly he looked tired and deflated. I knew it was time for me to go. Tomorrow was another day.

"Tomorrow" was today, and he had run out of time.

◻ *Preface*

In 1975 BUDDY Rich talked to me about writing his biography. We had been close friends since 1944. Occasionally we had suffered disagreements that strained the relationship, and that was all right. Those intermittent estrangements served to strengthen our friendship, and toward the end of his life we were closer than we had ever been.

While this book has been written from a personal perspective, I have tried to keep my presence in it from being obtrusive or obstructive. Buddy asked me to write his story because he felt I knew him as well as or perhaps even a little better than anyone outside his family.

If that is true, then my chronicling of the anecdotes, the vital statistics, the successes and failures, the trauma and travail that went to make up the life of this extraordinary man may be of greater value than a biography written by someone who did not know him and might, therefore, approach such an undertaking through research alone.

No pun intended, Buddy's life was rich with adventures in the music business as well as in his personal relationships. No one who ever played the drums, with the possible exception of Gene Krupa, achieved the popularity, respect, and adulation that Rich enjoyed. Rightfully so. Like a few other "originals," he stood out in *bas relief* as a genius-grade musician.

Cantankerous, abrasive, witty, charming, charismatic, sentimental, and loving, he was the stuff that authors' dreams are made of. Truly, one of a kind.

I hope this book does him justice.

Beverly Hills, California   M.T.
1990

☐ *Acknowledgments*

AS IN ALL books of this kind, there are many people to thank. My friend writer/ producer Rudy Behlmer has once again given of his time and expertise in the editing/annotating phase of this effort as well as having made some vital suggestions earlier.

Stacey Endres of the Academy of Motion Picture Arts and Sciences provided several key photographs of Buddy Rich and the films in which he appeared. She also unearthed numerous reviews about Rich from the voluminous files of the Academy library which were useful along the way.

Jack Maher, president, John Maher, publisher, of *Down Beat* magazine kindly gave me permission to quote freely from pieces and reviews about Buddy that appeared in his publication from 1938 until Buddy's death in 1987. Mr. Maher also allowed me to use some key photos of Buddy, without which this book would have been the poorer.

Needless to say, the participation of the entire Rich family makes this a genuinely personal remembrance of the great drummer. I cannot sufficiently thank Marie Rich, Cathy Rich, Buddy's sisters, Jo Rich Corday and Marjorie Rich Ritchie, and the late Mickey Rich, Buddy's younger brother.

I am grateful for the reminiscences of Artie Shaw, the late Georgie Auld, Jo Stafford, Paul Weston, Les Brown, Jack and Kim Jones, Ed Shaughnessy, Freddy Gruber, Louie Bellson, Johnny Carson, Frank Sinatra, Jim Chapin, Steve Marcus, Mousey Alexander, Jerry Lewis, Alvin Stoller, Roy Burns, Bob Bowlby, Ross Konikoff, Andy Gravish, and John Bunch.

The Official Buddy Rich Fan Club was extremely helpful, with special thanks to Charles Braun, John Titsworth, and Dr. Steve Piazzale. A bow to *Drum Tracks* for permission to use material from their Buddy Rich memorial edition.

ACKNOWLEDGMENTS

Sincere appreciation to Sheldon Meyer, senior vice president of Oxford University Press for his enthusiastic support and to non pareil copy editor India Cooper.

There is no discography at the end of this book. That would be redundant in light of the fine one supplied in Doug Meriwether's excellent volume about Buddy: *We Don't Play Requests*.

And a deep bow to the distinguished writer and critic Whitney Balliett for his insightful and interesting *New Yorker* profile of Rich, which later became a book entitled *Super Drummer*.

And then there is a nearly endless list of friends and well-wishers who have helped me in more ways than I can count: Harry Anderson of *Night Court*, P. J. Montrone, Leonard Tessler, my friend and manager Dale Sheets, my wife, Ali Severson Tormé, and all the Buddy Rich fans, family, followers, and friends who have stayed in almost constant touch with me, anxious to read this biography of the greatest drummer of all time.

🔲 *Contents*

I *Straight Ahead* 1

II *Sidebars* 183

Buddy and Drummers 185

Buddy and Drums 188

Buddy and Drumming 193

Buddy on Film 196

Buddy's Passions 202

Buddy's Pranks 204

Cathy Rich: I Remember Dad 208

I Remember Buddy 212

Buddy's Mouth 215

Buddy's Beliefs 218

Index 221

I Straight Ahead

◙   *Chapter* *1*

"One pocket—mine"
Robert Rich

WILSON AND RICH were doing all right. The blackface comedy-song-and-dance team was getting steady work, appearing in some of the better vaudeville houses around the country. Their position on the bill was usually the number two spot, but that was okay. Not every act could headline, and seventy-five dollars a week was respectable money early in the twentieth century.

Robert Rich had been a performer since he was fifteen. A handsome, genial young man, hailing originally from Albany, New York, he had found employment in the early 1900s with Dockstader's Minstrels, but he felt buried in that large organization and soon left Dockstader to join a smaller minstrel show. His membership in that group was also short-lived. He yearned to strike out on his own, to make an indelible impression on the audiences of America.

Still in his late teens, he partnered with Sam Wilson, who, like himself, had held down one of the important "end man" positions with the Dockstader show. Sam Wilson was the straight man and looked the part. Wilson sang acceptably well, but the real strength of the act was Rich, whose comedy timing was impeccable and whose tap-dancing abilities were hailed by audiences and critics alike.

In those early days, some of their dates were downright dangerous. While appearing in San Francisco, they were offered a week's work at a theater in Los Angeles, reachable by nothing less than a stagecoach ride. Bandits had been robbing this stage with monotonous regularity. Consequently Sam Wilson and Robert Rich were required to sit alongside the driver of the conveyance, each armed with a double-barreled shotgun and a Colt revolver. Happily, the trip was uneventful. They weren't at all sorry to head east to fulfill some dates where civilization flourished.

Both young men were good-looking, and there was no shortage of female companionship out on the road or in the Big Town. One evening in 1906, during a party at his cousin's house in Brooklyn, Robert met Bess Skolnik. She was a pretty young thing who took to the worldly vaudevillian immediately. Later in the evening, she was asked to sing. She had an attractive voice, an attribute Robert mentally filed away. They decided that night to begin keeping company.

There was a stumbling block. Bess's father was a very strict man who disapproved of Robert Rich. "What are you doing with an actor? A bum?" Bess's father did not reckon with one unalterable fact: Bess and Robert adored each other. Robert promptly married her and plunked her into Wilson and Rich's stage presentation.

Robert continued to work in blackface. He played a messenger boy. He would come out to deliver a package to Bess, and they would do give-and-take repartee. Then he would leave the stage, and Bess would sing two choruses of "Roses of Picardy." Robert and Sam would return to the stage sans blackface make up and all together they would finish their turn.

When Robert and Bess met, he was nineteen; she was eighteen. She joined the act in 1908 and worked until she found she was pregnant. This was a somewhat unexpected wrinkle in Robert's life. A new mouth to feed, and, frankly, the act wasn't doing that well or making much money.

Abruptly he quit vaudeville and went back to Albany to work in his brother's grocery business. On May 24, 1910, Bess gave birth to a pretty little thing they named Marjorie.

A year passed.

Robert was bored to tears. Albany and the grocery business had palled. After the life he had led on the road, rewarded by the applause of the crowds and the respect of his peers in vaudeville, living and working in a staid city like Albany was tantamount to being buried alive. The Riches packed bag, baggage, and baby and moved back to Brooklyn to live with Bess's parents. Her father was still unimpressed with Robert. However, he had married Bess. They finally declared a truce.

Robert went into Manhattan and made the rounds of the agents' offices. Shortly thereafter, he, Sam Wilson, and Bess were back in business, doing the same act that had sustained them, however meager the income, in the past.

All went reasonably well, and in December of 1913 Bess discovered she was once again with child. This time Robert firmly swore that the addition of another baby would not put him out of show business. He was actually jubilant about the upcoming event.

"It'll be a boy. I know it. A boy. We had a girl. Now it's time for a boy. As soon as he can walk, I'll put him in the act!"

Robert even picked his future son's name. Joe.

On July 30, 1914, Robert was on the road while Bess was having their second child. As Robert was coming off the stage, he was told there was a long-distance call for him. He grinned. Bess had given birth! He shot a glance into his dressing room. He had bought a kid's football, a tiny toy locomotive, and a little iron auto for his new son. He ran to the phone and heard an uncle of his on the other end say: "Well, you got your wish. You got a 'Joe.'" Robert yelled "Hooray," and Sam Wilson clapped him on the back in congratulation. "Gee, that's great!" he said into the old-style black mouthpiece.

"Wait a minute. Not so fast. You did get your 'Joe.' But you'll have to spell it 'J-O.'"

"What? What are you . . ."

"It's a girl, Bob. A beautiful little girl. A sister for Marjorie." Robert gulped.

Bess's mother was in the hospital room, holding Baby Jo, who was cooing contentedly. The registrar came in, wanting to know the baby's name in order to enter it on the hospital records as well as the birth certificate. At that moment Baby Jo did what all newborns do into a diaper. Grandma looked at the registrar in dismay. In her thick Yiddish accent, she announced: "Oy! Vet!"

The hospital official grunted "Mmm-hmmm" and wrote something on her clipboard.

A few days later, Bess was handed the birth certificate. She looked at it and frowned. Baby's name: Yvette. Yvette? What's going on? She summoned the registrar. What is with this Yvette business? The registrar shrugged. "That's what your mother told me when I came in here the other day. Yvette. That's what she said the baby's name was."

When Bess quizzed her mother, the mystery was solved.

"No, no, no, no," protested Grandma Skolnik. "I felt the baby's diaper, and I said 'Oy! Vet!' The diaper was vet and . . ."

"Yvette" (crossed out) still appears on Jo's original birth certificate.

Robert had wanted a son, and Jo, as she grew, became an active little tomboy. When she was two years old, in the great tradition of vaudeville performers, Robert put her into the act. What better way to keep the family together, all earning money that went, as Robert put it, into "one pocket—mine!"

Jo Rich Corday recalls her participation in the act of Wilson and Rich. "I danced. I sang. I did a recitation. It was called 'Mother.' Believe it or not, I still remember the first few lines:

No one but a mother knows
What this word really means

It plays the part of sacrifice
In life's fast-changing scenes

The hand that rocks the cradle
Rules this world in toil and strife . . .

She laughs and says: "That's all I can remember."

Marjorie had been sent to stay with Robert's family in Albany while Jo traveled with the act. Then, quite suddenly, Robert decided to pack it in once again and go back to Albany. This time he worked for a chemical firm called the Wander Company as a shipping clerk. The job was pure drudgery, but it was January 1917, and Bess was pregnant again. She and the kids needed the stability of a solid home life, staying in one place instead of traipsing all over the United States.

The decision was Robert's alone. He had once more tired of the constant rat race called show business and was determined to try being a "civilian" again. And so he and Bess and Marjorie and Jo lived the quiet life. Bess's belly grew with child. On September 30, 1917, she gave birth to the third of the Rich children. They named him Bernard. No middle name. Marge and Jo laugh when you ask them why none of the Rich kids had middle names. "We were too busy. We didn't have time for middle names!"

Robert Rich finally had a son.

Chapter 2

> *"Cut it out, for God's sake!"*
> Robert Rich to his son

RIGHT AWAY BESS and Robert knew they had a hyperactive baby on their hands. He crawled early, talked early, then stood on wobbly legs and walked early. He was a good-looking baby, favoring his mother's side of the family in facial features. And he was strong. He would grip his daddy's forefinger, and Robert would look up at Bess in surprise and wonderment. He would beam proudly and exclaim: "My God, this little squirt of ours is another Samson!"

As Bernard grew, so did his precocity. He ruled the roost, demanding constant attention from his parents as well as his sisters. He refused to be left with anyone. He would wail, stamp his feet, fall on the floor, and pound his clenched fists on the carpet until he got his way. "His way" meant being dragged everywhere by Robert and Bess. The kid was a handful.

In February 1918 Bess got a telegram that stunned her. Robert had not yet returned home from his day's work at the Wander Company. Bess knew how much this wire would upset him. She warned the girls not to tell him about it until after he had eaten his dinner.

A weary Robert finished his evening meal. Bess placed the Western Union envelope in front of him. He removed the message and read it. His eyes misted over. Sam Wilson had suddenly, unexpectedly, died. He had been in his early thirties, robust and full of life. A heart attack? A fatal disease? What did it matter? His best friend and partner for so many years was dead. Robert looked around at the little dining room of the small house.

"The hell with this!" he suddenly cried, throwing his napkin on the table. "I've had enough of Albany and the Wander Chemical Company. What do you say? Let's go back to Brooklyn and start all over again."

"You mean—go back into vaudeville?" Bess inquired.

"Yes. Right. Vaudeville."

"But—but Sam's . . . gone. How will we . . ."

"We'll start a new act. The two of us. With a new name. You'll see. It'll work."

It was the first time in months that Bess had seen her husband so animated, so interested in something. She suspected it was reaction to his old partner's passing. He seemed to be saying—Let's keep it going. The act. In Sam's memory. Let's not let it die.

Sam Wilson had indeed been Robert's closest friend. Sam's wife also shared in that friendship. She was dear to both Robert and Bess, although it was an unspoken fact that she had been in love with Robert for years. (She died in the early 1960s.)

Once more the family moved back to Brooklyn. And yet again Robert knocked on agents' doors, excitedly expounding about the "new" act. In fact, there was no new act, just the germ of an idea in the back of Robert's fertile mind. There was a new name, though. Henceforth, Bess and Robert would be billed as "Rich and Renard." Where the "Renard" came from is anyone's guess. It was alliterative. Sort of. And it was a fresh heading for the theater marquees.

In those days, it was the practice to change the name of an act almost as often as one changed one's underwear. Usually it was a double-edged ploy: a new name (or names) for the theater patrons to conjure with as well as the opportunity for theatrical agents to rebook itinerent performers in their old, established stomping grounds camouflaged in new songs, jokes, and costumes.

Little Jo, four years old by now, was part of the plan. A hardy and talented youngster, she added a piquant flavor to her parents' presentation. Unfortunately, Jo contracted polio, became dangerously ill, and had to be hospitalized for seven months before recovering. During her illness, she had completely lost her power of speech and had to be taught how to speak again. The process was painstaking but finally successful.

Rich and Renard, of necessity, became a "two" act. At one point, Robert considered conscripting Marjorie into the family "business." It was merely a passing thought, never given any serious consideration. Marjorie was— Marjorie. The first-born. Petite, slender, feminine. A delightful little girl with no apparent talent for performing. Little did they know that she, too, had the strain of talent that ran through the Rich veins and genes.

Marjorie Rich—mainly known as Marge—found her way to Broadway by the time she was fifteen and, completely on her own initiative, became a chorus dancer in *Gay Paree* along with Barbara Stanwyck and Winnie Lightner. Jack Benny was also a cast member. When the show closed on Broadway, Marge went on the road with it for eight months then returned to New York in a show called *Temptations* at the Winter Garden. She danced in *Hit the Deck* and "doubled" at clubs such as the old Everglades.

By 1933 twenty-three-year-old Marjorie Rich saw that opportunities on the Broadway scene had diminished, so she switched to vaudeville. She got a job in a new act called "Blondes and Brunettes" that consisted of a troupe of shapely girl dancers, a comic called Shavo Sherman, and a young boy dancer, Carl Ritchie. Six months later, Marge and Carl Ritchie were married and doing their own dance act in theaters and night clubs all over the country.

"But," Marge remembers with a grin, "I was never part of my parents' act. Never part of Rich and Renard."

In 1918, when Rich and Renard first trod the boards in vaude houses, the family was once again separated. Back went eight-year-old Marge to the relatives in Albany: Jo remained in the hospital, fighting for her health, watched over by Bess's family. And their son?

He went on the road with his parents. The very mention of leaving him behind sent him into paroxysms of howling and stamping. Bess and Robert looked at each other and shrugged. He *was* the baby of the family, after all. Not even a year old yet. "He needs us," Bess rationalized. "We better take him along."

In each town in which they appeared, they set up light housekeeping, even though the engagement sometimes ran a mere "split" week (three or four days). They carried a portable high chair for their baby boy. He drove both of them slightly crazy when he sat in that chair. He would pick up knives, spoons, forks, anything he could get his little hands on, and beat on the high-chair tray. Once or twice, when Robert took his fingers out of his ears, he thought he heard the semblance of a genuine rhythmic pattern emerging from those seemingly random, childish hammerings.

No, he would finally shake his head. I'm hearing things. He would shout at his kid, "Cut it out, for God's sake!"

The tot, oblivious, would continue his high-chair concert.

The beat(ing) went on.

And then, in the spring of 1919, something extraordinary happened. Something that would change the lives of the entire Rich clan forever.

Chapter 3

"Lordy! That little fella is just wonderful!"
Theater owner, Fort Wayne,
Spring 1919

RICH AND RENARD, with their eighteen-month-old offspring in tow, traveled west to Fort Wayne, Indiana, for a week at the Bijou. As was the custom, they arrived at the Bijou on the morning of opening day, passed their music out to the orchestra, and prepared to rehearse. Robert Rich set his son down on the stage near the pit drummer. As Robert and Bess began to go through their paces, a sudden commotion came from the general direction of the drummer. Robert's low boiling point bubbled up quickly. He waved to the leader to stop the music and was prepared to tear strips off the offending percussionist.

The drummer told Robert to hold his water, begin the music again, and keep an eye on his kid. As the orchestra began to play again, the baby began tapping the stage, with a pair of drumsticks the drummer had given him, in perfect rhythm. Each time the tempo changed, the tiny hands adjusted to the new pace without missing a beat. The musicians were astonished. So was the theater manager.

"Hey, Rich," he cried. "Your kid is really something! Why don't you put him in the act?"

Robert's first reaction was resistance. His baby son was . . . well, a baby. Would it be right and proper to . . .

The band shouted encouragement. The theater manager shrewdly suggested: "Look, why not try it for the first show? The theater owner always watches a new act. He'll love it."

Robert reluctantly agreed. He borrowed a snare drum and a bass drum and worked out a little piece of business with the band. Little Bernard Rich, whose family always called him "Pal," was about to make his show business debut.

That afternoon, Rich and Renard went onstage and did their usual turn. Toward the end of their "spot," Robert Rich stepped to the wings, stage left, and reached offstage. As he turned and walked back to center stage, the audience saw a snare drum in his right hand and, hanging by the seat of his pants from Robert's left hand, baby Pal Rich.

Robert set him down and turned him loose on the drum. Pal paralyzed the Indiana audience. When the band finished the number and the toddler laid down the drumsticks, there was bedlam in the theater. The audience rose in a body and cheered, whistled, stamped, applauded. Robert Rich was stunned. What was happening here? Certainly, little Pal *had* banged on pots and pans around the house. Sure, he had shown a . . . well, talent for having a sense of rhythm. But this? This!! People shouting, demanding more from his—his *baby!*

The manager and theater owner came back to the dressing room.

"Lordy," said the theater owner, in his broad Indiana drawl. "That little fella is just wonderful! I have kids of my own, and I can't wait for them to see your little tyke . . ."

"Whoa, whoa, hold it!" Robert interrupted. "My kid's not a regular part of . . ."

"Uh, Robert," the theater manager interjected quickly. "I . . . uh . . . I think it would be a good idea if he went on for the evening performance as well. Sure gives your act a real boost. And," he added pointedly, "there'll be a little something extra for you and the missus."

Robert was still unconvinced. Vaudeville audiences thrived on novelty. The unexpected appearance on stage of Pal had created quite a stir, admittedly. One performance, one audience. A fluke? Go know. However, his objections were once again overcome by the manager. That evening the "baby" did it again. The response was positively explosive.

Now "Pop" Rich took a hard look at what had happened. He and Bess were working, earning a living, to be sure. But the fact that they were constantly playing the smaller towns, the "lesser" theater circuits, had always rankled. They were due for bigger and better things. Damn it, they had paid their dues. They *deserved* a break. Maybe—just maybe—their baby son would provide that necessary element, that unpredictable push that would shift their act into high gear and the "big time."

The next day the manager once again prevailed upon Robert to "put the kid into the act." This time Robert cannily agreed, reminding the man that "something extra" had been promised at the end of the week's run. Word had spread around the relatively small city of Fort Wayne about this incredible tot at the Bijou, and the house for the final four days of the engagement was packed. The little drummer simply wowed the citizens, and Pop Rich envisioned an unlimited future for his act, thanks to the addition of this amazing boy of his.

And at the end of the engagement, there *was* "something extra" in Rich and Renard's pay envelope—twenty-five dollars. Robert was mildly bitter about that, but, philosophically, he knew it was nothing compared with what the future might bring.

Bess was put slightly off-balance by what happened that week. Of course, she *shepped nachas*—took great pride—in seeing her little boy literally worshiped by the Indiana audiences. Indiana was Indiana, nonetheless. Provincial. Hicksville. Was Robert serious about building a whole new act around their baby, who still fell down when he tried walking? Would he impress big-town audiences—New York, Chicago, Philadelphia, where they'd seen everything? Would they go crazy over Pal or shrug collectively and say: Just another novelty vaudevile act with a kid in it?

"Hey," Robert informed her. "First we gotta get booked in those towns. Then we'll worry about how the kid does with the audiences."

"Yes, but don't you think . . ."

"Bess, I think we've got some kind of little genius on our hands. I don't know how or why he got this way."

"Well, it's in his blood, isn't it? Look who his father is."

Robert grinned. "You could be right. All I know is the Fort Wayne date was great. I think we should capitalize on Pal's talent."

When Rich and Renard showed up at the next theater on the circuit, the theater manager had already heard about the sensational week in Fort Wayne and immediately insisted Pal be part of the act. Once again Robert was promised that he would be "well taken care of" financially. Robert, who had been known to make the same mistake twice, trusted the manager to be as good as his word. Little Pal was once again a smash hit, and Robert once again was treated to a paltry twenty-five dollars in the pay envelope. He chose to take the long view: with Pal in the act, the possibilities were exciting.

Robert rushed back to New York and confronted his booking agent. He spared no adjectives in describing how successful the act had been with the inclusion of his little boy's drumming. He then instructed his agent to ask for more money. Much more money.

"How much do you want?" asked the agent.

"Er . . . I don't know."

"Well, if you don't know, how the hell am I supposed to know?"

Robert stormed out of the man's office, leaving the agent wondering whether he was still booking the act or not. He had never seen little Pal in action. He had taken Robert's word that the kid was great. And the news had filtered into the Big Town about how well the moppet had gone over with the Hoosier audiences. So okay. So he would ask for more money. But how much more? The volatile Robert Rich hadn't given him a clue.

Robert did not call him; he did not call Robert. After fuming and fussing and stewing for more than six weeks without a single offer, Pop Rich grudgingly called his agent. A booking was arranged. The fee: the usual plus twenty-five dollars extra for "the kid."

Robert Rich was in a frustrating situation. It was as though he had suddenly acquired an uncut diamond potentially worth a fortune, yet he did not know how to cut that diamond properly so that its enormous value could be realized. He forced himself to be patient. There had to be a way. It would come; it would come. First and foremost, a good piece of special material had to be written so that Pal would fit more naturally into the act. Robert began to haunt the music publishers' offices in Tin Pan Alley, looking for the right tunesmith to come up with something clever.

In those days, the likes of George Gershwin, Irving Berlin, Jerome Kern, and dozens of other hopeful young songwriters could be found in the Alley, writing new songs and occasionally "special material" for stars like Al Jolson and Helen Morgan. Unfortunately, the Rich pocketbook had been depleted by the long layoff, and Robert had to find cheaper music labor than theirs.

He finally settled on a piano player he thought (hoped! prayed!) could come up with what the act needed. The song (?), when it was finally finished, was not that original, and the piano player posed no real threat to Kern or Gershwin. But the little ditty served its purpose well enough, corny though it sounds today.

On the very next date Robert and Bess unveiled their new specialty song.

MOM & POP:	Whose baby are you, PAL?
POP & MOM:	Whose baby are you?
MOM:	Whose lovey dovey?
POP:	Whose bunch of love?
MOM:	Who buys you gum, dear?
POP:	Who bought you these drums right here?
MOM:	Who eats Mother's cooking?
POP:	Who gets all the bookings?
BOTH:	Who will never be content
BOTH:	'Til you become the President?
POP:	Who's Daddy's boy?
MOM:	Whose pride and joy?
BOTH:	Whose baby are you?
PAL:	(with Jolsonesque gestures) I'M EVERYBODY'S BABY! DUMDADADUMDUM . . . DUM . . . DUM!

The audience thought the song strictly ho-hum. It didn't matter. Pal proceeded to play the drums (a borrowed bass drum, a snare drum, and a cymbal). He tore the house down.

Had the audience paid closer attention to that special song, they would have realized it was structured as a competitive piece, with Mom and Pop vying for the affections of Pal. In the not-too-distant future, life would begin to imitate art.

◫ *Chapter* 4

> *"If you break my drums, I'll sock you in the eye."*
> "Traps" to newspaperman, 1921

ROBERT NOW SET about in earnest to "dress up" the act. He contacted the Ludwig Drum Company in Chicago and ordered a good snare drum, a cymbal and cymbal holder, and a bass drum that stood higher than his son. "It'll make the kid look even tinier. Good showmanship," he confided to Bess. Next he bought an arrangement of the famous Sousa march "Stars and Stripes Forever." "Patriotic," Pop intoned. "Military. Pal'll knock 'em dead with this one." Most important, he came up with a new name for the newest member of his act. "From here on in," Robert commanded, "Pal will be known as 'Traps.'"

The word "traps," as applied to drummers, seems to be a contraction of "trappings." Indeed, the large assortment of cymbals, cowbells, wood block, temple blocks, gongs, tom-toms, triangles, whistles, and the like that were the standard equipment of percussionists in those days certainly qualified as "trappings." "Traps, the Drum Wonder" became part of the huge roster of vaudeville performers of the time.

Traps's hair was given a Buster Brown cut, a hairstyle that the Beatles would affect decades later. He wore a natty white sailor suit and patent leather shoes. Bookings began to come in. The word was out. Rich and Renard had a brand new wrinkle in their act, their baby son who played the drums as well as (some said better than) most adult, seasoned drummers. Pop Rich was elated. "Our time has come," he cried. "It's finally our turn."

His timing couldn't have been better. America was entering the Jazz Age. The Great War had been over for almost two years. A wild and wacky decade was about to commence, filled with colorful sports and entertainment figures, gangsters, crooked politicians, silent-movie stars, band leaders, and a public intent on—no, *obsessed* with—having fun. The flapper and the Charleston became symbols of the day. Bathtub gin flowed freely in private homes and speakeasies. Gang wars erupted. The wicked snouts of Thompson submachine guns, "the gun that made the twenties roar," were poked out of the windows of Lincoln Phaetons, barking at rival bootleggers.

Ex–World War I aviators were buying up surplus Jennies and flying them under bridges. Wing walkers were a common commodity, as were flagpole sitters, high-wire daredevils, and "slide-for-life" crazies who slid down a thin wire from a high place to the street by their teeth, by their legs, and in one case, by the hair.

Child performers were very much a part of the Roaring Twenties, and "Traps, the Drum Wonder" was soon to become the highest-paid child performer in the world, topped only by Chaplin's protégé, Jackie Coogan, a few years later.

Josephine and Marjorie were still with the grandparents while Mom, Pop, and Traps toured the country. They were well cared for but lonesome for the three Rich nomads zig-zagging all over the map, reaping fresh plaudits thanks to the Wonder Child. The reviews were awesome; a scrapbook was growing thick with glowing notices. An early paragraph of praise went:

> Everyone fell in love with Traps and marveled at his ability. He surely is a prodigy and what he cannot do with a pair of drumsticks is not worth doing.

Yet another critic (obviously in love with his own special brand of prose) wrote:

> Another perishable product is in town. Little Traps, the baby drummer, is thumping at Keith's. It is another case of "Coogan," for the youngster shoots skyward apace. . . . It won't be long until he will be a spindling smarty and not a cute kid who could keep house in his own bass drum. Just another growing boy, sneaking out behind the garage, to try his first Camel.

By 1921 "Traps, the Drum Wonder" had become a seasoned vaudeville veteran, having played extensive dates on the RKO-Keith circuit, the midwestern Balaban and Katz houses, and the seemingly endless string of independent variety theaters that dotted the country. Those houses—the Palaces, the Strands, the Bijoux and the Colonials and the Princesses, in towns like Erie, Pennsylvania, Baltimore, Maryland, and Wilmington, Delaware—were where Traps honed his craft, although each successive press rave seemed to indicate he had been born with his craft already honed. Whether he came by his extraordinary talent genetically or environmentally, or whether it was simply mysteriously God-given, was moot by that time. He was an instant star, easily overshadowing his fellow performers, as the reviews unanimously testified.

> Traps, the tiny drummer of the fourth act, runs away from the other acts on the bill. . . . He was well worth the price of admission alone.
>
> *Baltimore News*

> The boy drummer, Traps, received more individual applause and more curtain calls than any other performer on the stage last evening. . . . at Keith's, Wilmington, Del.
>
> From unidentified news clipping

Reportedly, the youngster did not endear himself to his adult coworkers. In one very early interview he made a remark that was, perhaps, a presage of things to come:

> "If you break my drums, I'll sock you in the eye," remarked Traps, three, the world's youngest drummer. It is rumored that Traps is temperamental.

This was probably true. Adulation was pouring over him like barrels of sticky maple syrup. The famous drum company Ludwig and Ludwig dedicated a full page to him in a contemporary catalog, an unheard-of honor in those days before Gene Krupa revolutionized the drummer's image and became a household name. He was a handsome little guy. Women wanted to cuddle him; grown and accomplished musicians regarded him with awe and respect. He had become the darling of his family (not to mention the biggest breadwinner), and each day seemed to bring new offers, better money, greater triumphs.

Robert Rich, always mindful of the fickleness of the theater owners, the bookers, and the public, now informed his agents, Fox and Considine, that he was changing the name of the act. Henceforth it would be called "Rogers, Bennett and Traps." How he pulled those names out of the blue (or a hat) is a complete mystery.

At the same time, Robert placed ads in various show business periodicals: "Rogers, Bennett and Traps: Always working. There's a reason." The reason, of course, was Traps. The youngster was "news." Any stunt Pop dreamed up was dutifully reported by the press. During a date at the Palace in Bridgeport, Connecticut, the house bandleader bet Traps could not break his drumhead. He won that bet. The boy's playing was so "correct" that despite his best efforts he could not break the head. The papers reported, nonetheless, that "his drumming was so distinct from the orchestra in a rendition of the Sousa march, that the youngster scored sensationally."

At the Tivoli (probably on Chicago's South Side), the kid appeared on the stage with Jack Dempsey, whose oft-broken nose had just been reset for the umpteenth time. Little Traps, clowning around, tagged the champ with a random Sunday punch. Every newspaper in the country reported the accident, and the Manassa Mauler had to have his nose attended to once again.

If Traps was basking in his newfound fame, his father was beset by problems because of his son's high visibility. In those days, there was legal provision for the appearance in vaudeville of child singers, dancers, and actors. Conversely, there was a law, strictly enforced by the Geary Society, an organization protecting children in the entertainment business, against child musicians appearing in stage shows. Robert chose to ignore the law; the Geary Society began to make trouble for him.

CHILD ACTOR'S FATHER HELD

Robert Rich, an actor of 38 Ellory Street, Brooklyn, was arraigned in Harlem Court this week before Magistrate William A. Sweetzer and held on $100 bail for trial in Special Sessions on charges of permitting his three-year-old son, Bernard, to appear on the stage of a vaudeville theater.

Robert grudgingly paid the fine, only to have it happen again in a few short weeks:

Traps, the three-year-old son of Rogers and Bennett, and appearing with them in vaudeville when [*sic*] the boy, a drummer, was taken off the stage at Loew's Yorkville last week, and the parents summoned to court. Judge McQuade fined them $50. A child's stage permit is not issued in New York for the playing of musical instruments. The father said the boy was not happy unless drumming, and he wanted him to be happy, so he let him drum.

What Robert omitted to say was that *he*, along with the whole family, would not be happy if the star attraction of the act were denied the right to dazzle the crowds and contribute to "one pocket"—Robert's. This was perfectly natural and sensible. Many vaudeville acts were brightened by youngsters; in many instances, those youngsters were the chief draw. Not to capitalize on Traps's great talent would have been foolish and unrealistic.

Robert Rich was part dreamer and part realist, and realistically he began to see that the intelligent thing to do was concentrate on his little son's solo future—especially when a 1921 review in the show business Bible, *Variety*, exclaimed:

> All there is to the act of Rogers, Bennett and Traps came right at the end of it. That was Traps, and that was enough. A nice looking boy in his neat sailor suit, this turn can go anywhere with him, but it's still wrong to have the kid in a three-act. A boy of four who can drum in this manner should be heavily featured as a single. This boy Traps is the best novelty vaudeville could purchase, secure or buy for he can't be duplicated except by pure accident. Rhythm in a boy this young can't be taught. It's a gift.

Of course, Robert had his pride. He had been a blackface performer since the early part of the century. Audiences had responded to his comedy timing and dancing with enthusiasm for years. Still, while he enjoyed working, his young son's genius was inescapable. He was determined to think big, to move out of the vaudeville houses and into the mainstream with his child prodigy. Broadway was what he had in mind. A major break.

Happily, he found that break in the form of Raymond Hitchcock's *Pin Wheel Revel*.

Chapter 5

"Traps, a crafty Hebrew infant . . ."
"Traps, a six year old girl prodigy . . ."
Australian press, 1924

RAYMOND HITCHCOCK WAS one of the most successful producers on Broadway in 1922. His forte was musical revues, and Pop Rich heard about a forthcoming production of Hitchcock's to be known as the *Pin Wheel Revel*. Auditions were being held in the spring, and Robert, through his various show business contacts, arranged to have his four-year-old do his stuff for the producer. Hitchcock was bowled over. Instantly he determined to present the diminutive drummer boy in his show. Traps was signed on the spot.

To no one's surprise, the youngster won the evening on opening night. Unfortunately, the rest of the show did not come up to the standard of previous Hitchcock productions, and *Pin Wheel* was short-lived. Traps, at any rate, had made his mark on Broadway. Almost immediately another Broadway revue paged him, and Robert signed on for the *Wunderkind*. *Greenwich Village Follies* was the name of this one.

A huge toy shop set was constructed. A special set of drums was ordered from the Ludwig company, with an even bigger bass drum than Traps had been working with in vaudeville. The drums were placed in an oversized dollhouse in the toy shop set. The shelves in the shop were occupied by dancers in soldier uniforms and dolly dresses.

After the dancers did a chorus-line number, the dollhouse was wheeled to center stage. The door opened, and facing the audience was the huge bass drum. Slowly it revolved on its pedestal to reveal Traps, the Drum Wonder, wearing a white sailor suit and bashing away like mad on a snare drum, cymbal, and bass drum while the band played "Stars and Stripes Forever" and the "dolls" and "toy soldiers" danced around the toy shop. The audience cheered, and the reviews were breathtaking.

> The climax of the first half is made by a tiny little actor who looks as if he were about three years old. As the orchestra thunders out the finale, he chews gum with enthusiasm, beats a tatoo with perfect art but utter weariness, and from time to time he gives the cymbal a vicious swipe with his drumstick, revealing a malicious enthusiasm beneath his air of contempt and *sang froid.*
>
> *World Telegram,*
> September 13, 1922

> The best applause getter of the evening was the finale of the first act in which the Village Toy Shop is brought to a conclusion with a talented little boy manipulating the trap drum and effects with remarkable skill. The little chap plunged into his task in the most unconcerned manner and alternately grinned and chewed gum while he tapped the drums and crashed symbals [*sic*] with the ability of a veteran jazz drummer. The number was good for several encores.
>
> *Variety,*
> September 1922

Traps was a smash on Broadway. On many Sundays he also doubled at the Winter Garden, where he was cast in a supporting role to the likes of Al Jolson and Will Rogers. While the ill-fated *Pin Wheel Revel* folded after only four days, *Greenwich Village Follies* ran seven months, and Traps was firmly entrenched as a major attraction on the Great White Way.

During the *Follies* run an important agent saw the kid drummer perform and began making plans to book him on an extensive tour of Australia. The proposed tour would have to wait its turn, however. When *Follies* closed, Pop Rich and his son went right out and played many of the same vaudeville theaters in which they had appeared several times before. This time out, thanks to Traps's newly achieved popularity, the act was placed next-to-closing, traditionally the star spot in the vaudeville world.

Bess Rich did not accompany her husband and son on that tour. The act now qualified as a "single," although Robert did appear briefly at the beginning of the turn to set up his offspring's solo spot, the now inevitable "Stars and Stripes Forever."

But Bess did not go along for yet another reason: she was expecting her fourth child, a boy born November 24, 1923. They named him Martin. Again the Riches were blessed with a genuinely beautiful baby son, who would grow into a handsome young man nicknamed Mickey. When Bess was fully recuperated, she and Robert decided she would once again go into the act. They would revive the mock tug-of-war "Whose baby are you, Pal?" but now "Pal" would be "Traps."

The Australian tour had taken shape. The plan was to sail from San Francisco in April of 1925, breaking the long sea journey with stops in Honolulu and Pago Pago. They would perform for a few evenings in each port of call and then proceed to Sydney to begin their Aussie tour at the famed Tivoli Theater in that city. Dragging fourteen-year-old Marjorie and eleven-year-old Jo halfway round the world was unthinkable; the girls would stay with the two sets of grandparents. Seven-month-old Martin was too tiny and in need of his mother to leave behind. He would accompany Mom, Pop, and Traps on the trip.

Bess had a new wardrobe made for the tour Down Under. On the way to Australia she became quite ill and went into the hospital once they landed. She never again rejoined the act. Upon her return to the States, she had her spanking new dresses cut down to fit her daughters and from that time on remained a firmly retired vaudevillian.

Happily for Robert, the Australian authorities were not nearly as devoted to child labor laws as his nemeses in America had been. When Traps had appeared in the *Follies,* Robert had to have the boy's permit renewed every Saturday so that he would be "legal" the following Monday. In point of fact, he was never "legal." The Geary Society hounded his hapless father, who saw the inside of jails several times. If Robert was not "jugged" it was usually because he had found a way to grease some palms. Brother Mickey recalls that, while his older brother was making significant money in those days, much of it was spent in bribes so that the little musician could keep working.

Spreading the wealth was not, however, a problem in Australia. Relatively free of such hassles, Robert Rich and his son blossomed. The moment the sailor-suited little boy put drumsticks to drumheads, he electrified the impressionable Aussie audiences. Not surprisingly, the reviews were excellent (if occasionally strange). One writer, madly keen on being clever, wrote:

> There is Traps, a crafty Hebrew infant, who thrashes drums, bangs cymbals and converses in rich American. . . . An expression of gloating pleasure shines in the child's face as he prepares to bring down his instruments [drumsticks?] upon the towering flanks of the big drum itself. How many other small boys are encouraged to turn the place into a blast furnace?

And, incomprehensibly, another review ran

GIRL JAZZ PRODIGY APPEARS

> Traps, a six-year-old girl prodigy with an American reputation, provides the star turn with jazz selections on various instruments.

Whatever show *that* critic saw (or obviously did *not* see), it certainly wasn't the Tivoli presentation, since Master Rich was nothing if not a rugged little boy and played only one instrument.

While the Australian tour was long and successful, there were other bookings awaiting the act in the States. On the way back, they played Hawaii and Pago Pago once again, but Robert and Bess were restless, homesick, and missing the girls. They literally raced off the boat in San Francisco and took the first available train eastward to be reunited with Jo and Marge, as well as their many friends in Brooklyn.

Traps had been feted, feasted, fretted over, fussed about. Did he love every glorious minute of it? Was he having any fun?

Chapter 6

"He never had a childhood."
Marge Rich Ritchie

"HE NEVER HAD a childhood," says sister Marge. "I mean, he *never* had a childhood." A small, slim, vital woman of eighty, still attractive and articulate, she recalls her brother's early years with a tinge of plaintiveness in her voice: "He didn't even know how to play with other children. He had a terrible inferiority complex about the fact that he never went to school. No education at all. He was always intimidated by educated people, even though he may not have shown it outwardly."

Sister Jo interjects: "This was a kid who never had an electric train set. How the hell could he? There was no way to schlep toy trains on the road. And where was he supposed to play with them? Backstage, in a tiny dressing room?" Jo, whose daughter Barbara produced the long-running series "Cagney and Lacey" and who herself was seen repeatedly on that show as The Bag Lady, is a hearty seventy-six with a ready smile and a great sense of humor. Not as petite as her older sister, she has a perpetual twinkle in her eye and a charismatic personality.

Drums. That's all my brother knew when he was a kid. Drums. One of the few toys he ever had was a pair of skates. One day he fell down and broke his arm. Pop was furious, since it meant the act would be out of action while Buddy healed. Buddy got terribly antsy, so Pop tried an experiment. He tied drumsticks to my brother's feet! It kept him from going nuts! And, frankly, it kept Pop from punishing him. Temporarily.

The day the cast came off Brother's arm, he fell down the front stairs and broke it again. Pop could have killed him, he was so angry. Weeks later, right after the arm healed, Mickey got scarlet fever and gave it to Buddy, and once again our main breadwinner was out of action.

We called that house the bad-luck house.

We moved to another house directly behind it, at 1777 East Twenty-seventh. With all those sevens, Pop figured it would be a *good*-luck house. And he was right.

A touchy situation had developed in the Rich household, and because of it Robert Rich became a martinet where his breadwinning son was concerned. Bess Rich, now out of the act, stayed at home in Brooklyn while her adored son and her husband went out on the road, sometimes for weeks at a time. She felt she was being left out of their lives, and that hurt and depressed her.

She began to resent little Traps. She believed that, if it hadn't been for him, she would still be doing a "double" with her husband. When Robert and Traps came home from a tour, her feelings surfaced.

She openly gave all her attention to Martin and let it be known that she had no room for affection for Traps. Whenever she could, she would air some complaint about his behavior and needle Robert with remarks like "That boy will be the death of me" and "Someday, he'll wind up in the electric chair!" Robert's already short temper would explode into a wild fit of anger, and the result would usually be a beating administered to his hapless son. It was Robert's way of assuaging his adored Bess's feeling of rejection. When the furor subsided, Bess would either threaten suicide or walk around the house moaning, a damp white washcloth tied around her head.

A catch-22. No one really to blame. The three of them caught in a whirlwind of frustration, anger, helplessness. Robert, an inveterate practical joker, a gregarious, likable man; Bess, pretty, gentle, caring, a good mother and wife; Pal, blessed with great talent and cursed with it at the same time. Robert's treatment of his son in those days was completely out of character. No one would have believed such behavior of him.

And yet he unquestionably abused his little son, and all three remaining Rich children believe that Robert's early harsh treatment of their brother molded and shaped him into the sometimes difficult man he became later in life.

If Robert vented his spleen by whipping his son, then Traps's outlet, more and more, was bashing his drums. Drumming was the boy's only refuge. His drumsticks became a surrogate "security blanket," and, to no one's amazement, his already monumental talent as a drummer burgeoned. The only other relief he enjoyed was an original curse he concocted. When he had enough abuse at his father's hands, and when the world seemed to close in on him from all sides, the little fellow would clench his tiny fists, raise his head, and bay at the top of his voice: "SISSYMARYFAIRYANNAQNILSSON!!!" Somehow, it seemed to help.

He hated the Buster Brown haircut. Robert insisted it was good for the act and made his son look younger than he really was. In those days, most performers lied about their age, and child performers were deemed more "phenomenal" if they appeared to be impossibly youthful. Many times Traps was advertised as being a year—and sometimes two years—younger than he actually was. The youngster would look in the mirror and pray for the day to come when he could shear away the detested bangs. For one thing, the kids on his block in Flatbush ragged him mercilessly about his "sissy" hair. On one occasion they gave him a good, sound beating, and he retired into his house, bloody-nosed. When Robert saw this, he administered his own beating, warning his son to "be a man and stand up to those punks!" These instructions were senseless to the boy, since his father had continually lectured him on the necessity of staying out of fights and guarding his precious hands against injury. But now, with his nose bleeding and his backside smarting from Robert's whipping, he turned in his tracks, went out into the street, and beat the hell out of the bully who had picked on him.

And then, for no apparent reason, things slid back to normal. With the remnants of Traps's earnings from the Australian tour, Robert bought the family a house (their first) in the Flatbush section of Brooklyn. A kind of normality settled over the family. Robert went into Manhattan every day to see about the bookings; Bess seemed relaxed and content now that her husband was spending more time at home. Marge, who had been sneaking out of the house trying to get a job in a Broadway show, hit pay dirt at age fifteen and landed in the chorus of *Gay Paree*. Sister Jo and brother Mickey were happy housekids, and Pal, believe it or not, was enrolled in the local grammar school—for about twenty seconds.

While on one hand he craved the company of his peers, the seasoned young performer and former Broadway star had a terrible time adjusting to the normalcy of everyday school life. He had grown up backstage, in an adult milieu. Grammar school seemed to him like life in slow motion as opposed to the fast-lane existence of a traveling vaudeville act.

When Robert got a booking for the act, he would have to go to the school and make extravagant excuses to get his son out of his classes so they could go out and earn their living. Pal was restless and unhappy in the classroom. The theater dates were like vacations for him. However, the novelty of the baby drummer had begun to wear a bit thin, and bookings were not as plentiful as they had once been. Bess and the kids were perversely happy over this turn of events. They were content to muddle through, to have the whole family together for longer periods of time.

Robert was worried. His son's career had begun like the proverbial house on fire. Suddenly the flames seemed to be cooling, and the elder Rich nervously contemplated the possibility that, brilliant though he was, little Traps might have been a flash in the pan and that the Rich family might find themselves out in the cold if the bookings did not improve.

◼ Chapter 7

God rest Traps!

BY 1929, IN spite of the fact that Robert and Traps were playing occasional dates on the Gus Sohn "time" as well as random "one-shots" for the midwestern Balaban and Katz circuit and a few Keith theaters, their string seemed to have run out. The Rich sisters admit that the end of the twenties was a lean time for the family. Yet, as sister Jo recalls:

> We never had more fun together than during that period of time. Pop was a compulsive practical joker and cut-up. If you were coming to dinner at our house, whether you were a friend or a total stranger, you had to be careful to show up after Pop had watered the lawn. Otherwise, the minute you came in sight, he would turn the hose on you and you'd get soaked.
>
> Or, if pie was the dessert, chances were Pop would casually pick up a piece from his plate and shove it into your face. That would start a chain reaction, and everybody at the table would take their turn at the pie-shoving contest.
>
> Everybody [Jo recalls affectionately] except Marge. She never got a pie in the face. She was always considered the ladylike member of the Rich family, whereas I was the tomboy, more like my brothers.

Jo also remembers her mother as being somewhat remote. "Mom didn't have much of a sense of humor. She never joined in the craziness. I really didn't know my mother very well. But," she added, "maybe that's because she and Marge were so much alike, and I took after Pop, Buddy, and Mickey."

In mid-1929 Traps, now a self-confident twelve-year-old, fought constantly with his father over the Buster Brown haircut. Reluctantly Robert finally gave his son permission to have his hair cut in a more contemporary fashion. He was thrilled. Free of those damned bangs at last. *And* the sailor suit.

Concurrent with this change in his appearance came an offer from Vitaphone to star in a one-reel short. With work in short supply, Robert jumped at it, thinking, quite properly, that the exposure would invigorate the booking situation. Sound films were the newest rage, Warner Brothers' *The Jazz Singer* having virtually revolutionized the motion picture business.

The short, filmed at the New York studio of Warner Brothers, was made late in 1929. Entitled "Buddy Traps in Sound Effects," it ran for seven minutes. It was the very first time the young drummer had been billed as "Buddy," although the "Traps" soubriquet was still retained. It opened at the Strand in New York on February 17, 1930, in support of a George Arliss film called *The Green Goddess*.

Variety reviewed Buddy's first cinematic effort like this:

BUDDY TRAPS

Sound effects
Boy drummer
7 mins.
Strand, New York
Vitaphone No. 949

Boy, hardly 14 [he was twelve], with a decided talent for drumming plus rhythmic feet. Scene is a music shop. Trying out a new pair of drumsticks, lad beats his tatto on vases, glass, cans and all sorts of wooden, metallic or noise-giving materials. Distinct advantage of being the only boy performer of and on [*sic*] novelty, okay for any average program.

Film Daily called him "Buddy Rich (as Buddy Traps), marvel drummer," and while this review is almost identical to the *Variety* review, it ends with the following: "It is diverting, particularly because it is unusual and also on account of the youth and versatility of the artist."

Not only does young "Buddy Traps" play his now standard version of "Stars and Stripes" as a finale in this little celluloid reel, he also dances up a storm and sings a tune called "Bashful Baby," complete with a "scat" chorus (and a damned good one). While the sound portion of this historic one-reeler still exists, the picture portion has not been found at this writing despite extensive research.

Unfortunately, the Vitaphone short did little to stimulate young Buddy's faltering vaudeville career. Then again, Black Tuesday had come and gone, and the nation, newly plunged into the abyss of the Great Depression, was tightening its belt and guarding its purse strings. The national mood was one of financial fear.

"Talkies," particularly optimistic little offerings like the Warner Brothers musicals, sporting unrealistically hopeful tunes such as "We're in the Money," were the country's shield against total despair. Vaudeville was by no means dead; yet many old troupers fell by the wayside, and the public, as always, looked to new faces for diversion.

"Traps, the Drum Wonder" was no longer a "kid" act. He was a handsome young fellow, true, and wonderfully versatile, as reviews of the day verify. But the novelty of the "kid" drummer, the "baby" marvel, had gone with the coming of adolescence.

Through Arthur Kraus, an agent and personal manager (who incidentally credited himself as the originator of the fox trot), Bernard played several vaudeville dates billed as Buddy Traps or Buddy "Traps" Rich. The reviews were, as always, glowing, but the uniqueness, the freshness, had faded. And there were now two other drum specialty acts making their way around the circuits that seemed to have taken a leaf from Traps's high jinks in the Vitaphone short.

Jack Powell was a slightly rotund fellow who came onto the stage dressed as a chef, complete with puffy white chef's hat. Pots and pans were his "traps," and he bustled all over the place with an oversized pair of drumsticks, hitting every single one of them again and again. (Traps had done this, of course, since infancy, and more recently in the 1929 Vitaphone one-reeler.) Powell at one point claimed that Traps had "stolen his stuff" and threatened a lawsuit, which was quickly withdrawn. Powell wound up his act playing on a toylike set of tiny drums in a presentation not far removed from Traps's famous "Stars and Stripes."

If Jack Powell was indeed the chicken, and Traps the egg, what was Charlie Masters? A tall, thin, mournful-looking individual, dressed in a carpenter/painter outfit, bib overalls and all, hauling a ladder on stage, a huge pair of clublike drumsticks in his back pocket, along with a red bandana, he proceeded to do an act almost exactly like Powell's, going up and down the ladder, tapping his sticks on the rungs, the sides, and the top in true rudimentary fashion, and ending up with the identical "toy" drum set that Powell was famous for using. Powell, the better drummer of the two (but not by much, and certainly not by any standard a "jazz" artist), was fortunate to have played the better vaude circuits; Masters played the secondaries.

Robert Rich, now acting as manager for his son, began looking around for a new idea, a fresh presentation. He found the solution during a visit to

Pittsburgh, where he ran across an organized band that had been stranded by its leader. The eleven-piece aggregation was comprised of good, solid musicians who suddenly found themselves marooned in the Pennsylvania city with nothing to do and nowhere to go.

Robert, never lost for words, convinced them that it would be a good idea to have his son Buddy front the band. He made several calls to New York and was able to interest Arthur Kraus in the project. Billed as Buddy "Traps" Rich and his Orchestra, the band played a string of break-in dates before heading for the Big Town. One review of their Broadway debut is worth quoting in its entirety:

> Since the advent of vaudeville on the Broadway stage, no feature act has received the marked applause that was given Buddy Rich and his band at last night's performance before a well-filled house. Youthful Mr. Rich and his group of musicians came to the Broadway stage with the praises of successful past performances ringing in their ears, and they lived up to their reputation to the letter.
>
> The band started up its program with a medley of popular dance tunes, but it was the ability of the leader that put the band across. In the closing minutes of the act, Buddy Rich handed his baton to another member of the cast, and proceeded to show his ability on the drums. In the short time that he handled the drumsticks, Mr. Rich did things with them that seemed almost impossible and still maintained a rhythm that sent the audience into prolonged applause.

Now, suddenly, Buddy was "fronting" an orchestra, waving a stick, counting off tempos, and generally taking charge. His drum specialty was viewed as a part, not the whole, of his appearance. The future for Buddy "Traps" Rich as a bandleader looked promising, at least on the surface. However, 1932 was a harrowing Depression year, and the golden era of music called the Swing Era was still a long three years in the future.

Buddy and the band went up and down the pike of vaudeville houses (usually once around), but inevitably the unique aspect of a youngster leading a group of grown musicmakers wore thin, and the band broke up. The experience had not been without dividends for young Buddy. He had tasted the wine of leadership and found it intoxicating. He had performed master-of-ceremonies chores with authority and humor, activities that would serve him well in the solo vaudeville dates he would play before abandoning that career and getting on with the business of being a jazz drummer.

He had become acutely aware of jazz. His playing since near-infancy had been primarily based on the pit drumming and military drumbeats he had heard. Yet his infectious singing and "scatting" in the Vitaphone short exhibited a real awareness of snycopation beyond what he had always displayed to the vaudeville-going public.

He began to listen to jazz artists in earnest now. And jazz drummers. Tony Briglia of the Casa Loma orchestra was one of his earliest heroes. Briglia was a master of the press roll, and Buddy, who had incorporated rolls in his performances all through his early years, marveled at Briglia's ability to press the sticks against the calfskin head of his snare drum so evenly that the "daddy-mammy" alternate contacts were indistinguishable from each other.

The tiny, sadly deformed whirlwind Chick Webb was becoming an enormous influence on aspiring drummers, and Buddy turned his incomparable musical ear in the direction of that worthy gentleman and soaked up what he had to say with his specially built Gretsch-Gladstone drums. Webb's free-wheeling approach to drumming was not lost on the up-and-coming young Gene Krupa, either. Krupa's early work with Mal Hallett's band and Benny Goodman reflects just how large a part Chick Webb played in the forming of his unique style.

The Benny Goodman "breakthrough" in 1935 was to have a profound effect not only on the public but on musicians of every sort. Buddy Rich was no exception. Jazz (or "swing," to be precise) became his obsession, although he wisely kept his newfound preoccupation a private affair. His father, as far as he concerned, was living in the past, still mentally entrenched in the business of vaudeville. To Robert, a band was just something that was necessary to accompany his son "Traps." But once the orchestra Buddy had fronted broke up, Robert was finding the pickings for the young drummer leaner and leaner.

Buddy found himself on excursion boats plowing up and down the Hudson, acting as master of ceremonies as well as novelty drummer. More and more he performed emcee duties in the increasingly sparse vaudeville dates Robert was able to secure. Buddy was restless. By 1936 "swing" was off and running. He wanted to climb aboard, shed the "Traps" image, and get on with becoming a jazz drummer. Having heard the records Krupa had made with Goodman, he knew instinctively that he possessed the talent to be a better drummer than Gene. Or Chick. Or anybody. He *knew* it. Period.

He had made friends with a neighbor, bassist Artie Shapiro, and together they would make their way around some of the little clubs springing up all over Brooklyn that catered to the kids who wanted to hear jazz. One of these, the Crystal Club, was particularly popular with the younger set, and Buddy cut his jazz teeth there, sitting in through the graciousness of house drummer Henry Adler.

Adler, a popular percussionist as well as a teacher and writer of drum books, couldn't believe his eyes or ears when Buddy Rich began to play. He had heard of this little kid "Traps," of course, but the young man borrowing his drums here at the Crystal Club was no novelty drummer. He was a driving, pulsing dynamo full or originality and fresh ideas. And he swung! No way around it. He swung!

That was for fun and for learning. There were still bills to pay, rent to meet, food to buy. Buddy played little clubs, the brim of his fedora turned up "wiseguy" style, singing, dancing, and delivering one-liners that "sucked" (his terminology), until he was covered in "flop sweat." Then they rolled out the drums and he finished to big applause, as usual. But life was tough now, depressing and at times, disgusting. He had been a genuine star act; now he was lucky to get work:

On April 1, 1987, Buddy remembered:

That was a hard part of life, once having been a star to a "who cares?" That was a tough transition for a kid to make. I had to go out . . . "Good evening, ladies and gentlemen, a funny thing happened to me. . . ." Bad fucking material! Bad material. On top of that, the brim [of my hat] pulled up, you know? Yuk, yuk, yuk! The embarrassment I was feeling . . . it lasted my whole life. To go out there in front [opening the show] was a very tough thing to do . . . for a kid that was once something and now . . . nothing. I was an opening act. "Hey, look at me! I got a new hat." You know?

I go to Chicago to be an opening act, introducing Jackie Osterman . . . MC, right? And your act is smart jokes and one-liners, and they all suck. There isn't a funny line in the eighteen minutes you're out there. You're dying—get me outta here . . . the audience is looking at you like—uh—get this bum off the stage . . . you're standing there doing bad material, trying to talk to people who don't want to hear you. . . .

I even degraded myself low enough one time to be a stooge. You know what a stooge is? [Buddy crying.] He's a guy who sits in the audience and has one-liners thrown at him. I stooged for a comic—you should know him 'cause he's from Chicago. Roy somebody. Funny guy. Tough guy. Played all the tough joints. He asked me if I wanted to be his stooge for a week in a club in Milwaukee. I was staying at the Croyden Hotel [in Chicago]. I said, "yeah." I was fifteen or sixteen. . . .

I was a stooge . . . not even human . . . you learn . . . [crying harder now] I'll tell you what you learn . . . [sobbing]. If you wanted to survive, you learned how to be humiliated in front of a lot of people . . . I did it . . . not very long . . . up to the point where I couldn't take it any more. I got ten bucks for the week. I took the gig because I needed the ten bucks!

In 1936 Buddy joined a touring government WPA (Works Progress Administration) show called *Oh, Say Can You Sing*. Once again he demonstrated his various talents: singing, dancing, doing comedy, playing drums. The finale of that musical shows Rich dressed in tails and white tie, a handsome twenty-year-old, "surviving."

Surviving was simply not enough for Buddy Rich. When he had had his fill of dying vaudeville theaters, dank little clubs, tatty hotels, sparsely attended performances, and humiliating experiences, he rebelled and finally informed Robert that he wanted to be a jazz drummer with a band—any band. Robert took the news badly. "He couldn't get over the fact that I was willing to [be] a . . . nobody in jazz," Buddy recalled in 1987.

For once, Buddy followed his own star. More and more he haunted the little Brooklyn jazz clubs, listening and usually sitting in. The Crystal Club became his hangout, and he was drawn to it like a moth to a flame. His natural sense of syncopation was overriding his early inclination toward military drumming. He thanked God that his father had been a tap dancer and had passed on that talent to him. The tap-dancing beats transmitted themselves into his hands—and feet—and he found himself becoming, through these near-nightly sessions at the Crystal Club, a genuine jazz player.

God rest Traps!
Long live Buddy Rich!

Chapter 8

"Did you ever think of playing with a band?"
Henry Adler to Buddy Rich, 1937

ROBERT WAS DISGUSTED. In his view, his son was throwing away everything they had built together. Sure, work was slow right now—nonexistent was more like it—and of course, Buddy, now twenty years of age, could no longer be looked upon as a "kid" novelty act. But vaudeville, *vaudeville,* was the backbone of show business. Vaudeville and Broadway. Buddy had been a star in both. And he would be again! Be patient. Give it a little time. The Depression would blow over and. . . .

Buddy turned a deaf ear to Robert. He was flatly determined to play drums with a swing band. His single-mindedness caused a short-lived rift between father and son. It couldn't be helped. Buddy Rich was about to realize his dream. On April 1, 1987, he talked to me about those earlier days.

Jazz, for some reason, affected me. Goodman's trio. Goodman's quartet. They were hot. When I stayed at the Croydon that time I mentioned before [early 1937], I met the Condos brothers, Nick and Steve, at the coffee shop there. We hung out. We used to play jazz records and dance to them. I learned a lot that way.

Then one time, my sister Marge was doing a dance act with her husband, Carl Ritchie, at Rocky Point, Rhode Island. There was a big band backing them that played all the Casa Loma arrangements. I used to faint. They played them pretty good. I used to stay near the bandstand and watch the drummer play. He had beautiful hi-hat cymbals, all shiny. We were friends. Anyway, he asked me to play . . . and I plaaaayed! "Casa Loma Stomp." I had the time of my life. I had always loved the Glen Gray [Casa Loma] band. They were so hot. And so hip!

They wore tails at night. My ambition was to meet that band. And particularly Tony Briglia.

HE NEVER PLAYED HI-HATS! Only press rolls on the snare drum. He was a bitch! I loved the way he played. Some of the tempos were so ridiculously fast; he had to be a speedball to play in the band. . . .

They played the Essex House in New York. Can you imagine? A staid hotel like the Essex House playing a big, loud band like that. They used to broadcast from there every night around eleven, eleven thirty. I'd be sitting downstairs in our house, with a pair of brushes in my hand, ready to play. Kick it off, Glen! [crying as he remembers] I played along with them. I was hot! I was hot! I played with the Glen Gray band. 'Cause I knew all the charts. All of them! "Go ahead. Kick it off! I got it! I want to play in your band!"

Actually, he had been playing almost every night at the Crystal Club, thanks to Henry Adler, who was becoming more astonished by the minute over the young man's technique and ideas. One evening, after Buddy had once again thrilled the customers at the Crystal Club, Adler took him aside and asked, "Did you ever think of playing with a band?" That, of course, was young Rich's current burning ambition, but now he played it casually and answered, "What's that mean?"

"I'll show you next Sunday," came Adler's reply.

On the following Sunday, Henry Adler and Artie Shapiro took Buddy in hand. It was time to cross the East River into the Apple. On that blustery October day in 1937, they made their way to Fifty-second Street, affectionately known as Swing Street. They passed the Onyx, the Famous Door, and the other now-famous little clubs and made their way into the Hickory House, a somewhat larger establishment, reknowned for Sunday afternoon jam sessions that starred the house band led by clarinetist Joe Marsala and featuring his wife, swing harpist Adele Girard.

The little group, cast in the Dixieland mold, was playing as the three Brooklynites entered, encouraged by a large audience of enthusiasts who were clapping, whistling, and snapping fingers in time to the beat being laid down by drummer Danny Alvin. Henry, Artie, and Buddy found a table and proceeded to enjoy Marsala's combo along with everyone else.

When the little band took a "ten," Adler got up and made his way to where Marsala was talking to other musicians who had come in to hear the band.

"Gotta talk to you, Joe," said Adler, who had known Marsala for some time.

Marsala, a fine clarinetist with a reputation for gentlemanliness, smiled at Henry and said, "Sure. What's up, Henry?"

"I brought along a kid you've gotta hear. His name is Buddy Rich."

"A kid?"

"Yeah. Well, not exactly a kid. He just turned twenty. He's a hell of a drummer. How about letting him sit in?"

Marsala knew Henry Adler to be an excellent musician, respected and honest.

"Kid's really good, eh?"

"Joe, he's better than good. He's goddam amazing! Wait till you hear him."

Joe thought about it for a minute. "Okay," he said finally. "He can play a tune with us during the final set, just before we break at six."

Adler smiled, thanked Marsala, and went back to tell Buddy, who took the news in stride. He knew he was ready. Sitting in with the likes of Marsala seemed to him a part of the natural course of things. He sat back, drank a Coke, and waited.

And waited.

At six o'clock, when the last notes faded and Marsala's musicians made their way off the stand, Adler, red-faced with embarrassment, confronted Joe Marsala, who was even more embarrassed.

"Oh, Jesus, Henry. I'm sorry as hell. Time just flew by. Forgot all about your friend. Listen, how about coming over again next Sunday? I'll get him up to play then, okay?"

If Buddy was disappointed, he kept it to himself. He had learned to take adversity in stride. Deep down, though, he was seething with hurt and his most recent bedfellow, humiliation. Adler and Shapiro had taken the time to bring him to the Hickory House. They respected his playing, and, because of his current lack of visibility and good fortune, respect was the most important element in his young life at that moment.

To be (in his mind) fluffed off by Joe Marsala was a very bitter pill to get down. When Adler informed him of Marsala's invitation to come back on the following Sunday, Buddy replied, with what he felt was righteous, injured pride, that Marsala could go screw himself. However, he knew that when Sunday rolled around, he would be right back at the Hickory House, chomping at the bit to sit in.

Once again he crossed the Brooklyn Bridge and headed for the jazz club. And once again he sat through several sets of music only to be denied the chance to play with Joe's group. This time he went back to Brooklyn in a cold fury. Goddam Marsala! How *dare* he brush him away like that, like he was some little nobody to push aside with no thought for his feelings? Fuck him! That did it! He would *never* go back to the Hickory House.

Artie and Henry worked on him all week. It had been another innocent error in judging the time. Joe had intended that Buddy would play the last tune of the last set, just before six o'clock. The next to last tune had run overtime, and the band *had* to stop playing. The slight had not been intentional or disrespectful. Marsala was an exceedingly nice guy, who genuinely felt terrible about what had happened again. Please, Buddy. Give it one more shot, okay?

Rich, with some effort, subordinated his ego and returned for a third Sunday. With misgivings. When he entered the Hickory House, Marsala smiled at him and waved a friendly hand from the bandstand. The afternoon wore on. Buddy looked at his watch. Five forty-five. No sign of being asked to play. Five fifty-five. The band was cooking, playing what was ostensibly their last tune of the afternoon.

Henry Adler got mad. He strode up to the bandstand at one minute to six, his face dark, his jaw set, and had words with Joe Marsala. Half of the band had already begun to make their way off the stand. Marsala called them back. It was after six, clearly a violation of union rules. Whatever Henry said to the bandleader, it was clear that he intended to play one more tune.

"Folks," he announced over the microphone to the crowd that had begun to disperse. "Gather back around. We're gonna do one more tune. We've invited a young man from Brooklyn to sit in with us on drums. We hear he's really something. His name is Buddy Rich."

Scattered applause.

Buddy, overtrained by now, virtually leapt onto the bandstand and bowed to Danny Alvin, who bowed in turn and handed the young drummer a pair of sticks.

"What do you want to play, kid?" asked Marsala.

Buddy, forcing himself to appear supercool and unconcerned, closed his eyes, raised his eyebrows, and made his mouth into a kind of who-cares grimace. "Suit yourself," he replied.

Marsala chose an "up" tune called "Jim Jam Stomp." Buddy was like a racehorse in the gate, waiting for the derby to begin. Joe counted off the rapid tempo, and Buddy Rich proceeded to stun both the Marsala band and the crowd. Danny Alvin used no hi-hat cymbals; consequently Rich played in a style that was half Dixieland, half swing drums. When he was called upon by Marsala to solo, he played thirty-two bars that brought a wall-shaking cheer from the audience, who were now eagerly gathered around the bar that encircled the bandstand.

When "Jim Jam Stomp" was finished, the Hickory House regulars not only stamped, clapped, cheered, and whistled loud and long, they refused to let the band leave the stand. Twenty minutes later, the Marsala group finally put their instruments away. The crowd was wrung out, their hands stinging from the prolonged applauding, their voices hoarse with cheering. This kid! This kid! Incredible!

There and then, Joe Marsala offered Buddy Rich a job. The story goes that Danny Alvin had planned to leave and that Joe was actually looking for a replacement. Buddy, not even a member of the musicians' union, said a grateful yes to the clarinetist, and this time he returned to the family home in Brooklyn with a skin-splitting grin on his face.

Bess and Marge, Jo and Mickey were happy for him.

Robert was not.

He groused and grumbled. Bad move. Wrong move. Dumb. He was Buddy Rich. "Traps." Throwing it all away to become a friggin' drummer in a band. Unbelievable.

◙ *Chapter* 9

> *"He can't read music. Not a note!"*
> George Auld to Bunny Berigan,
> 1938

EARLY THE NEXT morning, Buddy Rich made his way to the musicians' union in Manhattan. Having been a "novelty" act up to that time, he had never had to become a member of the union, but with the Marsala job in his pocket, membership in Local 802 was mandatory. He sat down in front of a couple of stone-faced older men who looked like they might be members of the Mafia and proceeded to play an impeccable roll. His audience didn't know a press roll from an onion roll, but he passed his "test" easily.

Now, suddenly, he had a place to go at night: the Hickory House. Over the next few months, he not only impressed the "regulars" in that house of jazz, he also played drums on an Andrews Sisters record that was to become a runaway best-seller, "Bei Mir Bist Du Schön." It was the first record on which he played drums. He did a recording session with the famed musician Adrian Rollini at the beginning of 1938, as well as a few sides with the Marsala group.

Trouble was brewing despite (or perhaps because of) the notoriety Rich was getting with Joe's band. The older, more seasoned musicians resented Buddy's seeming lack of respect for them (he wasn't terribly thrilled to be playing Dixieland music; he yearned for a berth with a swing combo or big band). His youthful arrogance plus his increasing popularity with the Hickory House crowds did little to endear him to the likes of Joe's brother, trumpeter Marty Marsala, or tenor saxophonist Babe Russin (who was fond of Buddy but finding his attitude hard to take).

Obviously, Buddy was getting a lot of attention, and he loved it, particularly after so long a drought in the press. He had forsaken his old drum company, Ludwig, and had sought a set of drums as an endorser for Slingerland. Ray Bauduc, the preeminent Dixieland drummer of the day with Bob Crosby's band, was the shining star in the William F. Ludwig firmament, and Buddy *was* more inclined toward the brand of drums that Gene Krupa played with Benny Goodman. Slingerland happily gave Buddy a white pearl outfit similar to the one Krupa played. It was the first complete set of drums he ever owned.

He was also enjoying newfound popularity with the ladies.

He admitted to me that when he first auditioned for Marsala, he was not "the sharpest, hippest looking guy in town." That soon changed. While he was never tall (he was fully grown by 1937), he was perfectly proportioned, with a muscular, rangy frame and the sort of dark, rough good looks that John Garfield later became famous for. He set about dressing himself in the fashion of the day. With his newfound freedom from Robert's overwhelming influence, he bought the kind of "threads" worn by the sharpest musicians in New York, becoming something of a clotheshorse. He had great appeal for the young girls who came to see him. They sensed his physical power through his dynamic playing, and there was something dangerous about him that struck strong chords in them.

He had always been opinionated. Now that he was playing in a famous combo at a popular Fifty-second Street location, he was not exactly reticent about his views. In a profile of the Marsala band (*Down Beat,* February 1938), he was described as the "youngest man in the band. All wrapped up in his work and glad he forsook a tap dancing career [?] for that of pounding sheepskin. Kinda likes Jimmy Dorsey's band for his kicks and thinks all sweet bands are unnecessary, especially those that ripple. Absolutely kills the cash customers."

Slingerland ran an ad on him in *Down Beat* that made him laugh a lot. They threw together a set of drums and plunked him behind them. The setup was silly and unplayable, but it showed off the Slingerland product to great advantage.

By mid-1938 Rich had had enough Dixieland and quit Marsala. He had gotten his feet wet in the jazz fountain; that's what was most important. He did a brief stint at CBS with conductor Leith Stevens on the "Saturday Night Swing Session" and then took his own small combo into the Piccadilly Hotel for a short run. But he was dissatisfied. He felt a bit like Popeye, with astonishing strength running through his body, waiting for the spinach to unleash it. In short, he ached to play with a big band after the more restrictive experiences with small groups.

The "spinach" came in the form of a formidable tenor saxophonist named Georgie Auld. Georgie had known Buddy since he had seen him play an isolated date in the Catskills years before. Georgie, born John Altwerger in Toronto, Canada, began playing alto sax at ten. "I ran away from home at an early age with forty-one dollars in my pocket." He headed straight for his aunt's house in Brooklyn. She took him in, and he began to gig around, even at that tender age.

He discarded the alto for a tenor sax after he heard Coleman Hawkins playing a tune called "Meditation" on a record. He worked with several small groups until one night in 1938, when a nondescript guy in wrinkled black pants and a dirty white shirt heard him at Kelly's Stables on Fifty-first Street and beckoned him with a crooked forefinger. Auld thought, who the hell is this jerk?

The "jerk" turned out to be Bunny Berigan, one of Georgie's musical heroes. He offered the tenor saxophonist a job with his new eleven-piece band. Georgie jumped at the chance.

In August of 1938 the Bunny Berigan band played Brighton Beach in Brooklyn. After the first set, Georgie came off the bandstand to find Buddy Rich waiting for him. They embraced affectionately, after which Buddy fervently remarked to Auld: "Jesus, Georgie, I'm in big trouble."

"What's the matter, Bood?" asked Georgie, using his favorite nickname for the drummer.

"I'm starving to death," came the reply. "I need a job."

Georgie, who had heard Buddy play many times in recent months at the Hickory House when Auld had played around the corner at Kelly's Stables with Roy Eldridge's little band, went to Bunny Berigan and recommended Buddy for the drum chair. George Wettling had been the Berigan drummer for a time, but as Auld tells it, "he had a beef with the piano player, Joe Lippman. We were driving along the highway. Lippman stopped the car, got out, and beat the shit out of Wettling, who had made an anti-Semitic remark. We left him there on the highway, in the middle of nowhere."

George had forgotten the name of Wettling's replacment, but apparently Berigan was unsatisfied with him.

"One thing, Bunny," Georgie informed the bandleader. "This kid, Buddy Rich, is the greatest drummer in the world. But."

"But? But what?"

"He can't read music. Not a note."

"For Christ's sake, Georgie. What good is he? We play five acts of vaudeville in a theater. What am I gonna do?"

"If he hears a thing once, you'll never find a drummer who'll play any better. Just let him get up on the stand. Play a few things with the band."

Bunny invited Buddy to sit in. After the first tune, as Buddy began to rise from the drums, Bunny held out his hand like a cop stopping traffic and said: "Don't move. Stay right where you are." As he had with Joe Marsala, Buddy got the job immediately.

Shortly after Buddy joined Berigan, the trumpet player had a falling out with Auld. They had been very close friends since Georgie had joined the band. Unaccountably, they had a knock-down-drag-out hassle at an RCA record session, during which Berigan's band was making an album in tribute to Bix Beiderbecke. Georgie Auld tells the story:

> Bunny wanted me to play alto and tenor on this album. I hadn't touched alto in a long time. I squeaked a couple of times. [Bunny] took his trumpet and threw it up against the wall, cursed me out, said, "Blackie [Bunny's nickname for Auld], you sonofabitch, you're doing the squeakin' so we can go overtime." It broke my heart. Those were the first out-of-the-way words we ever had.
>
> I go back to the Forrest Hotel [most musicians' favorite hostelry in New York City] and run into Billie Holiday and Tony Pastor. They say, "Artie [Shaw] has been looking for you all day. Where have you been?" They were working at the Lincoln Hotel. So I said: "I'll come by there tonight." I went by that evening, and Artie hired me.
>
> Next evening I went back to RCA to finish Bunny's album. I walked into the men's room to take a leak, and there's Bunny in there, taking one. He looked at me and said: "Jeez, Georgie, I was overtrained last night. I never should have done what I did. I hope you'll forgive me."
>
> "I forgive you, Bunny. I hope you'll forgive me."
>
> "Why? What'd you do?"
>
> "I joined Artie Shaw last night. I'm going with the band in two weeks."
>
> He says: "You make a move and I'll knock every one of your fuckin' teeth out." One minute later, he's hugging me and saying: "No matter who's in your chair with my band, if you're not happy with Shaw, that chair always belongs to you."

I loved that guy. When he died, I went to the funeral parlor before they had
gussied him up, took my comb out, and combed his mustache. He was like—
like my godfather.

Now Buddy's mentor with the Berigan band was gone, leaving the young
drummer to play in an atmosphere beset by the leader's drinking, extensive
personnel changes, and a morale problem brought about by the fact that Bunny
Berigan was a born sideman, not a forceful leader/role model like George
Auld's new employer, Artie Shaw.

A few months after Auld had joined Shaw, the handsome clarinetist, who
had catapulted to the forefront of big band leaders, told Auld that he really
wanted to "turn the band around," make it a real "swing" band.

"I need a swinging drummer," Artie told him.

Once again Georgie found himself in a position to help Buddy Rich. "Well, I
know this kid who works in Bunny's band. I can have him come up and blow
for you. I think he's the greatest drummer in the world."

"What's his name?" Artie inquired.

"Buddy Rich."

"Isn't he a Dixieland drummer?"

Georgie laughed. "If he's a Dixieland drummer, I'll play the next four
weeks for you free of charge. Look, he can't read, but he'll do more for you than
any ten drummers who can." Artie agreed to let Buddy play a set with the band,
which at that moment was working once again in the Blue Room of Maria
Kramer's Hotel Lincoln in Manhattan.

Robert Rich, by now resigned to the fact that his one-time child-star son was
going to pursue a career as a jazz drummer, brought Buddy's drums to the
Lincoln and set them up during an intermission. Says Georgie Auld: "Buddy
got up on the bandstand, played one tune, and the same goddamned thing
happened: he completely turned the band around. It was a whole different
sounding band. He played "My Heart Stood Still." He knocked me out so much
when he played behind my solo."

Interestingly, Artie Shaw's account of how Buddy joined his band differs
from George Auld's. When I asked him about Georgie Auld recommending
Buddy for the drum chair. Shaw smiled and shook his head:

Buddy came around, I mean, I had been told about him. Georgie wasn't the
only one; everyone knew about Buddy's playing. He, at that time, had not
developed the discipline that he later did. He got so excited that he rushed, a
normal thing for young people. Anyway, he said to me: "I'd like to join the
band. I hear you might be looking for a change." I was about to let Cliff Leeman
go. It wasn't happening. Too heavy. [Leeman left Shaw, immediately went with

the romping Charlie Barnet band, and came into his own as one of the Swing Era's loosest, swingingest drummers.]

And so Buddy came on [the band]. We were sort of kindred spirits. We both had that disrespect for authority. I was never harsh with him. Tommy [Dorsey] was later on, but I never was.

There is some discrepancy about *when,* as well as *how,* Buddy joined Shaw. Georgie remembers distinctly that Buddy joined the band immediately upon playing that first night for Artie. Artie recalls that, when Buddy told him he could not read music, Artie had him "sit around" the Blue Room of the Lincoln for two or three nights "memorizing" the library before actually taking his place on the Blue Room stand.

When did he join the band? It has been reported as December 25, 1938. Artie says no, it had to be after he (Artie) returned from a week-long holiday in Cuba, just after the first of the year 1939. Buddy told me that he played his first night with Shaw on December 29, 1938.

Does it matter, other than for the sake of historical accuracy, when or how Buddy joined Artie Shaw's orchestra? Not really. What was and is important is that he did, indeed, "turn the band around," giving the already exciting band a new dimension, a new drive, a new personality.

▣ Chapter 10

"Buddy Rich, still a loud drummer,
is undeniably a good drummer."
Down Beat, May, 1939

IF THERE WAS an optimum Swing Era year, it was probably 1939. The country was emerging from the crushing grip of the Great Depression. Everyone was breathlessly awaiting the arrival of David O. Selznick's epic *Gone With the Wind.* Movie screens were also displaying MGM's *The Wizard of Oz,* as well as *Goodbye, Mr. Chips, Wuthering Heights, Stanley and Livingstone, Dark Victory,* and *Mr. Smith Goes to Washington.*

The youth of America was shagging, trucking, pecking, and Lindy-hopping with a collective exuberance not witnessed since the Charleston took America by storm during the Roaring Twenties.

The reason for this sweet mass hysteria among the saddle-shoed, angora-sweatered brigade was "swing." Benny Goodman had really started something back in 1935. His band of youngbloods had set fire to the teen and college kids during many "Let's Dance" broadcasts emanating from a Los Angeles ballroom called the Palomar and paving the way for a slew of similar musical aggrega-tions, some of which were original and exciting, many of which were copying the originals and making a buck in the process.

It didn't matter. Young people wanted to dance, to "jitterbug"—a new word someone had coined to describe the wild, erratic gyrations of the thousands of young "rug cutters" turning out in record numbers in ballrooms all over the country. Big bands had come into their own and were having a field day.

Among black swing bands, originality and musical magnificence reigned. Prominent, of course, was the elegant Ellington and his men. Duke had been a great favorite for many years, but the Swing Era was breathing new life into his already famous orchestra.

William "Count" Basie roared in from Kansas City, aided and abetted by the likes of Lester Young, Buck Clayton, Harry Edison, Jo Jones, and Freddie Green, and was hailed as musical royalty by jazz enthusiasts and critics alike. Dapper, handsome Jimmie Lunceford fronted a greatly gifted group of musicians and arrangers who created a style of swing that was to be copied in years to come by Tommy Dorsey (who snagged Lunceford's chief arranger, Sy Oliver), Stan Kenton, Boyd Raeburn, and, much later, Billy May.

White bands were almost evenly divided between the "swing" variety and those euphemistically referred to as "Mickey Mouse" or "sweet" bands, which played tame dance music exclusively and appealed mainly to older people. Kay Kyser, Blue Barron, Orrin Tucker, and Guy Lombardo were only a few practitioners of the art of playing "schmaltzy" for the people.

The kids thumbed their collective noses at the "Mickey" bands. They loved swing. Ate it up, thrived on it, and made it their personal musical religion. Just as the rock fans of the '90s know every single member of every heavy-metal group, so did the youngsters of 1939 glorify and hero-worship the big band musicians. Most of the kids I went to school with in 1939 Chicago could rattle off with ease who played hot trumpet with Jimmy Dorsey's band, who replaced Krupa with Goodman's tribe, or what girl singer had gravitated from Artie Shaw to Benny Goodman. (Helen Forrest, for the record.)

Since Benny Goodman's rise as undisputed King of Swing, other talented clarinetists—Tommy Reynolds, Jerry Wald, Joe Marsala—had formed their own orchestras and were doing fairly well, following in the great man's footsteps. Only one really gifted man had emerged to challenge the king's domain. He was no mere pretender to the throne but a downright opponent: good-looking, intelligent—intellectual, actually—and he could play the clarinet as excitingly as Benny.

In 1938 Artie Shaw had recorded an obscure song of Cole Porter's as an afterthought. The "A" side of the record, a romping version of Rudolf Friml's old chestnut "Indian Love Call" complete with a sassy vocal by saxophonist Tony Pastor and shouted answers by the Shaw bandsmen, was pegged by the wiser heads at RCA Victor as a surefire jukebox hit. The "B" side, something called "Begin the Beguine," took off and against all odds screamed skyward to become one of the best-selling records in big-band history.

By the end of 1938, Shaw's band had climbed to the top of the *Billboard* charts, the *Esquire* magazine jazz poll, *Down Beat's* yearly census, and just about everyone's "favorite band" list. The hysteria over the Shaw band had to be seen to be believed. Georgie Auld recalls:

In those days, we went into "Begin the Beguine" and played it four times during the night. They were dancing on top of tables. It was unbelievable. Never saw anything like it. One kid jumped off the front balcony [at the Strand in New York] and broke a leg. Every time we went into the theme ["Nightmare"], thirty, forty kids would jump up on the stage. Security would have to come up and put them out. One show we did, as the pit was going down, this little broad jumped on top of the pit, grabbed hold of Artie, and started to dry-hump him! He's holding his clarinet above his head; he don't want to break his reed. I must say, Artie was as on fire then as Sinatra was when he hit it big.

Artie viewed his success at that time with *Guinness Book Of World Records* ambivalence. "I was in total confusion," Artie remembers grimly. "I'm not cut out for that life. You know, I started out to live a quiet life as a writer, make twenty-five thousand bucks and buy a dairy farm." When his band became the rage, he just could not believe it.

"My God. Every night was like Life Goes to a Party. But I had a very poor self-image. I thought: the music is mine—it can't be much. No matter what people told me. I mean, I didn't think much of what *I* was doing."

Enter Buddy Rich.

His stints with Marsala and Berigan had gone largely unnoticed by the public and critics alike. Neither band had achieved what came to be known as high visibility. They languished in the category known as moderate popularity, and impatient, bursting-with-talent Buddy Rich had languished with them.

Now he was perched behind the drums propelling the hottest big name band in America. In talking about his year-long run with the Shaw band, he grinned one of his famous toothy grins at me and said, laughing: "They were all in shock when I came on the band. No drummer had ever punctuated brass licks with the bass drum before. Always with the snare drum. Mostly rim shots. All of a sudden, I come along, kicking the band right up its ass with bass drum accents. They couldn't believe it, but they liked it."

Buddy was not without his predilection for rim shots, however. The critics sometimes took him to task for his heavy-handed snare drum work. In the May 1939 issue of *Down Beat* a reviewer wrote: "Buddy Rich, still a loud drummer, is undeniably a good drummer." And in the June issue of *Down Beat* the reviewer, commenting on Shaw's new record of "One Foot in the Groove" and "One Night Stand," complained: "Buddy Rich's annoying rim shots ruin this issue [recording]."

Still, as Artie has pointed out, Buddy began to discipline his playing, and in a review of a September 1939 RCA Bluebird release of Shaw's "I'm Comin', Virginia," *Down Beat* crowed: "Note the improved, less noisy drumming of Buddy Rich."

Incidentally, Buddy came in Seventeenth in the 1938 *Down Beat* poll. In 1939 he jumped up to fourth and was soon to dominate that reader/musician poll.

Rich was having the time of his life playing with the Shaw band. Artie had secured for the band and himself a CBS half-hour weekly program sponsored by Old Gold cigarettes called "Melody and Madness." The show was hosted by Artie himself, who delivered his lines well, and announced by actor-announcer Warren Hull. Rich's drumming was prominently displayed on a number of those broadcasts now available on an independent record label, and they remain some of the most effective and exciting in the entire Shaw musical litany.

The band went before the movie cameras at Paramount studios in early '39 to make a short subject; they would make a similar one for Warner Brothers that same year. Since the Shaw band was on a perpetual tour, most of the Old Gold programs were broadcast directly from locations around the country. In April 1939 Artie and the boys settled into the famed Palomar ballroom in Los Angeles, where they broke the opening night attendance record, attracting 8,753 Shaw devotees.

Disaster in the form of a strep throat infection kept Artie off the Palomar stand for most of the band's run there and nearly cost the clarinetist his life. He endured three blood transfusions and finally recovered from agranulocytopenia, the medical name for what had laid him low. The band had been fronted during this time by Tony Pastor, and Artie's solos had been split between Pastor and Georgie Auld.

Air checks of this engagement indicate that the performances did not suffer from Artie's absence, testimony to the fact that Shaw was an unusually protean leader-tutor. The "Melody and Madness" show during that six-week period also maintained its high quality. Buddy's infectious shouting over the band's driving arrangements, written mainly by the talented Jerry Gray, Rich's hard-kicking gusto behind the Slingerlands, Bernie Privin's warm, open trumpet excursions, George Arus's Teagardenesque trombone interludes, Georgie Auld's gutty tenor solos, the nonpareil singing of Helen Forrest (possibly the best big-band singer of all time), and Tony Pastor's rib-tickling, jazz-infected vocals saw the band through this period with all banners flying.

When Artie returned to the Palomar just prior to the band's closing, he was greeted with wild cheering by the capacity crowd gathered to welcome him back. There was talk of extending the engagement, which, even without Shaw, had been spectacularly attended, but Artie had signed for two feature films at MGM, the first of which was to begin shooting in June.

It was called *Dancing Co-ed*. It starred Richard Carlson, Ann Rutherford, Roscoe Karns, Artie Shaw, and Shaw's future wife, Lana Turner. Artie's band is heard mainly as background music, playing some of their best charts, including "I'm Comin', Virginia" and "Lady Be Good." There is one featured Shaw number, "Traffic Jam." It is well shot, with a few close-ups of Buddy.

Buddy was out and about the town in the evenings, escorting some of the best-looking women in the city, frequenting jazz clubs in Hollywood and Santa Monica and on Central Avenue, L.A.'s Harlem. He had made an indelible mark on jazz lovers, musicians, and the female contingent during his Palomar stint. He was enjoying enormous personal popularity all around the town. He was *persona grata* at every jazz club he visited and usually was called upon to sit in with the local musicians. He was especially graceful in these situations, with a particular affinity for black musicmakers. He had been widely quoted as having said that "colored" musicians were at the forefront of jazz, leading the way, innovating, swinging, and that most white musicians were "followers." He did favor Basie, Lester Young, Roy Eldridge, and Basie's drummer, Jo Jones, over most of the white players.

His playing improved minute by minute. What many people failed to realize was that he was able to "get around" his drums with great ease because his arms were quite long. He never appeared to have to reach for the cymbals or the tom-toms. Additionally, his hands were large and graceful, not unlike the hands of another rhythm expert, Fred Astaire. He was very conscious of his hands, keeping his nails well buffed, manicured, and polished at all times. When we became friends, the relationship was a bantering one. With his longish arms, slightly protuberant, large teeth, and general dark, good looks, I nicknamed him "Kong." He would regard me with narrow eyes, make his hands into fists, and beat his chest with them, gorilla-fashion, in an "I'll get you for that, Tormé" warning.

On June 16, 1939, Chick Webb died from complications of liver ailment and tuberculosis of the spine. Buddy was depressed for days. He had been allowed to sit in with the mighty Webb band on several occasions at the Savoy ballroom in Harlem and had not only learned much from watching the little drummer but come to love him as a friend.

Work proceeded on *Dancing Co-ed,* and Lana Turner's talent and charm, not to mention her wholesome yet sexy good looks, were not lost on Buddy. She seemed to be smitten with Artie Shaw for the moment, and Artie with her. Buddy shrugged his shoulders and went on his merry way, eliciting envious whistles and catcalls from the Shaw bandsmen whenever he showed up with a gorgeous girl in tow.

The band continued to make some memorable Bluebird discs for RCA, and, while moviemaking was boring, the extra money was very welcome. They looked forward to Artie's second feature film, *Broadway Melody of 1940,* with

Fred Astaire and Eleanor Powell. That film was made, but without the Artie Shaw band, for the simple reason that within a few months of finishing *Dancing Co-ed* there would all of a sudden be no Artie Shaw band.

◨ Chapter *11*

> *"The music business stinks, and you can quote me."*
> Artie Shaw in a *Down Beat* interview,
> November 1939

SOMEWHERE IN THE Great Nowhere there must be a Graveyard of Lost Orchestras, a melancholy repository filled with the rotting musical arrangements and rusting instruments of groups that had to disband because of scant bookings, economic problems, dwindling popularity, and/or general discontent. There has never been an instance of a band breaking up at the very pinnacle of its popularity. Well, that's not exactly true; there was one glaring example: the 1939 Artie Shaw orchestra. (No—*two,* counting Stan Kenton's 1947 abandonment.)

By midyear Shaw fronted the number one dance band in the country; yet it was more than just a dance band. It was a genuine jazz band, a close-knit organization of superb players led by a virtuoso clarinetist. Despite the fact that Artie ran a tight ship with meticulously rehearsed charts, fun was abundant and morale was high. Why not? The band was making good money, the bookings were plentiful, and the future seemed rosy.

Critics raved about the Shaw sax section. The two-alto-two-tenor combination of Georgie Auld, Tony Pastor, Hank Freeman, and Les Robinson was being hailed as the greatest ever. That may still, to this day, hold true. Artie's dogged insistence on dynamics had produced a brass section that actually phrased, bending the notes when necessary, paying careful attention to the instructions on the parts: diminuendo to crescendo, forte to pianissimo, and so on. The brass players were especially adept at manipulating the plungers and the even more cumbersome derbies, an art that is mostly lost on today's young musicians.

And the rhythm section composed of Al Avola on guitar, Bob Kitsis on piano, Sid Weiss on bass, and, of course, Buddy on drums had come into its own. Where Basie's rhythm section was loose and rangy, the Shaw counterpart created a tight, driving force that kicked the horn players in their collective backside and lifted them off the ground musically.

Bassist Sid Weiss was the band's home-movie Boswell, and one of his efforts with a 16mm camera shows a playful Artie Shaw in an unnamed park with a cluster of musicians seemingly content with their jobs and their fame. All the Shaw men had nicknames, which were printed on the fronts of their music stands: Tony Pastor was "Emcee," Georgie Auld was "Killer" (no doubt alluding to his ladykiller status), and so on.

Buddy, as previously mentioned, regularly appended to his dynamic drumming shouts of encouragement to the various soloists. He also interspersed what amounted to "spoken scat singing" in the spaces between the band's "block" figures. For instance, in a recording of a performance of "The Carioca" at the Café Rouge of New York City's Hotel Pennsylvania, the band plays an ensemble figure, then the rhythm section alone fills two bars, augmented by Buddy's shouted "hi-hi-hi."

Throughout his year with Shaw, Rich continued to be a cheerleader of sorts and his infectious yelling caught on with other members of the band, who also began to be enthusiastically vocal at times. Shaw did not discourage such behavior. It added to the fiery personality of his newly famous orchestra.

Buddy's backing of the soloists was accomplished mainly with snare drum and/or snare drum-hi-hat timekeeping. The beauty of such playing was that it did not intrude on the featured player. Rich used deep-cup eleven-inch Zildjian cymbals on his hi-hat stand, and he devised a unique way of playing them— barely spread apart, with his left hand guiding the angle of the cymbals while his right hand manipulated the drumstick in a manner that produced a thicker, fuller sound from the "choked" hi-hats, rather than the "tip-ta-tip, tip-ta-tip" response that most other drummers elicited from their sock cymbals.

During the "bebop" era, percussionists favored the less demanding manner of backing soloists by applying the stick head or "bead" to a "ride" cymbal, usually mounted on the bass drum, and "ting-a-linging" away behind a featured player. The "overring" from this type of backing often obscured and occasionally obliterated what the soloists were trying to say musically. Buddy always respected the horn player being featured. Listen to his tasty background drumming on Artie's record of "Softly, as in a Morning Sunrise" or his gentle brush strokes on the Shaw version of "I Surrender, Dear." He never resorted to the "top cymbal" vogue until the postwar years, when he formed his first band and that kind of stick work was considered SOP.

The great hi-hat cymbal experts of the '30s and '40s—Ray McKinley, Gene Krupa, Chick Webb, and Jo Jones, among others—had a far more difficult time physically with that kind of playing. The right hand holding the hi-hat stick is unnaturally turned in order to attack the cymbals, whereas "bop" drummers enjoyed a more natural application by addressing the "ride" cymbal mounted directly in front of them. Often the hi-hat player's right hand collided with the protrusion of the snare drum. The "boppers" suffered no such obstruction. Still and all, the pleasure of hearing a trumpet solo or the flight of an alto saxophonist without a madly ringing "ride" cymbal blocking the way was refreshing and enjoyable during the big band era.

By the fall of 1939 the Artie Shaw band was riding higher than ever. Artie had tumbled Benny Goodman as King of Swing in the annual *Down Beat* poll. The Old Gold radio show was enjoying healthy ratings. The band's Bluebird records were big sellers. All seemed well, but looks can be deceiving. Artie Shaw was becoming increasingly disenchanted with the band business. He had no patience with "jitterbugs" who cavorted all over the dance floors but did not seem to pay attention to what the band was playing.

The August issue of *Down Beat* listed Artie's band as having begun location work on Warner Brothers' *Dancing Co-ed*. (A mistake—it was an MGM movie.) That was the very least of Artie's annoyances. In the early autumn he crossed over from Canada into New York to play a one-nighter at the Crystal Beach ballroom near Buffalo. Customs and immigration authorities delayed his arrival at the ballroom until 10:00 P.M. The band jumped off the bus, raced onto the bandstand, and began to play. The promoter, Tick Smith, was ticked off. He raged at the band from the sidelines.

At intermission, the irate Smith informed Shaw that he was not going to pay him. Artie did the only thing he could possibly do: he had the band pack up and walk off the stand. The capacity crowd was naturally unhappy, but before Artie departed, he explained what had happened, and his fans cheered him. The incident, reported in all the music magazines as well as newspapers from coast to coast, germinated in Artie's heart and mind, another prime example of how rotten the band business was and how much he detested it. If the Buffalo fiasco was the beginning of the end, then the real death knell was sounded when Artie, with all that anger festering inside him, gave a startling interview to Michael Mok of the *New York Post*.

"I hate the music business!" he cried hotly to Mok. "I'm not interested in giving people what they want. I'm interested in making music. Autograph hunters? The hell with them. They aren't listening—only gawking. My friends, my advisors tell me that I'm a damned fool. 'Look here,' they shout at me. 'You can't do that. . . . These people MADE you.' you want to know my answer? I tell them that if I was made by a bunch of morons, that's just too bad."

Mok adds: "What isn't known is that Artie is fed up with the whole business and is honest enough to act as he feels."

The interview appeared in the *Post* on October 15. In the November 1939 issue of *Down Beat,* a front-page editorial further amplified Artie's feelings when it quoted him as having said: "I like music—but I don't like the damned music business. The music business stinks—and you can quote me!"

As a result of the foregoing, Old Gold dropped Artie Shaw from the "Melody and Madness" CBS radio show. His life became even more turbulent, and the band feared the end was in sight.

🔲 *Chapter* **12**

> *"I want you to meet another pain in the ass"*
>
> Tommy Dorsey introducing
> Frank Sinatra to Buddy Rich

ON NOVEMBER 18, 1939, Artie Shaw walked off the stand at the Hotel Pennsylvania's Café Rouge. He never returned. The next thing anyone knew, he was in Mexico, apparently having washed his hands of the music business.*

The "deserted" Shaw bandsmen tried to carry on at the Café Rouge with Georgie Auld fronting the orchestra. Soon it was obvious that Artie, the closest thing to a matinee idol in the band business, was the essential ingredient necessary to draw the paying customers. The band ceased to be.

---

* After a few weeks of R and R south of the border, Shaw returned to the States with two songs he had heard in Mexico City; "Frenesi" and "Adios, Marquita Linda." He formed a new band supplemented by a string section, graduated from the lower-priced Bluebird label to the more prestigious RCA Victor side of that company, and proceeded to make hit records all over again.

"Frenesi" became one of the biggest-selling records of that time, as did his recordings of "Moonglow" and "Star Dust." The new band included Billy Butterfield on trumpet, Johnny Guarneri on piano, Nick Fatool on drums, and the great Jack Jenny on trombone. Artie's little band-within-a-band, the Gramercy Five, also proved to be hit-makers.

Buddy Rich moved on to the Tommy Dorsey orchestra. Just when he made that move—before or after Artie's defection on November 18—is unclear.

Memories are fragile things. In a conversation with Buddy on May 9, 1975, he emphatically recalled that Artie Shaw walked away on opening night at the Café Rouge. In Rich's own words:

> We came back to play the Café Rouge, and we had opening night. That's when Shaw disappeared. [He] left during the first set. He didn't show up on the bandstand. "Where's Artie?" The room was packed. I sat down behind the drums, and I waited. We all started looking around at each other. Everybody in the brass section looking at me. I'm looking at them. Finally after about . . . five minutes of waiting, Tony Pastor got up in front of the band and called a set.
>
> Artie never came back. We came in the next night. Artie was not there.

What is fascinating about Buddy's recollection is that he insists he was still playing with the Shaw band the night Artie left. Yet *Down Beat* reported him joining Dorsey prior to Artie's leavetaking. Since Shaw's actions were of great significance during that period, it would seem unlikely that Rich would forget an episode as startling as Artie walking away from his own men.

Tommy Dorsey's orchestra had enjoyed immense popularity for several years by the time 1940 rolled around. He had employed a pair of attractive singers—Edythe Wright and Jack Leonard—as well as several first-rate musicians, and his band never wanted for bookings. He had his string of hit records, like most other big band leaders of the day. Jukeboxes seemed to endlessly emit "Song of India," "Marie," and several other Dorsey evergreens to the delight of kids and grown-ups alike all over America.

And, like so many other leaders, he had organized a little band-within-the-band known as the Clambake Seven, strictly a Dixieland combo, since Tommy, whose forte as a trombonist was his seamless ballad playing, also dabbled in gut-bucket-style jazz on his horn. Realistically, in early 1940, he knew that his band was out-of-date, stagnating, badly in need of a solid shot in the arm.

Tommy had heard Buddy help turn Shaw's band around. He was sure Rich would be a vital element in doing the same thing for him. He invited Buddy to come to Chicago, at his expense, to hear the band. Buddy, out of a job now that Shaw had quit, made his way to the Windy City with misgivings. He did not like what he had heard of the Dorsey crew. It seemed to him a mushy, rather lifeless dance band. Period. After the excitement of the year he had spent with the swinging Artie Shaw gang, he did not want to get stuck playing the tired arrangements he associated with Dorsey or reverting to the Dixieland mode with the Clambake Seven. That would be a step backward, as far as he was concerned.

By coincidence, Buddy's older sister Marge was doing a dance act in Chicago with her husband, Carl Ritchie. As Marjorie Rich Ritchie recalls:

> We were staying at the Croydon Hotel in Chicago. We [Buddy, Marge, and Carl] all left the hotel at the same time. He went to hear Dorsey; we went to do our show. [Later] we started to walk down Dearborn Street, and we bumped into Brother.
> "Where are you going?" we asked him.
> "Dorsey's not playing my kind of music. I'm going back to New York."
> He had already called my father and said, "I'm not staying with this band."

He was prepared to leave Chicago the next day when he got a call from Dorsey.

"What're you doing? Come on back. I'm telling you, we're changing the book. I've hired Sy Oliver to write for us."

Reluctantly Buddy went to an afternoon rehearsal of the band. Sy Oliver was there with a couple of new arrangements. Oliver, one of the most talented, original, and respected of all arrangers, had helped mold the musical character of the great Jimmie Lunceford band for years. Tommy had lured him away from Lunceford with a tempting financial offer as well as the challenge to "Luncefordize" his band.

That rehearsal changed Rich's mind. The Oliver charts were thrilling to hear, and Buddy knew they would be great fun to play. Tommy also promised Buddy feature billing as well as a pair of drum specialties to be penned by Oliver. Buddy joined Dorsey on the spot.

Tommy was also on the verge of hiring a young singer named Frank Sinatra, who hailed from Hoboken, New Jersey, and had been appearing at the Rustic Cabin in Jersey when Harry James heard him and signed him to sing with his fledgling band. Sinatra's record of "All or Nothing at All" with James raised eyebrows in the music business. He had a fresh, original sound, astonishing breath control, perfect intonation, spotless enunciation, and a warm vocal quality that impressed the paying customers.

Harry James had put together a fine bunch of musicians, but in 1939–1940, prior to the addition of strings and the hit records that followed ("You Made Me Love You," "Sleepy Lagoon," etc.), his stringless jazz band suffered from undercapitalization. In short, it was close to being what was commonly known in those days as a "panic" band.

When Sinatra got the call from Tommy Dorsey, it was like being summoned from the bench by the head coach. Harry James unselfishly released Frank, who joined Tommy's clan early in 1940. James replaced Sinatra with a snub-nosed young singer named Dick Haymes. Not too shabby.

Coincidentally, Buddy had replaced Cliff Leeman with the Shaw band, then turned around one year later and replaced Leeman with Dorsey. Haymes eventually replaced Sinatra with the James band and a few years later replaced Sinatra again with Dorsey when Frank embarked on a solo career. Talk about musical chairs.

On April 5, 1987, Sinatra recalled with amusement the first time he actually met Buddy. Dorsey introduced Frank to the drummer with the remark; "I want you to meet another pain in the ass!" Frank laughed. "That's what we were in the band. Between Buddy complaining that the tempos were not quite proper and my saying that there weren't enough ballads in the library, we drove the old man crazy. But with all of that, he loved both of us. We really were the pets of the band."

Besides Buddy, Frank, and Sy Oliver, Dorsey had signed a splendid vocal group known as the Pied Pipers, featuring the most in-tune singing lady of all time, Jo Stafford, who also knocked everyone out performing some of the solo vocals. As an added attraction, he hired a peppery little Southern belle named Connie Haines to sing.

Buddy's old boss, Bunny Berigan, had given up bandleading and joined Dorsey in the "hot" trumpet chair. Bunny's health was sadly failing and Tommy, who loved Berigan personally and musically, knew he would eventually have to replace him.

Don Lodice on tenor sax and Johnny Mince on clarinet were two good reasons to acknowledge the Dorsey band's transformation from a fine dance ensemble to a roaring, kicking, entertaining show band that could play the jazz-oriented Sy Oliver arrangements in neo-Lunceford style and make you know it.

Buddy had his work cut out for him now. The Shaw orchestra had been a lighter load for the drummer, having merely six brass and four saxes to backstop. Dorsey carried five saxes and, when he played in his trombone section, eight brass. Rich, with power to spare at his fingertips, was well up to the task. The new Dorsey sound needed the punch he gave it, and, just as Tommy predicted, Buddy was a major force in turning the organization into the behemoth it became.

Rich's first roommate was Frank Sinatra. Early on, they became friendly. Both were feisty, independent, singularly talented, attractive to the opposite sex, and wildly popular with the fans. Buddy confided to me that he enjoyed Sinatra's companionship enormously and that he admired Frank's singing more than he would admit back then. Frank's only drawback as a roommate, as far as Buddy was concerned, was the singer's penchant for cutting his toenails in bed. "That damn clipper used to drive me nuts," Buddy laughed. "Two o'clock in the morning. I'm trying to sleep. Frank's clipping away."

On April 5, 1987, Sinatra recalled the early days with roommate Rich.

When I did my first one-nighter with the band, we all got on the bus. There was one seat empty, and it was next to Buddy. I sat down, we chatted for a while, and then we stopped somewhere. I asked somebody: "How come that seat was open?" They said: "Because he's a pain in the ass. Nobody wants to sit with him!" But [Buddy] said to me: "I like the way you sing."

I sat down in the chair next to him, and once you sat in that chair, it belonged to you. We began to talk about our childhood. I told him about the hokey places I played. After that engagement we became "married" and shared a room together.

Frank made no mention of the nail-cutting episodes, but he did remember another problem.

I was a reader. I'd put the bed light on and read, and I'd hear the rustling, the moving around in the other bed, the shaking from one side to another, and I'd say, "What's the matter? Warm or something?" and he'd say, "No. The goddam light. Don't you ever sleep?" That went on for a while, but we had a wonderful time together for many, many months.

Buddy was reunited with a few of his old Artie Shaw bandmates in the Dorsey band. Sid Weiss on bass, George Arus on trombone, and later the powerful trumpeter Chuck Peterson all shared the bandstand with the young drummer. Tommy's band as a whole, though, was an entirely different cauldron of seafood from the somewhat more restrained Shaw troupe. In fact, it would not be exaggerating to say the Dorsey band was "off the wall," thanks in no small part to the peccadilloes of the leader himself.

Dorsey had gone for years without drinking. Now that the band had turned a corner and was swinging, he fell off the wagon, and the results were sometimes humorous, sometimes near-tragic.

Example   Bassist Sid Weiss agonized for days about whether or not to ask Tommy for a raise. Finally, while the band was playing the Astor Roof of the Astor Hotel in New York, Sid took the plunge and made his pitch to Tommy during an intermission backstage. Result: Tommy chased Sid the complete circumference of the ballroom three times threatening to kill him.

Example   One night on a train siding in Texas, Tommy and a few of his drinking buddies in the band got smashed and began to throw water on each other. When the sleeping car's cooler ran out of water, they substituted whiskey. Then Tommy got a great idea. At four in the morning, totally bent out of shape, he tiptoed along the corridor of the Pullman, flung open the curtains of an upper berth, and doused the occupant with a tumbler full of Jim Beam. Trouble was, the occupant, Pied Piper John Huddleston, took the thrown contents directly in the face and was blinded. His wife, Jo Stafford, her hair in curlers, had to throw on a wrapper and lead her husband, his eyes bandaged, off the train, into a cab, and over to a hospital. Dorsey did not even remember the incident the following morning. Huddleston recovered his sight after a few days.

Example   One night the band bus broke down on the main street of a tiny Ohio village. It was a particularly lousy bus, and the Dorsey men were tired, cold, and disgruntled. At the rear of the bus were twin doors that opened outward, and at seven o'clock in the morning Buddy set up his drums in the street and, along with Ziggy Elman, Sid Weiss, and a few other Angry Young Men, began to play jazz. Loudly. It was a scene worthy of a Mickey Rooney–Judy Garland musical ("Gee, gang, this is a swell barn. We can put the show on right here!"). Surprisingly, no one in the little Ohio hamlet called the cops.

Arranger Paul Weston recalls that, during his tenure with Dorsey in the mid-thirties, Tommy was totally teetotal. Like all reformed drinkers (for the moment, at least), he had no use for the musicians in his band who drank, especially when it affected their playing. One night on the bus, when he was particularly mad at trumpet player Sterling Bose for that very reason, he ordered the bus driver to stop and then proceeded to throw Bose off the bus into a deep snow bank in the very center of nowhere.

"Tommy," he pleaded, "don't leave me here out in the boondocks."

Dorsey sniffed and closed the bus door, and the lumbering vehicle pulled away, leaving the hapless musician stranded. An hour later, the Dorsey bus was passed by a huge, modern Greyhound. In the rear window of that bus Sterling Bose could be seen, thumb to his nose, wagging his fingers at his former fellow Dorsey employees.

Chapter 13

"Tell 'em all about it, Bon Bon"
Buddy Rich to Frank Sinatra,
1942

RICH HAD A sleek Lincoln Continental convertible delivered to the Astor Hotel in New York City when the Dorsey band appeared at the Paramount in March of 1940. He posed proudly in the driver's seat for a photographer. In the rear seat sat Frank Sinatra. They were still buddies. As time wore on, the storm clouds would gather.

Buddy was miffed no end when Frank informed him that he did not feel he could share a dressing room with him at the Paramount because the Sinatra fans would undoubtedly be showing up in droves and he needed his own "space." Now Rich refused to play behind Frank onstage. He would sit with his arms folded, lightly tapping the bass drum with one foot, on the beat, and closing the hi-hat cymbals with the other, on the offbeat.

The friendly rivalry became a deadly one.

Buddy's relationship with the rest of the band, for that matter, was not exactly felicitous. Jo Stafford recalls: "You know, it's the strangest thing. Being in a band with somebody like that for three years. It's like living with him twenty-four hours a day sometimes, especially if you're on the road. And, my God, I don't know who Buddy Rich was! Who he loved—or why. I didn't know the man!"

Buddy kept mainly to himself. Pop Rich was around a great deal of the time, and Buddy was content with his company and that of his sisters, his brother Mickey, and his mother.

He was a nondrinker who simply didn't "hang out" with his fellow musicians. If they were playing in Manhattan, as soon as the evening's performances were over with, he would head across the Brooklyn Bridge to the family home where a night lunch awaited, prepared by the sisters or Bess. They would sit around the kitchen table while Buddy related the evening's happenings. This musician or that arranger had come in to hear the band. Yes, he had played a good solo; of course, the applause was thunderous.

He was not exaggerating. In a short period of time he had become one of the two undisputed stars of the Dorsey organization, the other, of course, being Frank Sinatra. Both of these volatile young men were getting the bulk of attention from fans, girls, critics, musicians, and a good cross-section of the public at large. Both were vying for those attentions with undisguised zeal. Predictably, the rift between them deepened.

Frank complained to Tommy about Buddy's meager backing of his ballads. Buddy complained to Tommy that Sinatra's ballads bored him. Tommy stood back and laughed at his two young prima donnas. He actually enjoyed the conflict between them. One Saturday afternoon in 1941, at the Chicago Theater, I watched as Sinatra sang "This Love of Mine," while Buddy yelled "Tell 'em all about it, Bon Bon" at him in a voice loud enough to hawk peanuts. (Bon Bon was George Tunnell, a black vocalist with the Jan Savitt orchestra.)

After Dorsey's eight-bar trombone interlude, Sinatra came back to sing:

> I ask the sun and the moon
> The stars that shine . . .

At that moment Buddy turned to Ziggy Elman in the trumpet section and shouted: "Hey, Ziggy, let's go over to the Panther Room [of the Hotel Sherman] tonight and catch Duke [Ellington]."

Frank, infuriated, stalked off the stage.

Buddy's behavior surprised many people, in the band and in the music industry. He had had the benefit of more professional experience by virtue of his early childhood stardom than almost any member of the Dorsey orchestra, excepting Tommy himself. He had always been the ultimate pro, yet his escalating war with Sinatra was diminishing that professionalism in the eyes of many.

And the worst was yet to come.

The Dorsey band played a one-nighter in Clarksburg, West Virginia. For prank lover Rich, the evening had started promisingly. While having dinner in the local hotel, he and Sinatra, who was barely talking to him by then, heard four old Southern biddies berating them. The women, real Southern belle types, sat at a nearby table and, according to Sinatra, were "cutting us up pretty good."

When Frank's dessert came—it was apple pie and cheese—he got up and walked over to the offending table. "The woman nearest to me was doing all the talking. I took off her hat and put the pie and the cheese on her head, and I put the hat back. Buddy fell right on the floor."

The restaurant manager rushed over. "There'll be no check. Get out!" he demanded.

Frank's assertive act put Buddy in a good mood. The sets that night were particularly sparkling. After the job the whole band went to a diner out on the highway. Sinatra recalled, "That night was when our 'breakup' came." A man came over to the table. With him was a ten-year-old boy carrying a pair of drumsticks. The man said: 'Mr. Rich, I'd like to ask you a favor.' Buddy looked up and said: 'Can't you see I'm eating?'"

Frank got angry. He scolded Buddy: "Don't yell at him. He's got the kid with him."

"Yeah, but I'm eating my dinner." He looked at the man. "Okay, what do you want?"

"My little boy's a big fan of yours. He's getting the same equipment you use . . ."

"Yeah, yeah."

"I wonder if you'd sign one of these drumsticks—or both of them?"

"I'd rather you'd wait till I finish my dinner."

The man took his son's hand and walked away.

Frank said: "I got a little teed off at Buddy. I really did. I think that [incident] started the 'divorce.' I said to him: 'You've got no right to do that!' I mean, I was no great crusader for behaving, but I felt that was the wrong thing to do."

The relationship continued to deteriorate. A few months later, it shattered to pieces.

Buddy continued to grouse about all the ballads Tommy was cutting. From the moment Tommy had taken the band into the RCA Victor studio in New York and recorded an Axel Stordahl arrangement of "I'll Be Seeing You," the Sinatra legacy began. Frank's tender reading of the bittersweet lyric struck responsive chords in everyone who loved good music. Buddy turned up his nose. "Boring!" he pronounced.

"East of the Sun," recorded on April 23, 1940, wasn't so bad. Crafted in the "Marie" mold, it featured a smooth vocal by Frank with choruslike "answers" from the band. And Buddy had little to complain about when the band made a swinging Oliver confection, "The One I Love," complete with hip Pied Pipers–Sinatra contributions.

But he rebelled when, on May 20, 1940, the Dorsey orchestra recorded a song that was to become one of the band's greatest hits as well as one of the biggest-selling records of all time. The tune was "I'll Never Smile Again." It elevated Frank Sinatra into major star status, enthralled the entire female population of the United States, and effectively placed Dorsey's young singer center stage, as the main object of adulation.

"Ballads!" grumbled Buddy.

Then in short order came "Our Love Affair," "Whispering," "Trade Winds," and "Only Forever."

"Singers!" grunted Buddy.

Plus "Call of the Canyon" and "I Could Make You Care," creamy, romantic ballads, every one.

"Shit!" protested Buddy.

Never mind that several Sy Oliver cookers were being committed to shellac, among them "Losers Weepers," "Hallelujah!" "Make Me Know It," "Another One of Them Things," "Swing High," "Swanee River," and most important, the solo feature chart that Tommy had promised Buddy when he joined the band. "Quiet Please" was recorded on June 13 with a small Dorsey band-within-a-band Tommy dubbed the Sentimentalists (not to be confused with the vocal group that sang years later, with his orchestra). For some reason, that first attempt was never released. "Quiet Please" was redone on July 17. It comes at you at breakneck speed, a familiar "riff" pattern instrumental that stops almost before it begins to allow room for a straight-ahead Rich solo. Buddy's forceful, syncopated work is on perfect display here, neither plain nor gaudy; a solid rhythmic drum solo. It was released on RCA's less expensive Bluebird label and sold well.

In spite of this sugarplum that Tommy had handed him, Buddy remained disgruntled and disenchanted. He had thought he was joining a genuine jazz band when Dorsey lured him, back in November of 1939, with promises of stompers galore. Then came Sinatra and all the goddam ballads. It is true, upon examining the 1940 recorded efforts of the Tommy Dorsey orchestra, that ballads overwhelmingly take precedence over the quick-tempoed instrumentals. It must be remembered, however, that these slow, lush tunes served dual purposes: fodder for Sinatra and solo trombone opportunities for Tommy. Much as he enjoyed the jazz side of the coin, he capitalized even more on the sweet side, and Sinatra was his vocal alter ego on these outings, a match made in heaven.

Sinatra's success with the fans rankled Buddy. Never mind that he was also lionized by the hordes of young jazz lovers whose enjoyment of the Dorsey band came from the Sy Oliver charts and, mainly, Rich's own exalted presence behind his white pearl Slingerlands. And from the standpoint of his importance with the band, Rich had nothing to complain about. Indeed, several theater marquees of that period proclaim: "Tommy Dorsey and His Orchestra featuring Bunny Berigan and Buddy Rich." Sinatra's name is absent from many of these theater billboards. Still, Buddy bitched.

What might have been another disturbing element for Rich occurred in April of 1940 when Joey Bushkin joined the band on piano. Apparently some friction had developed between them when they had worked together in the Bunny Berigan band and even before that, when they had been employed by Joe Marsala. Rumors were rife that Buddy was leaving Dorsey because of his antipathy toward Bushkin. When *Down Beat* braced him for a quote on the subject, his answer was not only suspect, it was uncharacteristic: "Tommy's the best guy I ever worked for. I'm staying with him." Despite Buddy's assurances, Dorsey had another drummer standing by "just in case." Tommy knew only too well that he was also a target of Buddy's ire. Employer and employee were engaged in a cold war.

After the band's second engagement at the Paramount, they hit the road for a series of one-nighters before coming to rest for eight weeks at the Astor Roof of New York's Hotel Astor, overlooking Times Square.

It was to be a memorable stand for several reasons.

◨ *Chapter* **14**

"Buddy Rich Gets Face Bashed In"
Down Beat,
September 1, 1940

ON MAY 21 Tommy moved his troops into the Astor to begin a record-breaking run. Many of the Dorsey musicians were New York–based and were happy to be in one place for a while. Buddy drove his beloved Continental home to Brooklyn every night. Pop Rich, for all intents and purposes still Buddy's manager, listened sympathetically while his son poured out his heart nightly about the shortcomings of his job with Dorsey.

Was Buddy merely a born malcontent? Not really. Ballads *are* boring for drummers. A drummer is made up of equal parts of adrenaline and nervous energy. Sitting behind a set of drums patting the snare drum and the cymbals with a pair of wire brushes is not a jazz drummer's idea of heaven. Some brush-wielders in those days were quite content to play the ballads and not work up a sweat. To that breed of timekeeper, playing with a dance band was a job, employment—nothing more.

To Buddy Rich drumming was a career, the single driving, creative force in his life. He was savvy enough, through years of experience in vaudeville, to realize that "pacing" was all-important in the repertoire of a band. Certainly not every number could, or should, be a "killer," a "swinger," a "cooker." But to Buddy's way of thinking, the "pacing" scales were badly unbalanced in favor of the sweet side of the Dorsey book. More and more, the Sinatra vocals had become prickly thorns in the young drummer's side.

On the plus side, Buddy was doing quite well financially with the band. Nothing, of course, like his bonanza days as Traps, the Drum Wonder. Still, with the money from record dates as well as his weekly salary, he was able to afford a nice new wardrobe (always in the height of current fashion, occasionally trend-setting), and his elegant Lincoln Continental, as well as being the chief breadwinner for his family.

Then the Dorsey band was paged to become the summer replacement for the popular "Bob Hope Show" on NBC, commencing June 25. More extra money. It didn't hurt. And as the Astor date wore on into late June, Buddy had to admit that the scales between the jazz charts and the sweet charts were balancing a bit more to his liking.

His favorite Dorsey employee was Sy Oliver, who would watch Rich closely when he brought new arrangements to rehearsals. Buddy's uncanny sense of embellishment and punctuation astounded Sy. On occasion Oliver would make a suggestion to Buddy ("How about a Lunceford two-beat on this one, Buddy?"), and Rich, who normally fumed when anyone told him how or what to play, would courteously accept Sy's ideas and apply them to his playing. He liked and respected Oliver that much.

Other than Oliver, though, he "buddied-up" with no one—a confirmed loner. His one pal had been Sinatra, but that relationship had effectively gone to hell by the time the Astor engagement was in full swing.

The Dorsey organization was breaking all records at the Astor Roof. The July heat gave way to the smothering humidity of August, and still the band held forth at the Manhattan hotel, the engagement having been extended because of the land-office business.

Nightly the jam-packed Astor Roof collectively swooned to the Sinatra magic. In fact, the word "swooner" was first applied to Frank. Buddy dominated the attention of fans who pressed against the rim of the bandstand to watch, fascinated, as he continued to perform his own brand of drumming magic.

It was very hot, very humid. Tempers flared. Harsh words were flung, the harshest being those between the two former friends, Buddy Rich and Frank Sinatra.

Jo Stafford recalls: "It was a perfect example of a love-hate relationship. They were both young, mercurial people. Their personalities clashed. Yet they were both fine enough and great enough at their craft so that there was no way each of them could not admire and respect the talent of the other."

Respect or no, the whole band held its breath, waiting for the inevitable. The balloon finally went up one oppressively muggy August night. What actually precipitated the blowup has never come to light. I asked Buddy about the incident several times over the years; he swore he didn't remember what the "beef" was about. What took place? Jo Stafford says:

> I can tell you about that. I was there. I got splattered! What caused the fight? I couldn't tell you. They were always bickering.
>
> I was sitting at a table backstage, writing a letter home. Across the hall was another table with three or four of those big, tall glass pitchers full of ice water.
>
> Frank was there. Buddy was in the doorway of the room across from me. They were yelling at each other, about what I don't know. I wasn't even listening. Suddenly, out of the side of my eye, I saw Frank pick up one of those pitchers and hurl it at Buddy. It crashed into the wall right over my head. For years after that, when we played the Astor, one of the Pipers, Chuck Lowrey, used to write little things around the pieces of glass embedded in the wall.

They went at each other then, all the pent-up bad feelings exploding into curses and swinging fists. Luckily they were separated by members of the band before any real damage could be done. But it wasn't over.

A few nights later, Buddy had gone over to Child's restaurant, just south of the Astor, for a bite between sets. As he was returning to the Astor, he felt a tap on his shoulder. He turned, and the night exploded.

The front page of *Down Beat,* September 1, 1940 trumpeted:

BUDDY RICH GETS FACE BASHED IN

New York—Buddy Rich's face looked as if it had been smashed in with a shovel last week as Buddy sat behind the drums in the Tom Dorsey band at the Astor Hotel.

No one was real sure what had happened except that Buddy had met up with someone who could use his dukes better than Rich. Members of the band—

several of them "tickled" about the whole thing—said that Buddy "went out and asked for it."

It is no secret among musicians here that Rich's behavior at times has been open to criticism. Only a few weeks back, Frank Sinatra, Tommy's vocalist, belted Buddy around as if he were a punching bag. Sinatra is smaller than Rich. It was not Frank who gave Buddy the latest beating, however.

Down Beat's reporting in this instance was erroneous, at least where the alleged beating by Sinatra was concerned. The backstage incident is well remembered; only a few ineffective punches were thrown before Frank and Buddy were pulled apart.

As far as Buddy having met somebody who could "use his dukes better than Rich," that somebody, according to Buddy himself, was *two* somebodies. When he turned around in response to the tap on his shoulder, he was smashed in the face by a total stranger. Down Buddy went. Immediately a man he had never seen before jumped on top of him and held him down while the deliverer of the first blow straddled his chest and slugged him in the face and stomach several times. Then, just as quickly, the two thugs jumped up and disappeared into the Broadway crowds.

Rich staggered into the Astor, made his shaky way up to the Roof, and played the final set of the evening, looking like walking wounded.

Buddy had a pretty good idea why the attack had taken place. Robbery was certainly not a motive; nothing was taken. The beating had been coldly efficient and professional. That it was a "put-up job" was a certainty in his mind. And he thought he knew who had arranged it. He told me that one night just before Sinatra left Dorsey (September 3, 1942) he quietly approached Frank and asked him point blank if the mugs who had flattened him two years before had done so at Frank's request. "Hey, it's water under the bridge," Buddy assured Frank. "No hard feelings. I just want to know." Sinatra hesitated and then admitted that he had asked a favor of a couple of Hoboken pals. Rich laughed, shook hands with Frank, and wished him good luck on his solo vocal career. The armistice between them at that moment would prove lucky for Buddy a few years later.

But now, in late summer of 1940, the war was ongoing.

Tommy Dorsey had sent Frank home right after the pitcher-throwing incident. "I can live without a singer tonight, but I need a drummer" was his practical explanation. Needless to say, Frank boiled.

Tommy, hitherto entertained by the sparring between his two lion cubs, was becoming less amused. He issued an edict: Enough of this crap! Cool off, you two! To some degree, his orders had an effect. The bad feelings continued between the drummer and the singer, but there were no more physical confrontations.

Jazz trumpeter Bunny Berigan left the Dorsey organization in late August, as the Astor engagement ended. His replacement was Chuck Peterson, Buddy's former Shaw bandmate. Within a few weeks Ziggy Elman took over the "hot" chair in the band, although, as Jo Stafford remembers, Peterson more than held his own against Ziggy, particularly on high notes. The addition of these two powerhouse trumpeters was yet another indication of how serious Tommy was about the jazz end of his orchestra. On September 22, the Dorsey crew ventured into Harlem to play a one-nighter at the famed Savoy ballroom. The uptown cats apparently loved the band, particularly Buddy and Ziggy's joint efforts on "Hawaiian War Chant."

Buddy, now using larger hi-hat cymbals to compensate for the juggernaut brass section, had opened up considerably. His playing was looser, his ideas more adventuresome than they had ever been before.

In mid-October, after a particularly exciting one-night stand in Rochester, New York, the band headed west to California to open the brand new Palladium ballroom on Sunset Boulevard in the heart of Hollywood. Also slated was a major appearance in a Paramount picture called *Las Vegas Nights*.

The Dorsey musicians made their individual ways to the Coast. Jo Stafford and her husband, John Huddleston, were invited to ride to California with Buddy Rich and his father in Buddy's Continental.

Jo reminisces: "Buddy liked me. We never had any problems, but there wasn't an obvious humanness, a closeness. We talked to each other along the way, of course, and I could talk a lot *about* him—except for really knowing him, the person." Miss Stafford recalls that trip as being strange and somewhat uncomfortable because of Buddy's—and Pop's—remoteness. Then she remembers, with a delighted smile, how Rich performed with the Dorsey band.

"Only way I can explain it—when he played a long solo—he played the melody. I knew where he was every minute." Then she adds, "But he was remote."

The band was to open the new Hollywood Palladium on October 16, but the ballroom wasn't nearly ready when Dorsey's group arrived in Los Angeles. The premiere evening finally took place on October 31, Halloween of 1940.

As anticipated, it was one of the great gala nights in Hollywood. Many celebrities attended the opening, including Bob Hope and Mickey Rooney. Rooney got up at Tommy's invitation and played drums with the band. The huge crowd loved it. Buddy wasn't impressed. He told me that Mickey had "gotten on" his prized cymbals and bashed them unmercifully, so that when the

Mick finished playing, the Zildjian gems Buddy had carefully chosen were bent way out of shape. (Months later, when the Dorsey band played a return engagement at the Palladium, Mickey again asked to sit in. As he made his way up to Rich's drums, Buddy held up his hand and said, "Ah, ah!" He then proceeded to remove all of his cymbals and, tucking them under his arm, said to Rooney, "Okay. Now you can play.")

The Dorsey band now embarked on a killing schedule. Nighttimes at the Palladium, daytimes at Paramount studios appearing in what was then known as a "programmer," *Las Vegas Nights.* The band would finish at the ballroom at one A.M.., sleep two or three hours at the most, and then report to Paramount for makeup at six A.M. The old-timers at the studio still remember with amusement how the soundstages looked during the making of *Nights*—Dorsey musicians scattered all over the set, sound asleep, waiting the interminable waits for the next "set-up"—and the next—and the next.

Buddy, with the ebullience of youth in his favor, didn't seem to be affected by the grind. He was having a great time nightly at the Palladium. All week long the spacious dance hall would play host to some of the biggest movie stars in Hollywood. Tyrone Power came in often. As did Judy Garland. And Errol Flynn. And Betty Grable.

And Lana Turner.

◨ *Chapter* **15**

"Lana . . . If only he could get next to her."
Buddy's dream

WHEN LANA TURNER and Artie Shaw had eloped to Las Vegas on February 13 of 1940, Buddy had taken the news somewhat despondently. While filming *Dancing Co-ed,* Buddy had been the object of Lana's attention more than once. He had secretly harbored notions of a possible romance with the MGM starlet. Well, he thought (prayed!), maybe the marriage won't last. And if it doesn't . . .

At least the Palladium gig was going swimmingly. The elegant West Coast ballroom had quickly become the most popular hangout for music fans, thousands of gyrating jitterbugs, and the great and not-so-great of the film colony. Plans to reopen the recently burned-down Palomar Ballroom had gone up in smoke, so to speak, and fans and musicians alike were grateful for the new, modern, conveniently situated Palladium.

The huge, domelike ceiling, with its soft, indirect lighting, looked down upon a well-kept dance floor that accommodated three thousand dancers and hundreds of band watchers. On both sides of the dance floor were raised terraces lined with tables where diners could enjoy the surprisingly good food the ballroom offered at even more surprisingly moderate prices. The bandstand was commodious, the backstage dressing rooms comfortable and attractive, and the entire facility reeked with its own special kind of ambience. It was a date the Dorsey band and its leader enjoyed, with plenty of remote radio "shots" every night.

In spite of being bugged over a *Down Beat* review that condemned his drumming as "too loud" and "tasteless," Rich was having a good time. A *great* time! Making movies by day, knocking out the customers at night, looked up to by the young drummers who came to stand and gawk, pressed against the rim of the bandstand at the ballroom. Not to mention the pretty girls who gazed with alternate shyness and boldness in his direction, his dark, young good looks not lost on them.

And a piece of news that gladdened his heart: he had won the prestigious *Metronome* magazine drummers poll, entitling him to appear with the other winners on a special recording to be made at the beginning of the new year. On January 16, 1941, with the Palladium engagement behind him, Buddy walked into RCA Victor's New York studios wearing slacks and a sweatshirt, sat down behind a scaled down set of drums, and along with Count Basie, Benny Goodman, Harry James, Coleman Hawkins, Ziggy Elman, Cootie Williams, Benny Carter, J. C. Higginbotham, Charlie Christian, Tex Beneke, Artie Bernstein, Toots Mondello, and his boss, Tommy Dorsey, proceeded to record Jimmy Mundy's arrangements of "One O'Clock Jump" and "Bugle Call Rag."

Fast company for most drummers, but not for Rich, who drove both selections with a clean, relentless beat that lifted the entire all-star band approximately three feet off the studio floor.

On the previous day the Dorsey horde had gone into the same studios to record a number of tunes, which mainly fell into the "pop" category. One Sy Oliver arrangement, however, was destined to become a classic, a Lunceford-like, insistent reading of Stephen Foster's "Swanee River." No critic could fault Buddy's restrained, careful approach to this chart, beginning with almost nothing more than bass drum and alternate hi-hats quietly compressed together on the afterbeats and then slowly, slowly building until, by the close of the record, the band is booted by Rich's strong, unswerving drumming, the connective tissue that glues the band together and makes the Oliver orchestration sing.

1941 saw the Dorsey orchestra performing almost entirely in the eastern United States, which was just fine with Buddy. Family-oriented as he was, he enjoyed living at home with Pop and Bess, sisters Jo and Marge, and little brother Mickey. Marge was working more and more with her husband, Carl Ritchie. They were doing their dance act in various night club ballrooms around the country.

Mickey, now a young man, had taken up the tenor sax and was sounding very good on the instrument. In a few short years, that endeavor would pay off where brother Buddy was concerned. Jo was not working steadily at that time, but in a sense that was good. She stayed close to home, helping her mother around the house, providing that peace of mind so essential to her home-loving "Brother."

The former estrangement between Pop and Bess had all but disappeared. Buddy had found his niche in the jazz world. Pop was home a great deal now, and torn fences seemed to have mended. The horseplay within the Rich family went on, some of it bordering on the childish, most of it harmless, good fun.

The Dorsey band had closed out 1940 at the New York Paramount. Eastern one-nighters and a return engagement at the Meadowbrook in New Jersey were coming up. In late January 1941 *Down Beat* reported that Tommy had signed a young soprano, Marie Frye, to join his complement of singers. "That's just what we need," growled Buddy. "Another singer!" P.S.—Miss Frye was never heard of again.

Down Beat, generally critical of the Dorsey band as a "jazz" entity, was uncharacteristically complimentary in a January 15 record review of "Swing High": "Surprise! Tommy lets his hair down for the first time in a year, gives Sy Oliver free reign, and lets the band cut loose in a mad, wild bash with everybody blowing their brains out. Ziggy Elman blows the loudest and longest, but Buddy Rich and Don Lodice are in there hustling."

Well, thought Buddy, at least they're not bitching about how loud I play!

After a supremely successful run at the Meadowbrook during the entire month of February, the band toured around the Eastern seaboard, playing ballroom and theater dates. Buddy guffawed loudly when, during a weekend stand at the State Theater in Hartford, Frank Sinatra was arrested for jaywalking. No amount of threats, pleas, or promises could deter the Connecticut cop involved from doing his duty. Frank was taken to jail and held there until Dorsey himself, accompanied by a local lawyer, showed up at the jailhouse, and paid his fine. Sinatra barely made it back in time for his next performance.

After stands at the Capitol Theater in Washington D.C., and a week at the perennial favorite Steel Pier in Atlantic City, New Jersey, the band, having made several interim visits to the RCA recording studios, prepared to return to the Astor Roof, scene of the Rich-Sinatra championship fight. Tommy should have been happy as the proverbial clam, but there was a spot of trouble in paradise. The May issue of *Down Beat* headlined his woes:

BUM KICKS PLAGUE TOM DORSEY

New York—on more than one count, Tommy made news last week as his band played three theaters in preparation for its late May opening of the Astor Hotel Roof. Bobby Burns, manager of the Dorsey band for several years, quit suddenly. Frank Sinatra, vocalist, also left, but returned and now appears to be set with Dorsey.

Tommy, in the midst of personnel troubles, was also plagued with legal difficulties. "Toots" Dorsey, his wife, was reported suing him for a divorce and alimony (they have two children), amounting to more than $500 a week. In addition, the United States Government, through its treasury department, was said to be seeking more than $80,000 in income tax, which the govenment says he owes.

Obviously, life at that moment for the trombone-playing leader was not all fun and games. To add to the problems, a "Late News Flash" appeared directly under the foregoing article headlined DORSEY BOYS ESCAPE DEATH IN CAR CRASH. Ray Linn, one of Tommy's trumpet players, Heinie Beau, his featured clarinetist, and Lowell Martin, a Dorsey arranger, were on their way by car from the Steel Pier date to a one-nighter in Binghamton, New York, when the auto hurtled over an embankment, rolled over twice, and smashed into the bottom of a culvert. All escaped with minor cuts and bruises, but it had been a near thing.

Tommy's great strength during these adverse periods was—his great strength. Iron-willed and seemingly indomitable, he weathered these crises with humor and a sense of fatalism, fortified on many occasions with the products manufactured by Schenley or Seagram's. Undeterred, he survived.

The Dorsey band broke its own attendance records at the Astor Roof. The May 20 opening was memorable, and the ensuing engagement assumed landmark proportion, especially since the hotel business was in a temporary slump and the rival Pennsylvania Hotel was having a tough time attracting people to its Café Rouge, even though it featured name bands of the Dorsey stripe and equal fame.

It was a crazy summer, hectic for the Dorsey employees, yet enjoyable and profitable. Buddy drove his sleek Lincoln Continental to most of the gigs. Girls were attracted to him and his elegant car. He had never really enjoyed random dating. His mind and his upbringing ran, romantically, toward one girl at a time. *Down Beat* had reported a romance with Martha Raye, whom he met on the Paramount lot when the band had made *Las Vegas Nights*. Martha, a Paramount contract player, was perceived by the world as the funny lady with the big mouth. ("MMMMMM—oh, boy!") She was also an extremely attractive young woman, with one of the sexiest figures in the film business. Buddy reportedly flew to see her several times, and she allegedly returned the compliment. If it was a short-term romance for them, it was apparently an intense one. "She was great," Buddy admitted. "But she wasn't Lana."

During the spring and summer of 1941, some of the most impressive Tommy Dorsey records were cut and released. Sy Oliver was given a blazing green light now, and he shifted into high gear and took off. In short order he turned in superior arrangements of "Deep River," "Without a Song," and "Swingtime Up in Harlem" and contributed originals such as "Yes, Indeed!" "Serenade to the Spot," "Losers Weepers," and "Loose Lid Special" to the expanding Dorsey library.

Now Buddy was in his element. He actually improved on what had come to be called the "Lunceford two-beat," playing a double beat on the bass drum, adding to the kick of the genre that Oliver had actually created in his Lunceford days.

The Dorsey crew moved into the Meadowbrook yet again in late September of that year. The popularity of the band was at an all-time high, rivaled only by Glenn Miller's newfound prominence. Evidence of Dorsey's eminence can be seen by looking at a three-week period in October of '41. On October 8 the band did a "remote" broadcast from the Meadowbrook on MBS (Mutual Broadcasting System). On October 12 NBC carried the Dorsey music over the airwaves. October 19 found Tommy and team displaying their musical wares on CBS. All from the Meadowbrook. The major networks all vied for a crack at the Sentimental Gentlemen of Swing, and the Dorsey stock was pure blue chip in 1941.

In December the band headed west once more. On tap were several "Spotlight Bands" radio shows for the Coca-Cola Company, numerous record dates, a return engagement at the Palladium, and some Armed Forces Radio Services transcriptions. More and more, the big name bands were making these special records for the young people who had been drafted or volunteered for military service, preparing for what looked like the inevitable: war with Germany and/or Japan.

Buddy's thoughts at that time had little or nothing to do with his possible conscription into a branch of the services or the war now raging in Europe. He had other things on his mind, some pleasant, some not so.

On the plus side, he had won the 1941 *Down Beat* drummers poll. Overwhelmingly. His nearest rival, one of Buddy's personal friends and favorite drummers, Jo Jones, garnered less than half the votes Buddy received, testimony to Rich's great new popularity. (Gene Krupa was ineligible for the drummer's poll because he was a bandleader.)

Also, he planned to keep his eyes open for Lana Turner when they played the Palladium. Her brief marriage to Artie Shaw had ended (as Buddy had hoped it would), and Rich was determined to get next to her, talk to her, date her . . .

There were negatives plaguing the drummer as well. His relationship with Dorsey had further eroded over the past few months. Tommy had wearied of Buddy's temperamental outbursts. The latest words between them were precipitated by Dorsey's announcement of a possible addition to the band of a string section. This was a self-defensive, as well as a creative, move on the bandleader's part.

With Harry James and Artie Shaw using strings, Tommy felt he had to be competitive, and he had Axel Stordahl on hand to form beautiful string backgrounds for Frank Sinatra, now emerging as the greatest singing idol since Bing Crosby.

Dorsey's managers, agents, arrangers and most of his musicians thought it was a great idea.

Buddy Rich loathed it.

Chapter **16**

"Where's Artie? Where's Tommy? Where's Harry?
Where's Buddy? Where's Gene?"
                              Down Beat, June 1, 1942

LANA TURNER DID show up at the Palladium. Opening night, there she was, snapping her fingers to the Dorsey music, dancing to the sweet and swing sounds of the Dorsey band, smiling appreciatively at the Dorsey musicians, not the least of whom, in her estimation, was Buddy Rich. He responded to her obvious attention by playing his heart out on that evening and on the ensuing evenings when she was present. They began going out together, casually at first and then, at least as far as Buddy was concerned, seriously.

Lana was an extremely open, friendly young woman in those days. Music-loving and music-oriented, she idolized musicians and bandleaders far more than she looked up to movie stars. Tommy Dorsey was one of her favorite musicians/leaders/friends.

On Saturday night, December 6, after the band had packed up, she invited Buddy, several Dorsey musicians, and Dorsey himself to her house in the Hollywood Hills for a late supper and drinks. Rich couldn't take his eyes off her. She returned the compliment, even though she kept busy being a perfect hostess, seeing that everyone had enough food and liquid refreshment.

It was a party to remember, starting at two in the morning and lasting until the winter sun slowly lightened the December sky. Several of the guests were invited to "crash" on Lana's sofas and armchairs and in her guest bedrooms. They accepted her invitation and slept through the day into the late afternoon. Consequently, Buddy, Lana, and a few Dorsey sidemen were probably among the last people in America to discover that, while they slumbered, Pearl Harbor had been attacked by Japan, and America was about to go to war.

Tommy and the band had been doubling once again, this time between the

Palladium and MGM studios, where they were engaged in making a movie called *Ship Ahoy*. The original title of this film, which starred Red Skelton, Eleanor Powell, Bert Lahr, and Virginia O'Brien, was *I'll Take Manila.* After Pearl Harbor, the MGM execs wisely changed it to *Ship Ahoy.* The movie was completed just after the first of the year, and Buddy, in particular, was pleased about it. He was heavily featured in an especially exciting segment opposite Eleanor Powell.

The Palladium engagement was a long one, ending in late February. The band remained in Hollywood to make several radio transcriptions, appear repeatedly on "Spotlight Bands," and cut more RCA Victor records, among them the Chuck Peterson/Ziggy Elman blockbuster, "Well, Git It!" and Sy Oliver's latest creation for Buddy, "Not So Quiet, Please." The latter was a howling, minor-keyed lament that gave Rich the best chance to show his tom-tom prowess since his Artie Shaw days and "The Chant" as well as Artie's "Serenade to a Savage."

"Not So Quiet, Please" was a hallmark endeavor for Buddy. It took him out of the conventional drum solo bracket and exhibited his talents in a far broader way. His early tap-dancing abilities came into play at the onset of "Not so . . . ," and the interplay of bass drum and tom toms is a first. His solo actually employs the bass drum as a third floor tom-tom. As a climax to this now-classic record, Rich plays a single-stroke roll that was unprecedented for its precision and speed. It is like the "brrrrrrppppp" of a World War II Schmeisser machine pistol; the beats are distinguishable because of their cleanliness, yet still impossible to fathom because of their enormous acceleration.

Buddy, however, was not happy. The dreaded strings had been added to the Dorsey band. Now, more than ever, he complained about it being nothing more than a dance band, having little to do with jazz. Of course, Dorsey's orchestra *was* a dance band. Its appeal to dancers was unquestionable and responsible for a great deal of the band's success. To damn it as merely a dance band, however, was to minimize and even denigrate the talents of Joey Bushkin, Ziggy Elman, Don Lodice, Heinie Beau, and Chuck Peterson as well as the tasteful, swinging charts penned by Sy Oliver.

Rich was further annoyed when, on March 9, 1942, the band recorded a creamy, lush arrangement of "Sleepy Lagoon," which featured Tommy's solo trombone. For Christ's sake! What the hell was Tommy doing recording this stupid tune? It was a Harry James hit. It belonged to Harry. Unneccessary, Buddy fumed. Frigging unnecessary. Rich would soon eat his words and actually be thankful for "Lagoon," since it provided the band with one of the funniest incidents in its long and wacky history.

Once again, Tommy brought his people into the Astor Roof in New York on May 3 for an eight-week run. Almost every night Dorsey trotted out "Sleepy Lagoon" and gave the Astor patrons a lesson in breath control, intonation, and tone quality.

One evening Tommy had been drinking too much. He began the opening, ascending melody line of "Lagoon." When he reached the top note he uncharacteristically fluffed it. As was his habit, he stopped the band and muttered, "Take it from the top."

Once again he reached for the top note of the first phrase and blew it. One of the musicians laughed. Tommy turned on him in a fury and shouted, "Get the hell off the stand. You're fired!" The musician shrugged and left the Astor bandstand. Dorsey once again ordered, "Take it from the top." And once again he could not negotiate the high note. Two of the violinists giggled audibly.

"You two! Get the hell out of here. You're fired!"

Four more times, Tommy Dorsey attempted to get past the jinxed opening notes of "Sleepy Lagoon." Four more times he failed, and with each failure the band became more hysterical with laughter. Whole sections were fired on the spot, until there were only six musicians left on the stand. Now the audience joined in the merriment, and the Astor Roof was awash in laughter. Tommy looked around at the nearly empty bandstand and finally saw the humor in the situation. Everyone was hired back the next day.

During the weeks in June at the Astor, Lana Turner came to New York to be with Buddy. She certainly gave every impression of being serious about him. She stayed with the Rich family at the Brooklyn house and even went shopping with the sisters. Marge Rich Ritchie remembers Lana getting dressed to go into Manhattan.

She put a little hat on, a little bit of makeup. She looked in a mirror and said, "Do you think anybody will look at me and stare at me?" If she was in her *blue jeans,* they would stare at her. A beautiful, beautiful girl. She finally moved out of the house because she had to have publicity pictures taken. She moved into the Mayflower Hotel in New York City. She used to meet Brother in the Walgreen's drugstore just across the street from the Astor.

It was a very serious romance. As a matter of fact, Brother thought she was going to marry him.

Sister Jo adds: "I kept praying to God something would happen to break them up. I had heard all kinds of stories about Lana's adventures with lots of men. I couldn't stand to see Brother hurt, but I knew it would eventually happen."

For the time being, the romance was in full bloom. Lana seemed to have eyes for no one except Buddy. Jo recalls with sadness:

Lana was the love of Buddy's life. And he was the only one that didn't know about her. It was strange. When she came to New York to stay at our house, she showed up with matching wedding bands and a watch for Brother. He went to pick her up at the airport. I redecorated the room she was going to stay in in our house in Manhattan Beach.

They had been on the phone every day while he had been working at the Astor and she was in Hollywood making a picture with Clark Gable. [*Somewhere I'll Find You,* MGM, 1942] I can't tell you how many calls. All hours of the day. He called her; she called him. While Brother was bringing her home from the airport, we all dressed up for her arrival. Mother, Marge, myself. Mickey was ordered to wear a suit.

Now, we hear the car pull up. We look outside. They're out of the car, laughing hysterically. Lana has dropped the rings, and they're both down in the grass looking for them. They finally find them, we open the door, and here is this lady in a gray sweatsuit, no makeup, with a kerchief tied around her head, a little chubby (as soon as she finishes a picture, she eats!) and she's gorgeous. GORGEOUS! Skin like a baby. Mickey looks at me, looks at Marge, looks at Lana, and says: "You know, I've got two of the ugliest sisters in the world."

Anyway, we'd been keeping this whole thing [between Buddy and Lana] a big secret. I don't think she'd been in the house fifteen minutes when there were people climbing up looking in the window, people walking back and forth in front of the house. Before you knew it, everybody in the area knew that Lana Turner was staying in our house.

Well, altogether, she stayed with us for about six days, and at the Mayflower in New York around four days, when she got a call from Hollywood. She had to do retakes on the Gable picture. Now came this tearful farewell between her and Buddy. "I'll call you as soon as I get there. We'll arrange the wedding and the marriage and this and that." She had given Brother the ring as well as the gold watch.

Two days after she got back to Hollywood, a telephone call, early in the morning. She wanted to tell him before he read it in the paper. She had just married Steve Crane. She told Brother that the studio made her do it.

Well, Brother was devastated. Absolutely devastated. Not just at the time, but for years! And every girl he met who looked like Lana, he went out with her.

The old saying "There are none so blind as those who will not see" certainly applied to Buddy at this point in his life. As a sharp-eyed Indian scout of the old American West might have put it—there was "sign" everywhere you looked. A blurb in *Down Beat* had reported Lana and Tommy Dorsey were "on the stove" (translation from *Down Beat*-ese: Tommy and Lana were having a heated romance.). The June 1 cover of *Down Beat* displayed a picture of Lana seated in a night club surrounded by Tony Martin, bandleader Richard Himber, and comedian Milton Berle. Below the photo, *Down Beat* slyly asks the question: "Where's Artie? Where's Tommy? Where's Harry? Where's Buddy? Where's Gene?"

Gene (Krupa) and Lana? Harry (James) and Lana? Tommy (Dorsey, for Christ's sake!) and Lana? Say it isn't so, Buddy had implored a coldly impartial God. And then the early morning phone call from the lady herself, smashing his dreams.

Consequently, no one was remotely surprised when the news of Buddy's enlistment in the U.S. Marines appeared in the August 15 issue of *Down Beat,* with further information that he would be allowed to complete Dorsey's next MGM project before reporting to Camp Pendleton at Oceanside, California.

Between the news of Lana's marriage and the presence of the dreaded string section, he had to fight to keep his spirits up, although it certainly did not show in his playing. Records and radio shots of the period show a stronger Buddy Rich than ever, propelling the Dorsey orchestra with that kind of forceful, positive drive for which he had become famous.

The draft was now seriously affecting all the bands. Danny Vane replaced Chuck Peterson, and "Well, Git It!" was never the same again. Milt Raskin came in to replace Joey Bushkin, who had enlisted in the Air Corps. The headline of the May 15 issue of *Down Beat* proclaimed in bold orange type: END OF ONE NIGHTERS IN SIGHT. The rubber shortage alone was enough to discourage bands from trying to drive cars or hire buses from date to one-night date. The Dorsey band was mainly unaffected by the war in that respect because of its ability to maintain long stands at the Paramount, the Palladium, and the Astor Roof and on the soundstages of Hollywood.

Buddy was unsettled and anxious to report to Camp Pendleton. Judo had become one of his hobbies, and he hoped to find a berth in the Marines as an instructor. Dorsey entreated him to wait a while. "It's going to be a long war." Dorsey also cast a commercial eye on the problem of losing Rich to the service.

The other of his two greatest attractions was about to go out and try it "solo." On the night of September 3, 1942, Frank Sinatra made his emotional farewell on Tommy's weekly radio show for Raleigh cigarettes. His final vocal with the band was a superbly sung "The Song is You." Dick Haymes replaced Frank, and while Haymes himself had become a favorite with the young crowds, he did not approach the popularity of Sinatra. With Frank's departure, Buddy became the main attraction, and Tommy was prepared to do anything it took to hang on to his drumming star.

1942 wound down. The war news was bad. The Philippines, Bataan, Midway, Corregidor, all had suffered at the hands of the invading Japanese army. U.S. losses were more than alarming, they were critical. More and more musicians were service bound. As did every other bandleader at the time, Tommy transported the band to army camps, naval bases, and USO centers to entertain the kids who were headed west across the Pacific or east toward France and Germany.

In mid-September the Dorsey gang began working at MGM once again. This time the extravaganza was a costume musical comedy, *Du Barry Was a Lady,* with Red Skelton, Gene Kelly, and Lucille Ball. Tommy saw to it that Buddy played a solo *in front* of "Well, Git It!" when the band performed that number in *Du Barry.*

Buddy looks strangely somber in a dark suit, seated on an MGM bandstand, playing with the augmented Dorsey orchestra. Even though his drumming maintains its usual excellence, he doesn't look like he's having fun. He had other things on his mind: the loss of Lana and the war. He had joined the Marines but was not due to report until completion of *Du Barry* in November.

Tommy, on the other hand, was doing a lot of laughing in those days. Even musician's union czar Jimmy Petrillo's recording ban didn't seem to affect the bespectacled bandleader. He had stockpiled enough RCA discs to last him (he believed) through the ban no matter how long it took. Movies and "soundies" were unaffected by Petrillo's tyranny, and Dorsey had plenty of offers in both areas, as well as more than his share of airtime.

Now, if he could only get Buddy to smile.

◨ *Chapter* *17*

"I was an all-around pain in the ass"
Buddy Rich on his time
in the Marine Corps.

BUDDY WAS FRUSTRATED. He had enlisted in the service, and his actions had been reported in all the music magazines as well as the general press. He had begun to get paranoid about people looking and laughing at him. ("So if he's a Marine, what the hell is he still doing in a Tommy Dorsey band uniform?") He probably imagined these slurs, given his current frame of mind.

The band had opened once again at the Palladium in Hollywood, scene of his original romantic encounters with Lana. To make matters worse, the opening took place on New Year's Eve. The ballroom reeked with an air of forced gaiety. Most of the male customers and many of their female partners were in uniform. America was still recovering from the defeats it had suffered in the Pacific. The majority of the servicemen present were on their way to fight the Japanese. Buddy recalled that evening as strangely reserved, not only on the part of the dancers but the Dorsey band as well.

He sat behind his drums and gazed out into the audience with unseeing eyes. Lana was not there, would not be there. Lana, who had brightened his life, captured his heart, promised to marry him. How could she have done this to him?

There are, in fairness, several accounts of the "beginning of the end" of the Rich-Turner love affair. Buddy admitted to me that he had "pressed" her to marry him. One night in Hollywood, he had forcefully insisted they drive to Tijuana, Mexico, just across the California border and tie the knot. Turner, half afraid to hurt him and half afraid *of* him, got into the Lincoln and sat quietly while Buddy headed south.

At one point, she asked him to stop at a restaurant along the way so she could use the powder room. Once inside, she headed for the public phone and placed a frantic call to George "Bullets" Durgom, Dorsey's majordomo.

Bullets was a much beloved character during the big band days. Short and prematurely bald, he was like a walking kewpie doll, with the personality to match. Lana, along with just about everyone else, was crazy about him, and they became good friends.

She dialed his number, and when he answered she nervously told him what was happening. "What should I do?" she implored.

"Let me talk to him," came the reply.

She called Buddy to the phone, and Bullets, who could charm an Iranian terrorist if he put his mind to it, reasoned and lectured and finally calmed Buddy.

Reluctantly, the lovesick drummer turned his Continental around and headed back to Los Angeles. Lana had been advised by Durgom to "let Buddy down easily," and she wisely took that advice. As they headed north, she quietly assured him that it simply wasn't the "right time" for them to get married. "Let's wait a while. Let me get used to the idea."

Judging from the later episode in Brooklyn and Manhattan, she was genuinely torn where Rich was concerned. Why the twin wedding rings? Why the New York trip itself, with the week-long stay in the Rich household? What did it matter now? She was married, out of his life, and here he sat on the Palladium bandstand, mindlessly playing drums, catching an occasional glint from the Patek-Phillipe encircling his left wrist. "Time for you always.—L." Why the hell did he still wear the damned watch? "I was still clinging to the memory of her. Of the two of us, you know?"

Once again the Palladium gig was a long one, a six-weeker. Time dragged for Buddy. He certainly gave his all outwardly, listless though his mind and heart were. However, he kept at Tommy about his due date at Oceanside. Tommy effectively kept putting him off.

The band had fulfilled another MGM commitment in the waning days of 1942. This was a Judy Garland vehicle called *Presenting Lily Mars.* Buddy's playing was evident on the soundtrack, but he refused to appear in the film. It is believed that it is Glenn Miller's former drummer, Moe Purtill, seated behind the drums in the movie, miming Buddy's playing.

Buddy hated being on the MGM lot, even if it was only for the purpose of recording on the soundstage. He couldn't bear the idea of running into Lana, now one of MGM's hottest properties. He avoided eating in the studio commissary and left the lot the moment his duties with Tommy were finished.

Upon completing *Presenting Lily Mars,* the Dorsey orchestra almost instantly began work on yet another MGM musical, *Girl Crazy,* starring Judy Garland and Mickey Rooney. Again Buddy's distinctive drumming is heard on the soundtrack, but he is nowhere to be seen. There are close-up shots of the band during the concert-style arrangement of "I Got Rhythm" featuring Mickey Rooney at the piano. (You heard me—Mickey at the piano, and yes, he absolutely played the arrangement himself—an amazing talent.)

Changes were taking place rapidly in the Dorsey band. At the end of the Palladium engagement, Ziggy Elman got caught in the draft. The Pied Pipers had already departed in January to go out on their own, and so it went.

Buddy was being seen on the nation's screens in a little Universal "B" picture called *How's About It?* starring the Andrew Sisters and Grace McDonald. His billing read "Buddy Rich and his Orchestra." He had moonlighted this bit of froth without the knowledge of his boss during a hiatus in Hollywood in late 1942. Rumblings around Hollywood and Vine were that Tommy was furious. Buddy was *his* property. Who the hell did he think he was, appearing in some frigging movie as a bandleader? The gap between Dorsey and Rich widened considerably.

In late February, when Dorsey took the band back east, Buddy stayed in Hollywood, having been replaced by Moe Purtill. I've joined the Marines, he thought. Why the hell haven't I been called up? He made inquiries. To his utter astonishment, he discovered that his enlistment papers had mysteriously disappeared. Vanished! No trace of them!

He pestered the recruiting office in downtown L.A. regarding his "misplaced" papers. He finally solved the mystery. When he had enlisted, both Dorsey and MGM asked a certain officer in recruiting to "hide" Rich's papers until *Du Barry Was a Lady* was completed. Buddy and I talked about this in 1975. He explained:

> The papers were hidden. The major who had hidden them died suddenly, and there was no record of my enlistment. I went down there every single day, insisting that they find my papers.
>
> They finally found them, and I went in immediately after the picture was completed. I'll never forget, we got on a USMC bus and then a train to San Diego. Then this special Marine Corps railroad car was backed up into the rear end of the Marine base. I got out. I was dressed sharp. I heard someone yell at me, "Hey, boy!" [Buddy does a "redneck" accent]. I looked around to see if I could take the train back to L.A.

From that moment on, Buddy Rich hated the Marines. "I would have rather been in solitary on Devil's Island." The drummer had never taken kindly to discipline or criticism of any kind. He had led a free, unregimented life until that day when he got off the train at Camp Pendleton. Briefly he regretted having turned down Chief Petty Officer Artie Shaw when the latter had asked him to join his fine service band. Rich had made his mind up he was going to do something constructive in the service, not simply what he had done with Artie and Tommy in civilian life.

He made few friends among his fellow "boots." However, one lieutenant, a former FBI agent, befriended him. When the lieutenant was transferred to the Marine Tank Corps, he offered to take Buddy along with him. Buddy said: "The minute I got into one of those things, I realized if you got hit, there was no way you could get out. That was not for me. Then I wrote out a transfer to the Marine Paracorps. But I was too light for that."

During basic training he was able to secure weekend passes to go into Los Angeles. He sought out clubs where little groups were playing, or he would hit the Palladium, trim and rugged-looking in his Marine greens. "It wouldn't make any difference what kind of band was playing. I would sit in with [Charlie] Spivak's band or Shep Fields, just so I could play. Once in a great while, there would be a show at camp, and if there was a band, I would play a number."

On one such occasion *Down Beat* reported that "when Al Sears brought his band and his revue to Camp Pendleton for a two night stint, Pvt. Buddy Rich of the Marines knocked himself out. The first night he sat in merely for a couple of sets, but the second night, Chris Columbus [Sears's drummer] was missing and Buddy thumped the skins for the entire session."

While this may seem contrary to Buddy's determination to do "something constructive" in the service, it is important to remember that while he turned down Artie Shaw's Navy band offer and steadfastly insisted that he be put on active combat status following basic training, he still loved to play drums and did so at every opportunity.

He was pressed again and again to organize a small band within his outfit. "It was kind of like the Monty Clift character in *From Here To Eternity,*" he laughed. "You know, play or else! I told 'em to shove it. I'd play for fun, when I felt like it. Period. I didn't go into the Marines to be a fucking drummer in a band!"

Time and again during 1943, he is noted in discographies and program listings as performing with the Dorsey band on an intermittent basis, Marines or no. While he is mentioned in the April 1 *Down Beat* as having obtained permission from the Corps to play with Tommy for one night on the band's weekly Raleigh cigarette show, he is also reported as having finished his "boot" training in San Diego: "'I've asked for duty with the Raiders,' Rich, who is 26 years old, said. 'I want to beat a tatoo on the heads of a lot of Japs with lead.'" Having known Buddy since 1944, I am willing to bet a substantial amount of money he never, ever, uttered those words.

His desire for active duty *was* genuine, all the same. He wanted to get overseas, to fight, to prove himself. It never happened. Yet he was valuable to the Marine Corps in many ways.

I was a combat instructor. I was a judo instructor. And . . . I was an all-around pain in the ass in the Marine Corps. This general—his name was Fagan, I believe—was a celebrity-conscious guy. He passed Glenn Ford through. Bob Crosby—he made him a second lieutenant. There was a great deal of resentment on my part, since I had gone through the toughest fourteen weeks of my life [basic training]. I was at one time part of the Fourth Marines. I was part of Colonel Hanley's hand-to-hand combat group. I was an instructor at the swimming tank—the high dives. You know, forty-foot jumps, like off a cliff into the ocean.

Anyway, my captain's name was Rosenthal. I remember his name because he was the only Jew I ever met in the Marines. I kept going into his office, two, three times a week, insisting that my name be put up on the overseas call. It would be accepted, accepted, accepted. It would go up to the general—and be rejected.

Buddy half ruefully, somewhat proudly admits he spent significant time in the brig. "I was insubordinate as hell. I would have taken orders and liked them overseas, but I hated being pushed around in Oceanside, California, and I let them know it. The brig? It wasn't so bad."

I asked the unaskable. "Did you really want to go overseas that badly? Was it a death wish? A macho thing?"

Very seriously, he answered: "I really wanted to go. It was pride of the country. Dig my attitude about it. When you saw a picture like *Wake Island,* and you watched a division of Japanese assault troops wipe out a small contingent of Marines, when you're in your early twenties, you're thinking, 'How can they do that to us?' Here I am, sitting behind a set of drums? I can't allow that! I gotta go out and do my thing!"

"I know you volunteered. What was your draft status at the time?"

"I was 4-F. The sole support of my family."

During most of 1943 Rich performed his prescribed duties with the Corps, although there is evidence to suggest that he played the drums on the weekends wherever and whenever he could. He is also mentioned as having played with the Dorsey band on many occasions that year in a variety of locations, not only in Hollywood, but in the East! It seems very unlikely that there is any truth to these reports since by mid-1943 he was immersed in Marine Corps life, at least during the weekdays.

Now, when he returned to Pendleton on Monday mornings after enjoying a weekend pass to L.A., it was in his beloved blue Lincoln Continental. "I would pull up to the front gate of Pendleton, and all the redneck asshole Marine boots would see me in it and whistle and give me the finger. I loved it!"

One weekend a famous Los Angeles disc jockey called Jack the Bellboy took Buddy up in his Waco biplane. The object was flying lessons. The third lesson became three too many for Rich. "While we were up, we blew an oil line, which promptly scared the shit out of me and told me that I should never fly again. While we were coming down, I looked like I had just shot down the Blue Baron."

"The Red Baron," I corrected him, laughing. "Blue Barron was . . ."

"Yeah, I know, I know. Anyway, my goggles were all smirched with oil, and once he got us down safely, I got out, got into my car, and that was that for flying lessons."

Weekend sojourns to Hollywood or no, by the time 1944 rolled around and he saw that his combat ambitions were a lost cause, Buddy Rich had had his fill of the Marines and wanted out.

Chapter 18

"Five hundred a week to rejoin Dorsey. I laughed."

Buddy Rich, 1944

BACK IN APRIL of 1943, Gene Krupa had stood before a judge in a San Francisco court and pleaded guilty to contributing to the delinquency of a minor by using his seventeen-year-old former band boy, John Pateakos, to transport marijuana from his hotel to his Golden Gate Theater dressing room.

Krupa, one of the most respected and admired of all jazz musicians and also one of the most visible, was fined five hundred dollars and sentenced to three months in jail. Making an "example" of him seemed to be uppermost in the mind of the judge as well as the minds of a surprising number of self-righteous folk in the music business.

While the sentence was appealed and overturned (or at least amended), Gene spent several unhappy weeks in jail. He came out with the stigma of a "tea" conviction pinned to his coattail and, for the moment, decided against reforming his own band. Benny Goodman, with whom he had played during the initial days of the Swing Era, immediately offered him the drum chair with his band. Gene gratefully accepted and stayed with Benny until after the first of the year, when an old problem surfaced. Benny had resented Gene's enormous popularity with the fans back in the early days of the Goodman-Krupa relationship, and the great drummer was still getting more than his share of attention every time he twirled a stick or hit a rim shot.

Gene, despite his trouble with the law, had won the 1943 *Down Beat* readers' poll, nosing out Buddy, who suffered from out-of-sight-out-of-mind now that he was not directly in the public eye. Tommy Dorsey sorely missed his ace drummer, difficult though Buddy had been. When Krupa left Goodman,

Tommy saw the commercial possibilities of adding Gene to his roster. Krupa was delighted with the offer and joined Tommy at the Paramount late in January, 1944.

The residue of the drug bust was a negative that Gene knew would drag him down on occasion. Sure enough, at one Paramount performance, as Gene stepped to the mike to thank Tommy for the opportunity to work with his band, a slimeball in the balcony began yelling obscenities at Krupa and then pointedly threw cigarettes at him from the safe, dark environs of the upper tier of seats. Dorsey, livid with anger, yelled, "I wish I knew who did that. I'd throw them right back in your face!"

Meanwhile, back at the Marine base, Buddy continued to suffer non-coms, officers, and his own peers, the lowly Marine "dogmeat" with whom he shared a barracks. Several more times during the spring of 1944 he was obliged to do an about-face and head for the brig. You might say he was incorrigible.

Then, in the June 1 issue of *Down Beat,* came unexpected news:

BUDDY RICH TO GET DISCHARGE

Los Angeles—Buddy Rich, former Tommy Dorsey drummer, is set for a medical discharge from the Marine Corps. For the past nine weeks, Rich has been at the base hospital in San Diego. Relatives said he has been told to expect his release around June 1. Friends in the music business here said Rich would probably organize his own band, following a short rest.

What his "medical" problem was remained something of a mystery. He certainly did not talk about the "why" of his discharge. Some believed he was simply too much of a handful for the Corps. Others swore he had gone in with chronic back trouble, so rigorous Marine life was physically intolerable for him.

On the Saturday in June following his discharge, he showed up at the Palladium. He was still in uniform. He looked happy, relaxed, and relieved. From the bandstand Charlie Spivak spotted him and invited him to come up and sit in with his band. It was a memorable evening for several reasons. It was the first time I had ever seen Buddy up close. It was the night he played Spivak's arrangement of "Hawaiian War Chant." Remember that. "Hawaiian War Chant." There is a chilling coincidence about that tune much later on.

Buddy had his special kind of musical sonar going that night. He had never before played Charlie Spivak's chart on "War Chant," yet he caught every brass figure, every shading, every nuance of that arrangement as if he had written it himself. When the cheering died away, I went backstage and introduced myself. He was polite but distant. I was to learn over the years that that was his normal defense mechanism. He sized up people carefully. He never made snap value judgments. "Don't trust anybody" seemed to be his initial MO. Then, when he felt comfortable with you, he was all smiles, warmth, and wisecracks.

Later in the evening, he came over to my table. I introduced him to my date. He smiled at her seductively. She smiled back. Uh-oh, I thought. I was wrong. He was merely being charming, and as I was to learn, when it suited him, he held the original patent on charm. In 1975 I reminded him of that night. "You had no hair at all," I kidded him. "*The* GI-Marine haircut of all time."

"That was probably right after I got out of jail."

"It was. You told me so that night."

"Right. It was the second day I was out [of the Corps]. Arthur Michaud [Dorsey's manager] was there at the Palladium that night. He saw me play with Spivak, came over, and insisted, there and then, that I rejoin the band."

"Tommy's band, right?"

"Right. He offered me five hundred a week to rejoin Tommy. I laughed."

When Tommy, through Michaud, upped the ante considerably, Buddy stopped laughing and took the offer seriously. He was torn. He had not forgotten the unhappy run-ins with the trombone-playing leader. He was still angry over Dorsey's meddling where his enlistment papers were concerned (although now that he had had his fill of the Marines, he would not have minded had those papers stayed lost permanently). And he still hated the idea of the strings in the band.

He was also broke. He had been earning thirty-three dollars a month in the Marine Corps. He wanted to begin to live the good life again. He wanted spending money. Lots of it. Buddy loved spending money in large chunks. On cars and clothes and anything else that took his fancy. He wasn't a saver. He rarely stuffed a bank account with an eye toward the future. "Live for today" was his credo. In later life his profligacy would nearly ruin him financially, but right now, at twenty-six, who gave a damn about what was in store down the pike?

He accepted Tommy's generous offer and became the highest-paid sideman in the music business. If he had any concern about displacing his friend Gene Krupa, he needn't have worried. Krupa had been testing the waters, and they were warm and inviting. Outside of a few widely isolated incidents like the nasty one at the Paramount, his popularity was intact with the public and had, in fact, increased during his four-and-a-half month stay with the Dorsey organization. He was ready to reorganize his own band and happy to relinquish the Dorsey drum chair to Buddy.

Rich went on a spending spree. He traded in his prewar blue Lincoln Continental for a bright, new yellow model. He ordered several suits, sports jackets, and pairs of slacks from famed Hollywood custom tailor Sy Devore. Collarless cardigans were the rage, and Buddy wore them, like the old song goes, "with style and grace." In my idolatry of the drummer, I couldn't resist having Devore make a few for me. I never looked as good in them as Buddy did. He had the physique of an athlete, and the clothes he wore hung on his frame the way they did on a young lightweight fighter. In fact, Buddy Rich always reminded me of Sugar Ray Robinson. He was the only drummer I ever saw who had the blinding speed, the perfect coordination, and the stunning "combinations" that were the equal musically of what Robinson had fistically.

In 1944 Rich's conversation was laced with occasional "hip" phrases. When Sy Devore fitted the first cardigan to his torso and he regarded himself in Sy's full length mirror, he grinned and said, "In there!" a variation of "in the groove." When he heard a new Sy Oliver original that pleased him, he would compliment the arranger with "That's a killer!" Mainly, however, he worked at improving his English. For someone who had never formally attended school, he acquired through reading and listening an enviable vocabulary—and, as almost everyone knows, he never had trouble expressing himself.

Tommy Dorsey had bought the Casino Gardens ballroom at Ocean Park, overlooking the Pacific ocean. Buddy would pick me up in the Lincoln, and as we headed out to the ballroom, we would sing some of the best of the current tunes or reminisce about the older ones.

"Some Other Time" was a new Sammy Cahn–Jule Styne song from Sinatra's second RKO movie, *Step Lively*. We exhausted the right to sing that one. Rich's favorite song, surprisingly, was an old Jerome Kern classic, "The Touch of Your Hand." He would nudge me with his right elbow as he drove the Continental toward Casino Gardens, and I would oblige by singing it for him. He got positively misty about that one.

Once settled on the Gardens bandstand, Buddy made a place for me alongside the drum platform. Dorsey did not seem to object. Rich would adjust the hi-hat cymbals, test the snare drum with a few gentle taps of his sticks, lightly press the bass drum pedal against the batter head, checking for tone quality, shift around on his drummer's throne behind the new set Slingerland had given him, and await Tommy's first downbeat.

As an aspiring drummer, there are no words to describe the thrill of sitting behind Buddy, watching him from that vantage point. The man was perpetual motion, filling the gaps with tasteful, sometimes explosive statements, bearing down when the dynamics of a chart called for strength, easing back for contrast, always totally in control, his mind playing musical chess, anticipating what was coming in any given thirty-two-bar chorus and executing his embellishments with astounding ease, never playing the same arrangement the same way twice, wonderfully improvisational in the best tradition of a jazz musician. I sat there night after night, eyes popped, head shaking in disbelief. Drum lessons from the master.

Late in the year, the Dorsey band began yet another MGM film. This time it was to star Esther Williams. *Thrill of a Romance* was the working title, and Tommy Dorsey was nearly eliminated from this one. The news media reported Tommy's dilemma, and it was a lot more serious than, for instance, a rumor that Buddy, who was warring once again with his former employer, was leaving to join Artie Shaw's new orchestra.

Tommy had been involved in a brawl at his Sunset Plaza apartment in Hollywood. He had had people in for drinks one evening, among them actor Jon Hall, who had become famous through his role as the bare-chested Terangi in *The Hurricane.* A lot of liquor had been consumed, and Hall allegedly made a pass at Tommy's beautiful wife, MGM starlet Pat Dane. Tommy, famous for his pugnacious exploits while under the influence, wrestled Hall out onto the balcony of the apartment, got hold of a knife somehow, and sliced off the tip of Hall's nose.

He had been aided and abetted by one Allen Smiley, a so-called man-about-town who was rumored to have mob affiliations. The police as well as an ambulance were summoned. Dorsey, Smiley, and Pat Dane Dorsey were arrested on felony assault charges. Hall walked out of the Sunset Plaza apartment minus a piece of his nose. The Los Angeles newspapers had a field day. MGM immediately made plans to eliminate the Dorsey band from *Thrill of a Romance* because of Tommy's possible imminent prosecution.

Buddy could not have cared less. He was having what he later described as the very best time of his entire professional life. While the Dorsey band had been doing preliminary work on *Thrill* in mid-September, the Count Basie orchestra had opened at the Plantation Club in central L.A. Around September 20, an agent for the FBI, posing as a Basie fan, approached the Count's famous tenor saxophonist, Lester Young, and his equally renowned drummer, Jo Jones. He smiled as appreciatively as any admirer would and handed them their draft notices. Apparently Lester and Jo had not exactly been eager to get their heads shot off in the war and had until then avoided Uncle Sam's invitations. Now they were ensnared and ordered to appear at the induction center the following morning. No amount of appeals by Basie himself, the band's manager, Milt Ebbins, or budding jazz entrepreneur Norman Granz could clog the inexorable wheels of the U.S. government. Within a month Young and Jones were wearing khaki.

When the papers were served on that September night, Basie was in a terrible spot. Who could possibly fill Lester's shoes? Who could properly take over Jo's drum assignment? Buddy Tate was summoned to occupy Lester's chair, and another Buddy, Rich by name, subbed for Jo Jones.

The Dorsey band was not working at night, and Buddy eagerly made his way to the Plantation each evening for two weeks to play with Basie, who publicly called him "my son."

Tommy Dorsey, beset with problems just then, gave Buddy his blessing. Tommy adored Bill Basie. So did Artie Shaw, recently discharged from the Navy, who also sat in with the Basie boys on a few AFRS radio shows. In fact, on September 30, 1944 (coincidentally, Rich's twenty-seventh birthday), Tommy Dorsey himself participated in an AFRS show called "Jam Session" that featured Basie, Buddy, Sgt. Ziggy Elman, Illinois Jacquet, Lionel Hampton, and Artie Shaw, as well as Jack Benny and Deanna Durbin.

Basie closed at the Plantation on October 1 and headed east, leaving behind a happy throng of West Coast fans and an even happier Buddy Rich. Closing night at the Plantation, he had presented Buddy with a blank check, which the drummer promptly tore up. A few weeks later, Rich received a gold watch inscribed "To Buddy From The Count. L.A. Thanks."

Buddy finally put Lana's Patek-Phillipe in a drawer and placed the Basie gift on his wrist. He wore it with great pride.

Chapter 19

"There are three rotten bums in the world—Buddy Rich, Hitler, and you—and I've had two of them in my band!"

Tommy Dorsey to Alvin Stoller, 1945

ON THE FRONT page of the January 1945 issue of *Down Beat* was a picture showing Tommy Dorsey and Pat Dane Dorsey laughing uproariously. Judge Arthur Crum of Los Angeles Superior Court had dismissed all charges against them in what had come to be known as the "Battle of the Balcony." Jon Hall had to pay for his own plastic surgery.

All had been forgiven and forgotten by MGM. The Dorsey band had made *Thrill of a Romance,* and in one hotel lounge sequence Buddy, working with a small group out of the band, played a longish drum solo. When the film was completed the band headed east for a number of dates at the Capitol Theater in Washington (owned and operated by MGM before the government forced the big studios to divest themselves of theater chains), the Meadowbrook once again, the posh 400 Club in Manhattan, and theaters in Albany, New York, Boston, Columbus, Cleveland, and Detroit.

Down Beat chronicled the Buddy Rich—Tommy Dorsey war during the first half of 1945.

TD Losing Two—Rich, De Franco

New York—Featured drummer Buddy Rich is pulling out to build his own orchestra. . . . Rich, who has been wavering in his decision to front an ork, had made up his mind to take the plunge, and is waiting only for his contract to run out on May 29th before taking up a baton. [The rest of the article has to do with clarinetist Buddy De Franco's leave-taking.]

Down Beat, March 1

Los Angeles—The Dorsey band arrived here for the June 1st opening [at Casino Gardens] virtually intact. Buddy Rich who was, as usual, reported to have left the band, was on deck at the tubs and seemingly happy. [The operative word, here, is "seemingly."]

Down Beat, June 1

TD and Buddy in Another Spat

Los Angeles—Tommy Dorsey and his star drummer-man, Buddy Rich, are at it again. Fly in the soup between the two, who never have exactly been in love, is Buddy's recording activities outside the TD band.

Rich recorded four sides waxed recently with the Herbie Haymer quintet for Eddie Laguna, who operates the Sunset label here. Tommy and his attorneys have threatened court action against Laguna if the sides are released, TD contending that he holds a contract with Buddy forbidding him to play or record with any other musical unit.

Laguna says he intends to issue the records anyway. By this time, the Rich contract may have expired, no one knowing just how long the agreement was for, anyway.

Down Beat, July 15

That Tommy had it in for Rich was no secret to anyone, and the Herbie Haymer sides were a perfect example of how selective Dorsey's wrath could be. Haymer, a fine jazz tenor sax player, had put together an outstanding clutch of guys for this session. On piano, Nat Cole was listed as "Eddie Laguna" because of his exclusive affiliation with Capitol records. Buddy was billed as "Buddy Poor," and trumpeter Charlie Shavers's listing read "Joe Schmaltz." The latter was now entrenched in the Dorsey trumpet section, but Dorsey took no action against him.

Buddy was the prime target of Tommy's ire. He was "worse than ever" since he had returned to civilian life, according to Dorsey. Of course, the bandleader meant that phrase to describe the personal side of Buddy Rich. Musically, he was better than ever. Despite his protestations about ill-treatment by Tommy and his ongoing harangue against the string section, he played marvelously well with the band during the spring and early summer of 1945. Critics and fans recognized this, citing his work as "more mature."

He was evolving, no question about it. His approach to playing drums had always been one of searching, probing, improving. More than ever, he was testing himself, playing "without a net." The results were dazzling, and he knew it. Now the Dorsey band seemed to him the musical equivalent of an older, used car: still serviceable, but out of vogue. He wanted to go fast, in an up-to-date "car," and he knew the only way to do it was to form his own band.

He met a girl. He had not been seriously involved with anyone since the Turner affair had gone bust. Her name was Jean Sutherlin, and she was uncommonly pretty. ("Life's too short to date ugly women," Buddy once informed me.) He was introduced to her by Pat Dane Dorsey. He thought he was in love with her. On July 16, 1945, they were married. It was a short-lived union, lasting only a few months.

Once again, in an August 1 headline in the *Beat,* we were informed BUDDY STILL WITH TOMMY, with Dorsey stating that Rich's contract didn't run out until July 1946. Tommy was still doing his love-hate thing: loving Rich's playing and hating him and the thought of losing him. Where could he find a suitable replacement for Buddy Rich? Impossible!

He kept trying to woo Buddy in his peculiar fashion, to make him believe he was firmly dedicated to the jazz idiom where his band was concerned. In addition to the electrifying trumpet of Charlie Shavers, he added veteran tenor saxist Vido Musso to the band. Musso, who had played the memorable solo on Benny Goodman's classic record "Sing, Sing, Sing," was regarded as one of the foremost players of jazz.

But when the band returned to the 400 Club in New York, the relationship was strained to the breaking point. Buddy showed up at night and did his usual superb work, but his gut churned every moment he spent behind his drums with the Dorsey ensemble.

He began to figuratively thumb his nose at his boss. On September 5, he walked into Columbia Records' recording studios in New York, greeted a famous bandleader whose drummer was ailing, sat down behind a borrowed set of drums, and recorded "Your Father's Mustache" with Woody Herman's Herd. (Take that, Tommy!)

On October 12 he showed up once again at Columbia, this time to lead a combo called "Buddy Rich and His V-Disc Speed Demons" featuring the independent and unafraid Charlie Shavers, Lou McGarity on trombone, Peanuts Hucko on clarinet, Al Sears on tenor sax, Buddy Weed at the piano, Remo Palmieri's guitar, and former Glenn Miller man Trigger Alpert on bass. Vocals were handled by the matchless Ella Fitzgerald, who shared responsibility for the group on her vocal sides, which were billed as "Ella Fitzgerald and Her V-Disc Boys." Buddy loved it. (Sue me, Tommy!)

By late October Dorsey had finally had enough. Contract or no, he decided he would not get an ulcer over the Buddy Rich situation. Buddy walked away from the band, claiming illness as the reason for press purposes and saying he would return, if only for a limited period of time.

Alvin Stoller, who had been playing with the Charlie Spivak orchestra, was paged to replace Rich. Stoller not only bore a startling resemblance to Buddy, he was visibly cast in Buddy's mold as a drummer. He possessed flawless technique and a keen sense of dynamics, and he kept good time. Tommy soon discovered another trait he had in common with his former star drummer; Stoller was as much an iconoclast as Buddy had been. In Dorsey's own words: "I lost one pain in the ass, and found an even bigger one when Stoller joined my band." And he once ranted at Stoller: "There are three rotten bums in the world—Buddy Rich, Hitler, and you—and I've had two of them in my band!"

Buddy took a deep breath, and the air smelled sweet. He was free! Finally! He kept his income alive by making a few records in the early part of December. The "Lester Young–Buddy Rich Trio" boasted pianist Nat Cole, this time bearing the unlikely pseudonym of "Aye, Guy." These sides were made for Clef Records in Los Angeles. Shortly thereafter Buddy flew to New York and got an emergency call from Benny Goodman.

Benny had always been his personal god. Outside of having played with Goodman on the 1941 Metronome All-Star record, he had never appeared on wax with the King of Swing. "I'm in a spot," Benny informed Buddy. "Davey Tough [Goodman's drummer of the moment—he was hell on drummers] is sick. Could you come in and do a record session with me?"

Buddy raced over to Columbia recording studios for the third time that year. To my ear, his playing on Goodman's "Rattle and Roll" is among his finest performances: tight, constrained, literally perfect. Ironically, Benny thanked him off-handedly and walked away. Buddy was never paid for that date. He called Benny about it a few times, then gave up.

A further irony: Benny came in to see me at Marty's, a night club in New York. The year was 1981. We sat and talked for quite a while. I mentioned how much I admired Buddy's playing on "Rattle and Roll." Benny got huffy. "Naw, naw. I didn't like that *kid's* playing. The only real drummer I ever had was Gene. Gene! He was the best!" While I was happy to hear Goodman praise the object of his once-frequent annoyance and envy, Gene Krupa, I was surprised and disturbed that he didn't hear what I, and the rest of the Rich admirers, heard on that recording.

As the end of 1945 approached, Buddy gathered together some of the best musicians in the business and herded them into one of the rehearsal halls at the famed Nola studios. He had been working on funding a band of his own. The money needed for arrangements, uniforms, rehearsal studios, and music stands came from as unlikely a source as one could imagine.

Frank Sinatra had decided to back Buddy Rich's new band.

Chapter 20

"Just because I'm paranoid doesn't mean he's not out to get me."
Mickey Rich, referring to Buddy, 1946

DESPITE THEIR CLASHES during the Dorsey days together, irrespective of their chronic bickering over their billing and/or status, and in defiance of the constant one-upmanship they had practiced on each other, Frank Sinatra was as much a great admirer of Buddy's drumming talents as any goggle-eyed fan standing in front of the bandstand watching Rich's superhuman pyrotechnics. When Buddy approached him tentatively about backing his own orchestra, Frank immediately agreed; never gave it a second thought. Well, perhaps one second thought: thumbing his nose at Tommy Dorsey.

When he had left the Dorsey fold, there had been strong rumors that the parting was not at all amicable. Dorsey had insisted on retaining a large chunk of Frank and his future earnings. Frank felt he had given his all to the trombone player while he had been in his employ. Enough was enough. He should be a free agent, allowed to pursue his solo career unfettered by indenture to Dorsey. But Tommy was a businessman as much as a bandleader. He stubbornly held onto a piece of Sinatra.

Frank decided to back Buddy with an initial twenty-five thousand dollars for two reasons: it was a good investment, and it represented a little "payback" to Dorsey for Sinatra's own problems with his former boss.

The band rehearsed every day for two weeks before opening at the Terrace Room in Newark, New Jersey, for a month, beginning Christmas night 1945. A string of theater dates early in the New Year would lead to an extended run at the Hollywood Palladium in the middle of March. For the first time, the "Where the bands are playing" section of *Down Beat* listed the Buddy Rich orchestra, opening at the New Jersey night spot. As much as he protested that he didn't read *any* of the music magazines, he admitted to me that he looked at that listing more than once, with pride.

While Newark was not exactly the garden spot of the Garden State, the Terrace Room was owned by Frank Dailey. Buddy now began thinking like the bandleader he had just become. Dailey's Meadowbrook was one of the class A major venues in the east. If the band did well at the Newark club, then maybe . . .

The band did do well. The reviews were more than encouraging. Rich had chosen his men wisely, and things began to coalesce almost immediately. Dottie Reid, a pert Helen O'Connell look-alike and a good singer who had formerly held the vocal spot with Benny Goodman, was hired. Buddy, at Sinatra's urging, began to do what he loved doing almost as much as drumming: sing.

He kept away from the ballads, vocalizing on the rhythmic tunes, "Aren't You Glad You're You" and "Baby, Baby All the Time" among them. Arrangers Eddie Finckel and Neal Hefti were contributing to the band's early library, as was bepop-influenced Tadd Dameron.

Now that the war was over, a new era in music had begun. Charlie "Yardbird" Parker and Dizzy Gillespie had created a firestorm with their convoluted, multinoted perambulations. While Stan Kenton and Boyd Raeburn had brought something decidedly different to the big band scene, Parker and Gillespie were the first truly original creators of a new departure from what had generically become known as "swing" music.

Bebop, as well as the new progressive jazz, had captured the minds, imagination, and ears of a large segment of the jazz-loving public. If the mercurial flights of Bird's horn or the rapid-fire complex clusters emanating from the angled bell of Dizzy's specially made trumpet were incomprehensible to the average listener, who cared?

In their thirst for something different, a great many jazz fans embraced the new music with breathless enthusiasm. Buddy, who never looked back during his musical life, whose motto was "straight ahead," was willing to bow to the new wave up to a point. He still clung to his roots, simplistically exemplified in Duke Ellington's old edict: "It don't mean a thing if it ain't got that swing." In particular, Rich was critical of the current crop of drummers who, in his opinion, were hamstrung in the bebop bag and did not swing.

He did like Max Roach's work, but in general he had no use for the kind of player who was "all arms and no technique." Four beats to the bar on the bass drum was still his idea of keeping time. "Bop" drummers generally ignored the bass drum, except to drop occasional, erratic "bombs" by way of accent or punctuation. Buddy also felt that most bebop drummers were too "busy" behind soloists. Their constant tapping away at the snare drum behind a trumpet or alto sax solo was disruptive, as far as Rich was concerned.

Some critics felt his criticism was hypocritical. He had, after all, been the target for just such swipes by music writers when he had played with Shaw and Dorsey. He was forever being damned in print during that period for throwing in "annoying rim shots" while backing a soloist.

"It's not the same thing," he countered when this was pointed out to him. "I never got in the way. Never. The hell with critics."

"Yes, but here you are, saying the same sort of thing about other drummers. You are, in effect, being a critic, aren't you?"

"Hey, man. I'm Buddy Rich." This always accompanied by a devilish grin.

His arrangers were staying up all night, thinking up clever titles for their original instrumental offerings. Eddie Finckel in particular turned in several charts with titles that were an obvious play on Buddy's name, among them "From Rags to Riches," "Poor Little Rich Bud," and "Rich-ual Dance."

The library was growing nicely. The band made its way, via several one-nighters, to the West Coast and a Palladium six-week stand beginning on March 19. There had been personnel changes in the short three-month existence of the Buddy Rich orchestra. The drummer-bandleader was a tough taskmaster. Like a good squad leader in the army he never asked anyone to do anything he wouldn't do himself. In terms of a squad of musicians, this meant giving 110 percent every minute they were on the bandstand. Not everyone was as dedicated or professional as Buddy, and the axe often fell, not only during his first venture as a leader but throughout his career fronting a band.

Buddy's brother, Mickey, joined the band at the Palladium on tenor saxophone. This was a mixed blessing. Buddy loved having his kid brother, handsome, quiet Mickey Rich, share the stand with him, but he realized he could not show favoritism. He was as tough on Mickey as he was on the rest of his employees.

Mickey had a personality diametrically opposed to Buddy's. He was sweet, friendly, almost diffident. A voracious reader, he kept to himself, although he was appreciated and respected by the band members. He had learned his instruments well and played with authority and confidence, a good, working saxophonist, if not a great soloist. He deferred to Buddy's position as leader. Sometimes it was painful for him. He felt that Buddy too often singled him out for unnecessary criticism. He laughingly told me on one occasion: "Just because I'm paranoid doesn't mean he's not out to get me."

Buddy was increasingly encouraged to sing with the band, not only by his own musicians ("Hey, B! I like the way you sing 'Baby, All the Time.'" "Sucking up to me will get you nowhere!") but by his fans, who commented on his gentle but hip reading of the lyrics to "The Frim Fram Sauce," "It's About Time," and "Surprise Party." Luckily, trumpet player Bitsy Mullins was a passable timekeeper, and when Buddy sang, Bitsy would slip out of his chair and slide behind Rich's drums.

Mullins left the band soon after the Palladium closing on April 28, and the Rich opening at the Panther Room of the Hotel Sherman in Chicago found a young man named Stanley Kay perched behind Buddy's set as a full-time alternate drummer. Later on, he became Buddy's personal manager. Currently, Buddy was being managed by his brother-in-law, retired hoofer Carl Ritchie.

The "bop" incursion grew almost daily. Tadd Dameron turned in an orchestration of Dizzy Gillespie's classic "Cool Breeze." "A killer!" Buddy cheered, and the band played it blazingly. In September the band recorded Johnny Mandel's romping arrangement of "Oop Bop Sh'Bam." Red Rodney, a close friend of Charlie Parker and one of bopdom's chief protagonists, joined Buddy's band briefly and played some memorable trumpet on this Mercury recording.

As usual, Buddy wore several jazz hats. Not content merely to perform with his own band, he appeared during 1946 at a Jazz at the Philharmonic concert at the Embassy in Los Angeles, backing Charlie Parker himself, along with Willie Smith, Coleman Hawkins, Buck Clayton, and Lester Young. In New York, while the band played the Aquarium, Buddy moonlighted on a recording with Billy Kyle's Big Eight in the company of jazz stalwarts Trummy Young and Buster Bailey.

And there were the *Metronome* All-Stars. By now the great drummer was almost jaded where the winning of jazz polls was concerned. He came in first with monotonous regularity. This time, instead of a big band of poll winners, it was a combo of Charlie Shavers, Lawrence Brown, Johnny Hodges, Harry Carney, and the ubiquitous Nat Cole on piano. Vocals were handled by Nat, June Christy, and Buddy's backer, Frank Sinatra.

At the end of 1946 Buddy Rich took stock of his situation. Musically he was happy. The band was tight, swinging, and respected by fans and critics alike. There was plenty of work, and the future looked good, even though singers were beginning to usurp the place of big bands in the public consciousness. By and large, everything seemed to be "straight ahead."

The trouble was—Buddy Rich wasn't making any money.

◙   *Chapter* **21**

> *"When it comes to my playing, I take no prisoners."*
> Buddy Rich to Mel Tormé, February 1949

DESPITE FINANCIAL AID from Frank Sinatra, who reportedly sank a second twenty-five thousand dollars into Buddy's band, the costs of transportation, several uniform changes, and arranging and copying were eating up what profits there were. Far from living the good life, Rich was beset by money problems. His single appearance with Jazz at the Philharmonic prompted promoter/producer Norman Granz to make him an offer he couldn't refuse. He disbanded and joined Jazz at the Philharmonic early in 1947.

Once again he found himself in heady musical company. Buck Clayton, Willie Smith, Flip Phillips, and Trummy Young were among the many fine players on this first, brief tour. Norman Granz, a former film editor, was viewed by many as a dilettante in the world of jazz. He also had an undeniably keen eye and ear for great players and singers, particularly those who had not received the recognition due them. Ella Fitzgerald and Oscar Peterson are two examples of jazz greats who might have remained "cult" artists had not Granz taken them under his managerial wing and guided them into becoming huge commercial successes.

Buddy enjoyed this first minitour but clashed with Granz over some diametrically opposed outlooks on the subject of music. In February he left JATP and went back to New York to reorganize his band. "I was a glutton for punishment, I guess," he admitted. "Having a band was a problem, for several reasons. First, of course, was the money end. It was tough. But also, the goddam beboppers. The minute you got a few in the band, they'd want to throw out all the charts except for the bebop ones. The other guys in the band were always fighting with the beboppers."

Despite these problems, Buddy realized the only way he would ever be free to play what he wanted, when he wanted, was at the front of his own organization. Even so, he was advised by his agents to lace his book with danceable arrangements. Thus when the new band, with an almost totally fresh roster, opened at the Arcadia ballroom in New York in early April of 1947, *Down Beat* reported it to have a "ballad-heavy book."

Buddy's reply to this observation was so uncharacteristic that it sounded as if it came out of someone else's mouth: "I certainly did learn my lessons with my last band. Long before we folded I realized I couldn't make a go of playing the way I felt like playing. But I was stubborn and wouldn't change. Now I'm sticking to melodic music playing at low volume. . . . We intend to feature standards."

This edition of the Buddy Rich orchestra *was* a dance band. It was also, unquestionably, a jazz band. To captain a group of fine musicians and play nothing more than tame stuff would have gone totally against Buddy Rich's grain. The perception of him by his fans as the ultimate jazz drummer was too strong, too important to ignore. Nightly, in addition to the ballads and the "danceable" selections, he and the band would cut loose with some of the Ed Finckel offerings. Allen Eager, one of the youngbloods of the new wave of tenor saxophonists, would stand and deliver, and the cats would roar. Buddy, uncaged from the prison of mediocre music he had been advised to play, would come on strong, giving his admirers what they came to see and hear. These jeweled intervals were pure disclaimers to the *Down Beat* remarks the drummer had allegedly made.

But the "standards," the dance orchestrations, kept coming, regardless of his attempts to show the world his prowess as a pure jazz artist. As badly as he wanted to "concertize," he simply was not at that time in an important enough position to have total freedom.

Rich had made a new drum deal that surprised many people. He had always had a personal aversion to William F. Ludwig, Jr. On many occasions in my presence he had spoken disparagingly about the young heir apparent to the Ludwig dynasty of drum makers. Bill, Jr., was well aware of Buddy's feelings about him, but he swallowed his pride. Now that Buddy was a leader, Ludwig knew how important his name would be to the company. He also recognized Rich's genius and promised to capitalize on it in the print media.

From Buddy's standpoint it was a good deal, especially because Gene Krupa was still the reigning star at Slingerland. A Slingerland executive told him: "As long as Gene is with the company, you'll always be one down."

When Bill Ludwig, Jr., offered Buddy an undisclosed sum of money as a bonus for joining up, as well as a promise of unlimited drums and accessories, Rich, who had been a Slingerland user for nearly a decade, signed. A WFL ad in the May 7, 1947, issue of *Down Beat* exhibits a photo of Buddy standing with a WFL snare drum cradled under his left arm. The copy reads BUDDY RICH—TOP STAR OF THE DRUM WORLD PLAYS W.F.L DRUMS.

Despite his willingness to conform to the dance band mode, Buddy remained plagued with money problems. In late September Rich and his boys found themselves stranded in Spokane, Washington, unable to muster the funds needed to transport them to Ione, Oregon, for their next one-nighter. Buddy appealed to his agents at MCA to forward some of the money being held by the agency, deposits that had come in for future dates.

MCA refused, saying that Buddy owed the agency seven hundred dollars. Buddy, in a murderous mood, missed the Oregon date. He went to the musicians' union and filed a complaint against MCA. The union ruled the agency had no right to withhold monies taken in from promoters for subsequent dates. It was a Pyrrhic victory for the drummer and a loss for the agency. Rich broke his contract with them and moved to the William Morris agency.

As far as "career moves" were concerned, the band seemed to be marching in place. As the calendar modulated into 1948, the aimlessness of the endless one-night stands was apparent and discouraging. One bright prospect was an upcoming two-week run at New York's Paramount. Buddy decided to go into the theater loaded for bear, with every musical gun he could summon. Bad luck in the form of an unexpected injury nearly turned the coveted Paramount date into a disaster. For any other drummer in the world it *would* have been just that: an impossible undertaking. But we're talking Buddy Rich here.

Mickey Rich, one of the few holdovers from the original band, remembers what happened. "The band was on tour in the midwest. Buddy and I would spend our free time at a local YMCA, trying to stay in some kind of decent physical condition, jogging or swimming or some such. . . . On this particular occasion we decided to play handball, and when we played, it was always for real. To win. I hit a particularly good shot in the corner, and when Buddy raced over to try to recover it he tripped over my outstretched leg and went sprawling." The result of that fall was a compound fracture of his left arm. "There was no way he was going to cancel the next six weeks of bookings while his broken arm healed, especially since two of those weeks were at the Paramount.

The April 7 issue of *Down Beat* reviewed Buddy at the Apollo in Harlem prior to the Paramount opening. The somewhat understated headline read ONE ARMED RICH FACILE AS USUAL. By all reports, he absolutely fractured the crowds uptown, singing, dancing in tandem with his old friend Steve Condos, and finally soloing on drums in a right-handed, right-footed version of "Not So Quiet, Please." The tough Apollo audiences cheered right into the accompanying movie. Jocular Jo Jones, one of Buddy's favorite drummers and friends, remarked, after seeing this unbelievable display at the Apollo: "If his left arm heals, somebody ought to break it again."

The fact that Buddy Rich and his orchestra played the Apollo at all is testimony to the fact that he was held in great respect and esteem by the black community. The Rich band was one of the very few "ofay" outfits to play the famed Harlem theater. ("Ofay was pig Latin for "foe," a word commonly used in those days by black people to describe white people—it caught on and was used by many music magazines to identify white bands.)

Buddy's crew was also welcome at the Howard in Washington, D.C., and the famed Regal at Forty-seventh and South Parkway in Chicago. Both of these landmarks were strictly "colored" houses, exclusively playing the likes of Lunceford, Ellington, Basie, and assorted black combos and solo artists. Buddy Rich was an exception to their rule. In the case of the Regal, I know that fact firsthand. My grandfather owned a clothing store directly across the street from that theater. In all the times I visited him at the store, I never once saw a white band billed at the Regal.

Buddy returned to play the Apollo again that year and several more times in his long career. One incident at that theater is perfect proof of his popularity in Harlem. On May 9, 1976, he told me that story again, with the same proud grin he wore the first time he recounted it.

It's one of the great stories of my life. They had just delivered a new Cadillac—this had to be in '48. For a couple of years I had driven nothing but sports cars, as you know. [Buddy and I had bought twin MG-TCs in 1947, and had been photographed in them at Frank Dailey's Meadowbrook on a rainy November evening. That picture appears on the back cover of our album, "Together Again for the First Time." A succession of sports cars followed this purchase for both of us through the years.]

I was appearing at the Apollo theater on 125th Street in New York. My band was only the second white band to ever appear at the Apollo. The other band was Charlie Barnet. The Apollo audience was a totally black one. Even though it was only 110 blocks from downtown New York, it was another world. The black audience's appreciation was so much greater than the cats who went to the Paramount theater, it wasn't funny.

Anyway, after the first show at the Apollo, I was told, "Hey, they just brought your new car over. It's out in front of the theater." I went out and looked it over—it was gorgeous—it had everything, radio and, you know, whatever was hip in those days. I went back inside for the next show, I guess it was the third show in the evening, and when I came back out [he laughs], the car was totally dismantled. I mean, they took the radio out, the wheels off, everything. It was just left standing there like that. It looked like it had just been through one of Rommel's invasions of North Africa. I remember the cat who was the stage manager backstage. He was six-foot-eight. He was a black Kojak. He had a totally bald head, and he was mean.

I went back to see him, and I said, "Man, somebody's ruined my car—stripped it clean. Come and look at it." He went out and looked at it—this was around seven in the evening. He put his arm around me, man, I almost sunk into the concrete, and he said, "Don't worry about it. It'll be straight." And I moaned, "Man, I haven't even driven the car. It's just been delivered." "Don't worry about it," he says again. "Don't worry about it? Man, that thing just cost me three thousand dollars."

Anyway, I came out after the last show. That car was put back together. It was polished when they had delivered it earlier. It was *Simonized* in the three hours since I reported the theft. What happened was, some of the cats did not know that the car belonged to Buddy Rich. When they found out it was my car, the car was put back in perfect shape—better, really, than when it was first delivered that day.

I can remember going up to Harlem after that, to the Savoy or the old Renaissance ballroom or Dickie Wells's club, and I could leave a thousand dollars on the seat of the car, I could leave my wardrobe in the car, my drums, and the word would get around, "That's B's car," and everything was safe. That was one of the greatest feelings, because I was accepted in Harlem, and to me that was the greatest acceptance of my career.

I have never had, to this day, a single disagreeable word with any black person, musician or otherwise. I readily accepted their lifestyle. It was beautiful. They were able to live the way they lived, and they were always happy for some reason or other.

Like, when you say hello to a white cat, it's always "How do you do?" or "Hello." When you meet a black cat it's "What's goin' on, my man?" There was always that letting down the facade, one on one, and I found that to be really marvelous. Two guys could walk up to each other and have a whole conversation in merely ten words. "What's goin' on?" "Nothin', my man. Things are, like, a drag." "Well, pick up on you later." I loved the informality of the black people.

Not only did the patois of the black community make its way into Buddy's everyday speech patterns, his pronunciation of certain words were a clear indication of how influenced he was by his friends and admirers up in Harlem. One of his favorite phrases was "It's a killer!" "Killer" came out "killuh." When he used the exclamation "In there!" it sounded like "In theh!" Definitely not Brooklynese.

And in Brooklyn, tragedy brought the Rich family to its knees with the passing of Buddy's mother. Bess Rich was fifty-nine when she died in the Rich home on Ocean Avenue. She had been a quiet woman all her life. Her early fights with Robert over the attention he was lavishing upon their talented offspring were behind them. The gap had closed, and they had lived together harmoniously for many years before she expired.

Buddy took her passing hard. In some strange, precocious way, he had known, way back, that he was the cause of friction between his mother and father. In recent years Buddy and Bess had been close, even loving. He was grateful for the upcoming bookings that would help keep him occupied and ease the pain.

His arm healed. He took the band west and played the Palladium. They sounded great, but it wasn't happening for Buddy. Good reviews, good reaction from the public. Good, not great. And it wasn't happening. He crossed over into the new year riddled with uncertainty.

Down Beat, January 14, 1949:
BUDDY GIVES BOOT TO HIS BOPPERS

Paving the way with a series of minor flare-ups, Buddy Rich finally cleaned house and put his entire band on notice. Explaining that a certain element was taking the style of the Rich music into its own hands, his firings backfired when it came time to board a bus to play at the Marine hospital on Staten Island. Not a single band member showed. Buddy, anticipating this, had contacted Count Basie and Oscar Pettiford to work with him [at the hospital] as a trio.

The "boppers" had made their position clear. Buddy countered with his own statement. "I like 'bop' as well as does any musician, but there are other things I want to play. These fellows want to play 'bop' and nothing else. In fact, I doubt if they *can* play anything else."

A large bramble in Buddy's side was a talking-to he got from Benny Goodman, who scolded: "What's the matter with you Buddy? You're letting these fellows run your band. Instead of their playing for you, you're playing for them."

The April 15, 1940, issue of *Down Beat* carried a picture of drummer Ray McKinley seated behind a pair of black pearl 12" by 24" Slingerland bass drums.

In the May 1 issue there is a Slingerland ad, again showing Ray behind his "Boogie Woogie" twin bass drums. Could this have been the inspiration for Louie Bellson's innovative double bass drum set-up years later? And could Buddy have seen this advertisement, storing the idea in the back of his mind for his own experiment with double bass drums?

In February of 1949 we played the Paramount together. I was excited for several reasons. I had just gotten married and was on my honeymoon. It was my third outing at the Paramount. And . . . it was Buddy's and my very first time on the stage together. We opened on a Monday. My bride and I had taken a train from Chicago right after our marriage ceremony in order to rehearse on Sunday afternoon with Buddy's newly reorganized band.

We checked into the Astor, and I crossed the street and entered the stage door of the Paramount. When I got off the elevator on the top floor backstage, the band was already setting up. I noticed some extra bass drum cases as I walked up to say hello to the maestro. "What's with all the bass drums?" I asked "B" by way of greeting. He growled, "Fucking Louie Bellson better learn to play *one* bass drum before he tries two!"

I knew he did not mean to disparage Bellson, one of the sweetest human beings in the music business and a close friend of Buddy's. Rich was merely exercising his prerogative as the world's greatest drummer to comment on the fact that, if *anyone* was going to play twin bass drums, the right was his as the feudal lord of percussion.

When we opened the next morning, a number of my fan clubs had lined the first few rows of seats on the main floor of the theater. "Mel's Belles" and "Mel's Angels" were two of the club names displayed on blouses, shirts, and T-shirts worn by these nice kids. Buddy looked down from the stage at my fans and smirked. He knew what was coming.

Just prior to my entrance onstage, Buddy uncorked an arrangement of "Old Man River." It was played at breakneck tempo, salted with several drum breaks, delivered with Rich's usual flair. In the middle of the chart, Buddy made his way down to center stage. Awaiting him down front were two bass drums and a stool. Nothing else. No snare drum, tom-toms, cymbals. Two bass drums.

He sat down on that stool and played the damndest drum solo I ever heard. With his feet. When he finished that solo, the house erupted into one of the longest ovations I have ever heard. Everybody in the theater, my loyal fans included, went crazy. My entrance announcement was barely noticed. It took me a good ten minutes to make any sort of impression on that crowd. ("Hey, look. There's Mel Tormé on the stage now." Hmmmm? Oh, yeah.")

"Thanks a lot, pal," I said to him in mock anger after the first show.

He shrugged and countered with "Hey, man, you know me. When it comes to playing, I take no prisoners."

During the rest of the engagement, we were both uneasy. The vicissitudes of the band business were getting to Buddy. He was less friendly than he had ever been before. We actually had a couple of go-rounds, unusual between us. I think he resented the fact that all those young kids out front were there principally to see "the Velvet Fog," a silly nickname that had been pinned on me by a disc jockey. I, on the other hand, resented the fact that I would never, ever, play drums within light years of this one-of-a-kind mucisian.

Another thing that was bothering the normally fun-loving Rich was the eroding status of his band. They had come to the Paramount directly from the Showboat Club in Milwaukee. Mickey Rich, whom I had taken to immediately (as had everyone else who knew him), confided to me that Buddy had had a tough time meeting the payroll and that the future of the Buddy Rich band was up for grabs.

In the face of the riotous reaction to his performance on the Paramount stage, I found it hard to believe that Buddy wasn't booked steady for the rest of the century. I was wrong.

On the cover of the April 22, 1949, *Down Beat,* just two months after we closed the Paramount, a headline announced BUDDY RICH QUITS AGAIN. Buddy blamed expenses as the main reason for throwing in the towel. He said he would seek bookings as a single—singing, dancing and drumming. Asked if he would organize a combo, he said an emphatic no. He admitted he did not like bebop and felt a small swing group could not be sold.

Once again the greatest big band drummer in the world had been forced to break up his sixteen-piece juggernaut. The second edition of the Buddy Rich orchestra was history.

Chapter *22*

"He cried like a baby."
Les Brown, 1949

IF HIS CAREER as a big band leader was currently up for grabs, Buddy Rich's personal life was thriving. Since the breakup of his brief marriage to Jean Sutherlin, he had dated a variety of young women without having had any strong attachments. When Buddy's band played the Palladium, his sister Marge had introduced him to one of her friends, Betty Jo O'Curran. As Marge Rich Ritchie explains:

> Betty Jo was married to dance director Charlie O'Curran. Betty Jo and Millie Castle [wife of choreographer Nick Castle] and I were very, very close friends. I invited Betty Jo to Buddy's opening at the Palladium. That's how she and Buddy met.
> She was a lovely girl, very quiet. Buddy took to her instantly, and when she and Charlie split up, Buddy and Betty Jo began to live together. As you know, Buddy was never a "chaser." He really cared for this girl and wanted to marry her. She was the one who didn't want to get married. Buddy needed stability, marriage. "Something of my own" was the way he put it.

Nevertheless, the Betty Jo O'Curran–Buddy Rich romance lasted for several years. If there was one major factor that finally brought about a parting of the ways, it was probably Buddy's nomadic existence. After the breakup of the second band, he was more itinerant than he had ever been before. While brother Mickey had had enough of the road life, opting for a career as a producer/writer, Buddy, unshackled from the responsibilities of being a bandleader, went off in all directions.

From early March until late June of 1949, he became a regular on an early

NBC-TV show called "The Eddie Condon Floor Show," hosted by the famed guitarist himself. Once again Buddy's versatility was on full display. The guests on that show ranged from Count Basie and Roy Eldridge to Dixieland players like Wild Bill Davison and Condon himself. Rich easily switched styles with a simple twist of his talented wrists.

Eager to kick a big band again, he signed a thirteen-week contract with Les Brown. Buddy and Brown got along very well. A headline in the July 29, 1949, issue of *Down Beat* proclaims LES IS THE GREATEST—RICH. In contrast to the squabbles and hassles that were prevalent in the Dorsey band as well as Buddy's own organization, the Les Brown band ran smooth as glass, thanks to its affable leader. Les not only found Buddy charming, funny, and friendly; he had never before, and rarely since, had his arrangements played with such finesse or spirit.

In early September the Brown band was involved in a series of shows in Hollywood for the U.S. Marine Corps. The dates frosted Buddy, who still bore mental scars of his term in the Corps. It is interesting to note that Rich cut out of the Les Brown band right after the last of these shows.

Brown recalled Buddy's last day with his band:

> It was Labor Day. We were playing some beach ballroom outside of San Francisco. The guys in the band told me and Buddy, "Hey, we have an intermission around midnight, right before we play the last set. Come backstage upstairs to the band room." I go up. The guys in the band, unbeknownst to me, had bought a cake. They brought it in to Buddy, and it had icing that said "Nice having you with us, Buddy." He cried like a baby.

"B" made his way back to New York, where Norman Granz was waiting with a new offer for Rich to appear with Jazz at the Philharmonic. Buddy signed but kept all his options open. In addition to his dates with JATP, he moved around town like a whippet, recording with such diverse groups as the Eddie Condon All-Stars, the Lester Young Quartet, the Charlie Parker Quartet (Buddy disliked bebop but recognized and admired Parker's genius), the Bud Powell Trio, the Ray Brown Trio, and a pair of one-shot versions of his own pickup orchestra.

In early May of 1950 he held forth at New York's Birdland with a band that included Allen Eager on tenor and Louis Oles on trumpet. In late May he appeared as a single on the popular "Broadway Open House" variety show on NBC-TV, hosted alternately by Jerry Lester, Morey Amsterdam, and Jack E. Leonard, three of the most popular comedians of the day.

Near the end of the month, he put together a scaled-down version of the Buddy Rich orchestra and once again invaded Harlem's Apollo. Harry Edison graced the trumpet section of this edition, and Buddy, who adored "Sweets" Edison personally and professionally, did a lot of beaming on the Apollo stage whenever Harry took a solo.

"Restless Rich" once again abandoned the idea of a big band and chose to rejoin JATP, this time at the forefront of a trio that included Hank Jones on piano and world-class bassist Ray Brown. He more or less stuck with JATP until the end of 1950.

In one of the strangest alliances of his career, Rich organized a band and toured with American expatriate Josephine Baker. Miss Baker had been the rage of Paris for years, having chosen to make her career on the other side of the Atlantic rather than in her native United States. She had been the toast of France during the '20s and '30s, starring at the famed Folies Bergere as well as the Casino de Paris. After World War II she had helped fund a home for war orphans in France and had received France's highest tribute, the Medal of Honor.

When her professional star dimmed somewhat in her adopted country, she decided to see whether her vast European fame had spread to America. Her manager sought out Buddy and asked him to form a special touring band to accompany Miss Baker. Buddy knew there was great anticipation on the part of the music business and the general public with regard to her American debut. He assembled a band that included "Sweets" Edison and the redoubtable Zoot Sims on tenor sax.

Josephine Baker needn't have worried about her reception in the United States. She was a smash, feted everywhere she appeared, and having Buddy Rich along was icing on a very sweet cake. When the curtain went up at the Apollo in Harlem and she stepped onto the stage, the crowd's roar nearly burst the walls. Buddy, of course, was a welcome "regular" at the Apollo by now, and once again the patrons cheered him boisterously.

When the tour ended in July, the band was so tight Buddy couldn't resist an offer to take it into Birdland in Manhattan. That was a banner week at the popular Broadway jazz club.

Rich was making money and spending money. He bought cars, tired of them, and traded them the way some kids trade baseball cards. To say his wardrobe was expensive and extensive would be a gross understatement. He loved giving presents to people he liked, and he did so with reckless abandon. His sisters and brother Mickey became concerned about his finances, with particular emphasis on possible tax problems in the future. Pop Rich was also worried. He lectured his talented son to no avail.

Robert Rich himself had never been particularly frugal during his own performing days. He wasn't a spendthrift, but he did believe in using money for what he felt it was intended for: living the good life. Buddy had learned well from his father. The drummer's spending habits didn't change.

Next up for Rich was a new venture: an all-star quartet. "The Big Four" contained tenor saxist Charlie Ventura, Marty Napoleon on piano, Woody Herman's former dynamo, Chubby Jackson, on bass, and Buddy on drums. The group lasted from early August of 1951 until November, when they all went their separate ways. Rich took a deep breath, gigged around New York, and plotted.

Early 1952 found him once again getting serious about leading a big band. He gathered up several of his old sidemen, added vocalist Jean Weeks, and lured Allen Eager out of the Fifty-second Street clubs, and all of a sudden a new Buddy Rich orchestra was a *fait accompli*. True, he had dabbled a bit in recent months with big bands, but these assemblages were purely fly-by-night, never intended for longevity.

Now here he was again, jumping into the pool feet first, ready and actually eager to hold his breath and hope to stay afloat. It was a good band, if not particularly original or impressive. Buddy took it touring into Canada after a shot at the Paramount backing Frank Sinatra. When the summer faded away, so did band number three.

That old standby, Jazz at the Philharmonic, was ready and waiting. In addition to jazz legends like Lester Young, Roy Eldridge, Benny Carter, and Ray Brown, Norman Granz had secured Gene Krupa for this tour. Ever the showman, Granz masterminded something called the Great Drum Battle between Gene and Buddy. Many fans and critics thought this an unfair contest.

Gene, onetime undisputed King of the Drums, sounded dated on these occasions, falling into set patterns with which he felt comfortable. His favorite ploy was to begin a run of triplets on the snare drum, cutting them into short bursts, and then, with these brief exclamations as prologue, he would launch into a long string of accented hand-to-hand triplets, eventually moving from snare drum to small tom-tom, a routine he had repeatedly done with Benny Goodman and his own band in the 1930s and '40s.

Buddy, at the height of his powers, had to hold back in these so-called battles, otherwise the "war" would have been blatantly one-sided. Gene almost certainly knew this. When we all appeared on a Canadian TV show together early in the 1970s, Gene watched Buddy play his featured solo, turned to me, and said: "God, he's amazing. Guy's the greatest drummer that ever drew breath."

I tried to suggest tactfully that Gene himself was a drumming genius, taking a backseat to nobody. Gene looked at me with those wise eyes of his, smiled, and said: "You don't have to stroke me, Mel. We've been friends too long for that.

Let's not kid ourselves, there is one—only one—Buddy Rich. God broke the mold."

A Carnegie Hall version of JATP took place on October 11, 1952. The Rich-Krupa drum battle was recorded and can be heard on an original Verve records release and several reissues. Rich's obvious deference to Krupa's contribution to the entire jazz experience, his influence on a whole generation of young drummers, and his downright sweetness of nature is apparent on this long-play record. Everyone connected with that tour knew that, had Buddy chosen to exercise his prerogative as the sole genius of the drum, the Krupa-Rich pairing would have been "no contest."

Gene, Buddy, and the JATP troupe headed for California soon after the Carnegie Hall date. On the evening they were to play the Long Beach Auditorium, something happened that changed Buddy Rich's life—for the better.

◨ *Chapter* **23**

> *"Marie, don't marry him!"*
> Gene Krupa to
> Marie Allison, 1952

WHEN BUDDY RICH pulled up in front of La Rue's restaurant on the Sunset Strip in Hollywood, he had no idea he was about to meet the young woman to whom he would be married for the rest of his life.

He had promised Gene Krupa he would collect him at the restaurant and drive him out to Long Beach for the evening's performance. Gene was waiting out in front. So was his dinner companion, a stunning blond who made Buddy's heart skip the moment he saw her. As she got into the car, Buddy couldn't help but notice that she bore more than a passing resemblance to Lana Turner.

She was an honest-to-God blond, blue-eyed, full-lipped, with even, white teeth and a fine, pert nose barely turned up at the tip. Her figure was nothing short of spectacular. Even though she was seated in back, Buddy could tell she possessed a fine upper frame and beautiful legs. He was smitten immediately.

Marie Allison had been a showgirl and a dancer on the stage and in films. She had been Gene Krupa's inamorata for several years. Gene had promised her again and again that he was going to break with his wife, Ethel, and make an honest woman out of her. He had not been able to keep that promise, and until that night at La Rue's Marie hadn't seen or talked with Gene in over two years. "Gene had called me and said he would like to have dinner with me. I was engaged to Hal March." Marie laughed, looked at me, and said, "I guess you never knew that, Mel. You were married to Candy [Toxton]. Funny how things work out." (Candy and I divorced in 1955, and she married Hal March shortly thereafter.) Marie continued:

Gene had told Buddy all about me, his California girlfriend. Against my better judgment, I decided to accept his dinner invitation. Hal himself advised me to. He wanted to set the date, and he had to make sure Krupa was completely out of my system. I was ready to get married. I wasn't doing anything with my career. I didn't have that dog-eat-dog thing you have to have out here to be an actress. Plus I didn't think I was very talented.

I was a contract player at MGM when I met you. I was working on *The Pirate* with Garland and Gene Kelly. [She laughed again.] "You and I actually had a date. We went to a movie together. [I had forgotten that date; I must be slipping, I thought. How do you forget having gone out with a beauty like Marie?]

Anyway, I met Gene for dinner, and he said, "By the way, Buddy Rich is picking us up and driving us out to Long Beach Auditorium." I remember Gene calling me, telling me he had screamed at MCA [his agents]: "Don't you ever book my band after the Buddy Rich band. He was here a couple of days ago, and he drummed everybody out of the place."

Then Gene said to me, "Well, I've been touring with him across the country, and he's really a nice kid, totally different from the way I thought he was."

So Buddy pulled up in front of La Rue's in his Cadillac convertible. He had his valet in the front seat with him. I got in the car and looked at him. He had this crew cut, and he looked like a college kid. I was so surprised.

As we drove out to Long Beach, every time I would look up, he was staring at me in the mirror. Why is he doing that? I wondered. I was getting very uncomfortable. When we got to the parking lot of the auditorium, I got out on Buddy's side. He helped me out of the car. I had to step over a canvas bag that had been in the backseat, and that was the first time I got an insight as to what he was all about. He screamed at his valet: "Why didn't you put that bag in the trunk? You made Marie uncomfortable," and so on. I assured him it was all right.

Buddy and his valet walked on ahead of us. Gene and I strolled toward the auditorium, and I asked him: "Tell me, which one of you is the better drummer?" Gene drew himself up rather stiffly and said: "Well, suppose I let you be the judge of that." I thought Whoops! What have I said? 'Cause I'd never seen Buddy Rich.

I saw Gene go on first. He had the hair flying, and he had the lights and, you know, all the tricks. Then Buddy came on, and all the time I'm standing in the wings watching Buddy, Roy Eldridge, who was part of Gene's group, was standing there with me. "See? There's no comparison," he said in my ear, trying to convince me of something I knew was wrong, because I could see that Buddy outdrummed Gene. It was ridiculous.

By the time I got up to the dressing room, Gene had already started on the scotch. Obviously he cared about what I thought about him. It was the first time I had seen Buddy work. The minute I came through the dressing room door, he turned on me and said, "Well?"

I lied. I mean, there was just no comparison, you know? After the concert we all went back to the Roosevelt hotel, where all the musicians were staying. I got out on Buddy's side again. His little valet kept Gene busy on the other side until Buddy could go around on that side and talk to Gene. Then the valet came over to me and said: "Buddy would like to have your telephone number." I said, "Oh, no. No, no, no. I don't go out with married men anymore."

"Buddy's not married," he said, and I said, "That's not what I heard."

He had been living with Betty Jo for six or seven years, but, as you know, they weren't married. Gene had told me that Buddy *was* married.

The valet then asked Marie if she had any girlfriends, since Buddy had not been out to the coast for a while and had lost track of former female acquaintances. Marie smiled at the valet and said: "I have a million girlfriends." Then the valet said: "Well, then. Can I have your number so Buddy can call you and get the number of one of your girlfriends?"

Pretty transparent ploy, which Marie saw right through, since it was now obvious to her that Buddy really wanted a date with her.

I gave him my telephone number, and Buddy called me bright and early the next day. He said, "Well, who do you know that would like to go out with me?" I mentioned a beautiful brunette I knew but told him I had to call her first to see if it was all right to give him her number. And then in this little tiny voice he said: "Won't you please have dinner with me?" I said, "No. I don't want to date married men. I've already been stung by Krupa. Besides, I don't think it would be very nice, because you two are touring together."

Buddy explained to Marie that he had broken with Betty Jo O'Curran several weeks before, that his belongings from the apartment they had shared were in storage, and that he was unencumbered by any relationship whatsoever with a woman.

"Tell you what," Marie said finally. "I'll call Gene and ask him what he thinks. I owe him that much."

When I called Gene, he said: "Go out with him. You'll like him." Well, I got real mad because he didn't care about me enough to say "No! Don't go out with him." Just before we hung up he said, very quietly, "Marie, don't marry him!"

Buddy and Marie had dinner that night at Tail o' the Cock, a popular restaurant on La Cienega Boulevard. She drank martinis with dinner, and Buddy, who was close to being a teetotaler, kept pace with his own string of martinis.

I didn't know he didn't drink. He got really smashed and didn't eat much. Neither did I, because we seemed to have so much to talk about. Later I had to drive his Cadillac; he simply couldn't. We went over to the Little Club on Canon to hear Kitty White. Well, we talked and talked, and he had a few more drinks. When we left the club, I drove his Cadillac up to my house, and we sat and talked some more. He kissed me goodnight and then reached for one of my boobs. I pulled his hand away, and he thought I was a real nice girl. Then and there he asked me to marry him. I looked at him and said: "Buddy, you're drunk. You don't know what you're talking about. Don't do this." He said: "I know everything about you. I've heard about you from Gene for thousands of miles. I know everything that I need to know about you. Will you please marry me?"

I said: "No! You're drunk!" Of course, my heart was racing. Nothing like this had ever happened to me before. I went in. I don't know how long he sat outside my house until he was sober enough to drive himself home.

He called and woke me up the next morning. He said: "I'm sober now. Will you marry me?"

Marie insisted they get to know each other before making any momentous decisions about marriage, children, or the future. She called Hal March and broke their engagement. Marie and Buddy began to date. Incessantly. When he returned from Hawaii after doing several JATP concerts there, he and Marie were a "couple."

Buddy flew back to New York, and Marie closed her apartment, gathered her belongings, and flew to Manhattan to marry Buddy.

I got a glimpse of what that temper was like the minute I got off the plane. I had taken so much hand luggage on the plane that the gentleman who sat next to me offered to help me with some of it. Buddy was standing there by the gate as everybody's getting off the plane. He sees this guy talking to me, coming down the steps. When we got to Buddy—well, I didn't introduce this man 'cause I didn't know his name. I didn't talk to him on the entire flight except when he offered to help me after we landed. He handed me my makeup case and my hatbox. Buddy threw a fit. He fought with me all the way into Manhattan.

I thought, my God, there's something wrong with this guy. I had never seen a temper like that.

Well, from then on, the fights just continued. We kept putting off getting married. Everybody back in California, including my mother, who lived in Sacramento, thought we *were* married. My trunks arrived from L.A. We were staying in a suite at the Warwick Hotel on 54th Street. I hung my clothes in the closet. I waited. We still marked time.

Buddy had found a new "home" in the Big Town: the Bandbox. In early 1953 he led, co-led, or merely played in a variety of small groups at that New York club. The Buddy Rich–Flip Phillips Trio, the (Chubby) Jackson–(Bill) Harris Herd, and the Buddy Rich Quartet appeared there during January through late March.

Buddy's quartet, with Don Elliott on vibes and mellophone, Curly Russell on bass, and Hank Jones at the piano, opened at the Bandbox opposite Harry James and his orchestra on February 27. On several evenings Harry sat in with the Rich group. Buddy returned the compliment by taking over the drums in the James band on occasion. Harry would look at Buddy playing with his band and think to himself: how ironic.

When Harry James left Benny Goodman to form his own band in 1939, he had one drummer and one drummer alone in mind: Buddy Rich. He had seen Buddy with Joe Marsala as well as Bunny Berigan's orchestra and, being a passable drummer himself, recognized Rich's great talent. He had made one mistake, however. He had raved to Artie Shaw about this kid named Rich. By the time Harry was ready to make Buddy an offer, he was employed in the Shaw rhythm section. Now here he was, fourteen years later, sitting behind the drums at the Bandbox, kicking the bejesus out of the current James crew.

Harry couldn't let this opportunity go by. He offered Buddy fifteen hundred a week, unheard of money for a sideman at the time, to join his band. Rich accepted, since one of the perks was a hefty advance on his future salary. He had had his eye on a rakish XK-120 Jaguar convertible. The moment the James deal was put to bed, he raced over to the dealer's showroom and drove the little sports car away.

He shipped his and Marie's clothes out to the West Coast, where he would be joining the James band on Easter Sunday. Then Buddy and Marie got into the Jag and headed for California. "Clear across the country," Marie recalls ruefully.

> He never put the top up. Never! We pulled into a glass-fronted restaurant in Oklahoma City and sat in a front booth so we could keep an eye on the car. All of a sudden there's a crack of thunder and lightning, and it came down in buckets! He went tearing out to the car and tried to get the top up. He hadn't checked it out in New York. The frame was bent. He got it halfway up, no more. We had to literally bail the water out of the car, just like a sinking boat.

By the time they reached Nevada, with the sun beating down on Marie's blond tresses, she was just this side of delirious. "I said to Buddy: 'Won't you please put the top up? I think I'm gonna faint!' P.S.—He never put the top up."

They reached Los Angeles and checked into the Beverly Hills Hotel. "We fought almost constantly. What were the fights about? Who knows? The men that I had dated in the past catered to me. I was used to being babied, you know? Buddy treated me like he treated everybody else. He was abrupt, difficult, temperamental. I had a knack for always opening my mouth and saying the wrong thing. He was extremely macho."

Why did she continue with Buddy?

"I've given it a great deal of thought lately," she said soon after Buddy died in 1987.

> Sometimes you're attracted to things you've never experienced before, be they good or bad. I had never known anyone that temperamental. But when he let all the barriers down, he was hysterically loving. Naive, wonderful, funny. That was the person I loved.
>
> He didn't have any money when we met. I knew that. I had even been warned in a phone call from Gene [Krupa]. He said: "Be very careful. Don't you know he's in debt? That he owes everybody in town?" I couldn't have cared less. Despite everything, I really loved him.

The first engagement with the James band at the Hollywood Palladium lasted from Easter Sunday through April 22. The first one-nighter Buddy played with the band took place in Yuma, Arizona, on April 24. Earlier in the day, something else occurred.

After six months of loving, fighting, trauma, indecision, and at times near-breakup, Buddy and Marie walked into an Arizona justice of the peace's office and were married.

Bess and Robert Rich, as
"Rich and Reynard," during
their vaudeville days, circa
1916.

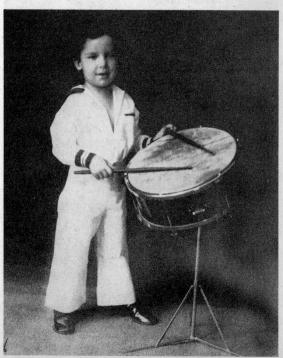

"Traps, the Drum Wonder,"
at twenty-two months.

Eight-year-old "Traps" in 1925. The Buster Brown haircut and sailor suit remained his "look" until 1929.

Publicity still from 1929 Vitaphone short, *Buddy Traps in Sound Effects.*

The "Drum Set That Never Was." The Slingerland Drum Co. signed Buddy as an endorser, then threw this cluttered set together, replete with Olde English bass-drum monogram, in order to get Rich to pose for an advertisement. Buddy never used this set. He pronounced the set-up unplayable.

ABOVE: Buddy's first steady gig as a jazz drummer, with Joe Marsala at the Hickory House in New York City, December 1937. *Left to right:* Artie Shapiro on bass; Louis Prima on trumpet; unidentified clarinetist; and Rich at the drums. Note absence of hi-hat cymbals, since Marsala's group was primarily a Dixieland outfit.

ABOVE: Artie Shaw plays, Lana Turner dances, and Buddy Rich grins. Could he possibly have known that, in the near future, he would be involved in a love affair with the beauteous Lana? *Courtesy of the Academy of Motion Picture Arts and Sciences.*

BOTTOM LEFT: A smiling Artie Shaw greets his adoring fans at the Strand Theater, New York City, 1939. The nicknames of his sidemen can be seen on their music stands. Georgie Auld, *left,* was known as "Killer"; John Best, trumpet, *back row,* was called "Colonel"; guitarist Al Avola answered to "Mouthpiece." Buddy is seen at the rear, his bass drum bearing a nondescript logo that soon disappeared.

RIGHT: Buddy and Ziggy Elman. Their numerous collaborations, particularly on "Hawaiian War Chant" and "Swing High," were highlights of the 1940–43 Tommy Dorsey Band (trombonist to Rich's right is George Arus). *Photo by Hugh Morton.*

LEFT: Buddy's dream! A brand new Lincoln Continental, delivered in front of New York's Astor Hotel, 1940. Frank Sinatra takes it easy in right rear seat. RIGHT: Buddy, in the rear cockpit of the Waco bi-plane belonging to famed L.A. disc jockey "Jack the Bellboy." During his third flight an oil line broke, and Rich abandoned plans to become a private pilot.

LEFT: Buddy and Eleanor Powell filming their electrifying duet in *Ship Ahoy*. Ziggy Elman sits behind Rich's drums, enjoying the action. *Courtesy of the Academy of Motion Picture Arts and Sciences.* RIGHT: How Rich inveigled Sinatra to pose in front of this billboard is one of those mysteries that will go echoing down the corridors of time!

A reconciled pair of Dorsey alumni, Buddy Rich and Frank Sinatra, discuss Frank's offer to back Rich's first band. 1946.

TOP RIGHT: The author and Buddy in their brand new 1947 MG-TC's on a rainy winter night at the Meadowbrook in New Jersey. BOTTOM RIGHT: A proud Buddy looks on as younger brother Mickey plays a solo during the tenure of Rich's second band. 1949.

Top Left: "Look Ma! No hands!" Rich's landmark double-bass-drum gambit at the New York Paramount. February 1949. Below Left: The second band, with an eight-brass complement. Later bands were shy of the fourth trombone. Above: Marie Allison with future husband Buddy enjoying dinner with Mr. and Mrs. Harry James (Betty Grable) and their daughters. 1952. *Courtesy of Bill Mark.*

Buddy, in a "Kata" stance. Karate was one of his great passions.

Rich was not fond of be-bop or be-boppers. Dizzy Gillespie was an exception. Buddy loved him and his playing. *Courtesy of John Titsworth.*

"One Night Stand," a Canadian TV special, hosted by the author, starring a multitude of great musicians including Gerry Mulligan, *right rear;* Buddy Rich, *left;* Gene Krupa, *center;* Mel Tormé, *right.* Lionel Hampton, on a fourth set of drums, is unpictured at far right of Rich.

Close friend and fan Johnny Carson convulses Rich with a joke.

A colorfully dressed Cathy Rich huddles with her doting dad.

Buddy Rich, circa 1980.

TOP RIGHT: The Rich siblings: Buddy, Marge, Mickey, and Jo in the 1980s.
BOTTOM RIGHT: A white-haired Rich behind his vintage set of Slingerlands at
New York's Blue Note. Mid-1980s.

ABOVE: Near the end. Buddy looks reflective and somewhat weary. BELOW: The Rich brood (*left to right*): grandson Nicky, Cathy, Grandpa, and Marie Rich.

Chapter 24

*"Without a doubt, the greatest drummer
who has ever lived."*

Dan Morgenstern,
Newport, 1965

MARIE RICH LAUGHED her husky, infectious laugh, remembering the how and why of her marriage to Buddy.

> The band closed the Palladium. They were about to go on the road. He wanted to leave the Jag with me, get on the Harry James band bus, and go touring. "But we were supposed to get married. Everybody out here thinks we *are* married. My mother thinks we are. You can't just dump me here and go off with Harry's band."
>
> "But, Marie, marriage isn't such a good idea, do you think? We don't get along very well. We . . ."
>
> "Well, you take your Jag and go. I live here. Everybody out here knows me. I can't take this anymore."
>
> So there he is, loading his things into the Jag, and I'm standing with my heart in my knees. We had been fighting. A lot. But I loved him, and I really thought he loved me. Finally he looked at me, grinned, and said, "Get in." I guess I had forced the issue. He would accuse me of that through the years, whenever we fought. "You forced this marriage," he'd say.

Marie laughed her tickling laugh again. "Anyway, that's how we went to Yuma and got married."

The marriage ceremony might have gone off without a hitch, had it not been for the minister. He had a broad English accent. Harry James, who acted as best man, began to giggle the moment the minister started reading the marriage vows. Buddy, an inveterate giggler, joined in. Harry's manager, little Pee Wee Monte, admonished them at first then fell prey to their contagious laughter. Marie was furious. "Why are you guys trying to louse up my wedding?" she yelled at them. They couldn't stop laughing. The minister cleared his throat and carried on, unperturbed.

Buddy's membership in the Harry James orchestra was on-again-off-again over the next several years. Certainly while he appeared as the featured member of the James band, he was never strictured by the kind of exclusivity Tommy Dorsey had demanded of him. To go through Buddy's discography is to discover that time and again he recorded with various combinations of jazz musicians, as well as playing occasional outings with JATP.

In August 1953 Norman Granz adroitly brought together Count Basie, Oscar Peterson, and Wardell Gray and Stan Getz, two of jazzdom's greatest tenor saxists, with Buddy on drums. These were memorable recordings, as was a "live" session with James's band for Columbia Records during a return engagement at the Palladium in December of that year. Buddy's tiptoe stickwork on "Palladium Party" and his alternate challenges with Harry on an updated version of one of James's original charts from his very first band, "Flash," are among the most highly regarded of all Buddy's work on record.

Buddy liked Harry enormously, but occasionally he would carp to me about Harry's desire to please him musically. "He knows how much I love Sweets's [Harry Edison's] playing," he would say derisively. "So you listen. He tries to copy Sweets. He'll play the same phrases, the same licks Harry plays. He'll do that 'fall-off' thing Sweets does. It makes me laugh. There's only one Sweets. And there's only one Harry James. Why the hell doesn't he just be himself?"

"Well," I argued. "You can't fault the man for trying to make you happy. Seems to me he's catering to you, trying to . . ."

"No, man. That's not the way. Harry James is an original. He shouldn't try playing like anyone else. It's wrong."

One thing Buddy Rich did prize was originality. He felt that too many—far too many—jazz musicians were vastly derivative. He understood "eclectic," being influenced by various artists and incorporating those influences into your own performances. But imitating another player—that's where he drew the line.

I kidded him. "Really? How about the bass drum and cymbal break you played on the Artie Shaw record of 'At Sundown'?" I illustrated with my mouth. "Boom-ching-ching-boom-chi-ching-boom-ching-ching-boom-ching. Right out of Krupa's repertoire, Kong. Heard him play it with Benny a hundred times before you came along." He balled his hands into fists and beat them against his chest. "One of these days, Tormé. . . . Anyway," he grinned, "I was young and impressionable at that time." He tossed his head in a grand gesture. "What did I know? If I copied a Krupa break, it was unintentional."

"Sure."

"I'm warning you, Melvin . . ."

His point was well taken all the same. James did seem to ape Harry Edison on a number of occasions. It *was* a nice gesture on his part. He loved keeping Buddy, his fifteen-hundred-dollar-a-week drummer, content and invigorated. He seemed willing to relinquish his own, famous brand of trumpet playing in order to simulate the Edison style just to please "Traps." He even had several arrangements written in the Basie tradition because of Rich's admiration of that leader and his band.

Given Harry James's vibrato, which remained almost identical to the one he had displayed with Goodman back in the thirties, and Harry's musical approach to the horn—a style that had been favorably compared to Louis Armstrong's on many occasions—his cloning of the Edison brand of jazz seemed out of place and awkward at times. Buddy's friendship with the trumpet-playing leader overcame his disdain for what he called James's "selling out."

On May 11, 1954, a little more than a year after Buddy and Marie were married, she gave birth to a baby girl. They named her Cathy. Buddy was wild with happiness. When he saw her for the first time, he whooped and cried: "Jesus! She looks like I spit her out of my mouth." A crude observation, perhaps, but right on the money. Baby Cathy did bear an incredible resemblance to her daddy. All of Buddy's most attractive physical attributes were evident in this lovely little girl. As she grew, she began to look like a young Jane Fonda, as well as a feminine version of her illustrious father.

Rich toured with the James band all through the summer and fall of 1954, even though he made several detours to record and perform with Lionel Hampton, Dizzy Gillespie, Harry Edison, Buddy De Franco, Roy Eldridge (who by now had obviously changed his mind about Rich vs. Krupa) and, rather interestingly, to play one week in Australia with Ella Fitzgerald and his old boss, Artie Shaw.

All this activity made him noodgy, and in the late autumn of that year he left James (for the first of many times over the next ten years or so) and joined, of all people, Tommy Dorsey, who had put together a band with his sometime sparring partner, brother Jimmy. The TD-JD combination was good, if undistinguished. Buddy looked around one day and said to himself: I've done this already. What am I doing here? What he was doing was collecting a hefty salary from the brothers Dorsey, but the money itself wasn't enough for him.

He split and once again joined JATP, where the air was more rarified and the jazz more spontaneous. In April of 1955 he talked Norman Granz (or was it the other way around?) into letting him make a vocal album for Granz's record label, Norgran. He had always loved singing, and the reaction to this album later encouraged him to accept an engagement at Larry Potter's supper club in the San Fernando Valley, in May of 1957.

It was fun, but it wasn't drumming, even though he did a number on drums in his "single" act. He could not command nearly the amount of money as a singer that he could make behind a set of drums, and "B" was a money player. Later that month, he flew back to New York with Marie and the baby, formed a dandy little sextet, and opened at Café Society Downtown, a club that had hosted jazz greats for over three decades.

"Gigging" occupied most of that year. Rich made what are now considered historic records with Lionel Hampton and blind genius Art Tatum. Most trios sound incomplete without a bassist. This one did not. In addition to the huge talents being displayed on these discs, the absence of a bass player is compensated for by the tuning of Buddy's bass drum. He detested bass drums that went "thud" or "plop," the sound most uniformly achieved by some of the foremost bop drummers.

"A bass drum is supposed to be resonant," he would lecture. "It's there for timekeeping, sure, but it should also blend with the band and the bass player." Rich's "blending" bass drum took up the slack on these fine Tatum-Hampton-Rich milestones.

In sharp contrast to this venture, Buddy appeared, late in 1955, in a Universal short called "Melodies By Martin," which featured the music of Freddy Martin and his orchestra. (Freddy Martin?!!!!) Buddy was finding married life with child somewhat more expensive than his previous single life. He set about picking up all the extra change he could, and that meant working in many varied musical situations.

In one of his periodic I-don't-want-to-be-a-drummer-anymore moods, he informed the world he was through beating the skins and would henceforth take up the role of balladeer. Nick Castle was slated to prepare his act, and he would open at a Vegas showroom at a reported figure of four thousand dollars per week. While that dream never materialized, he did diversify by appearing on a GE Theater presentation titled "From the Top," which also starred comic Jack Carter, in a serious acting role, and Broadway star Lisa Kirk. Buddy played a combination agent/drummer and pulled it off with his usual aplomb.

Rich's gift of gab and his quick wit had been instrumental in his being paged for an NBC-TV show that aired from New York. Starring dancers Marge and Gower Champion, the show ran through the summer of 1957. Buddy had several featured spots as well as large chunks of dialogue. It whetted his appetite once more for a career away from his set of drums.

Far from deserting the drums, though, he plunked himself back into the Harry James rhythm section. Reluctant as he claimed he was to play drums, he knew the timing was not quite right for his intended solo vocal career. One of these days . . .

For the next few years Rich marked time. He made some superb records with a wide variety of jazz musicians and show-biz personalities, but his career path seemed to be a treadmill. Some of the combinations with which he worked were:

Buddy Rich and the Howard Gibeling Orchestra
The Gene Krupa–Buddy Rich All-Stars
The Lester Young–Harry Edison All-Stars
The Buddy Rich–Buddy Bregman Orchestra
Buddy Rich with the NBC Orchestra
Buddy Rich with the NBC Impromptu Ensemble
The Buddy Rich–Harold Mooney Orchestra
The Buddy Rich Quintet vs. the Max Roach Quintet

This last was a Mercury LP recorded on April 7 and 8, 1959, in Manhattan. Both drummers had assembled some good players, and the jazz content on this record was first-class. The main attraction, obviously, was the head-to-head confrontation between swing's greatest drummer and the indisputable king of bebop drummers.

Roach's stylized playing had greatly influenced a whole new generation of young percussionists, some of whom had pronounced Buddy "old hat." Many were to change their minds after listening to this meeting. The "battle," no doubt inspired by the successful Rich-Krupa mêlée, was actually a far more diverse and interesting pairing, exhibiting the great contrast between Buddy's almost incomprehensible control and technique and Max's modern new combinations of bass drum "bombs," exclamatory interventions on the snare drum, and constantly ringing top-cymbal playing. Both drummers fared well, although Whitney Balliett in praise of Rich wrote: "There has been no contest: A sundial doesn't chance with a clock."

Rich's first serious health problem occurred in December 1959. He had been experiencing a disturbing pain in his left arm. Usually he minimized his aches and pains. Active as he was, he sloughed these off as normal occupational irritants, although he had gone into a New York hospital the previous July to have a kidney stone "crushed." This time, the persistence of the pain caused him to see Dr. Francis W. Fitzhugh, Jr., while he was appearing in Atlanta, Georgia.

Part of the doctor's report to an insurance company in Topeka, Kansas (Buddy was apparently applying for life insurance at the time), reads:

This 42 year old jazz drummer has . . . in the past 5–6 months . . . noted easy fatigue, nervousness and irritability. Because of his lack of energy, he has resorted to the use of an occasional Dekamyl spansule. . . . For approximately 48 hours he had noted an intermittent, dull pressure-type pain in the substernal region. Within a few days after its onset, he noted radiation of this aching into his hand, particularly the ring finger. During the night prior to admission, he was awakened approximately 4–5 times by this chest pain. It was associated with slight nausea and cold sweating. . . .

While the report praises Buddy's general physical condition, it ends: He was hospitalized at St. Joseph's Hospital [in Atlanta] on December 10, 1959, with the diagnosis of 'impending myocardial infarction.'"

Clearly Rich was headed for heart trouble. The moment he felt better and was discharged from St. Joseph's, he treated the episode the way one treats a visit to the dentist: you're in pain; the dentist alleviates the pain; you're out the door and on your way, the pain forgotten. Buddy minimized the doctor's report. Get back to the band, back to the road, back behind his drums. That's all the doctoring I need, he reckoned. The future would prove him wrong.

Marie and his family were worried about him. He was, like so many musicians and singers, a junk-food eater. He exerted himself unreasonably night after night. The Atlanta episode was a warning to be taken seriously. Buddy did not.

In early 1960 he once again experienced chest pains and sought out Dr. Arnold Treitman. The doctor promptly admitted Buddy to the Bone and Joint Hospital in New York City for a prolonged rest and prescribed anticoagulation medicine.

Several weeks later he was out of the hospital. The doctors had thrown a healthy scare into him. Play drums and you could die. This time he took it to heart. He had his agents book him into the Living Room, a small East Side club. He forsook the drums entirely and worked as a standup singer. This engagement has been reported as having taken place in October of 1959. Marie Rich remembers it as being in the early spring of 1960.

He asked me to come hear him. It was a pleasant evening of music. Afterward we strolled west on Fifty-second toward the jazz clubs. We walked in silence for a while. Finally he asked: "Well, what did you think?" I looked at him and replied: "Let me put it this way. I'm not your favorite drummer, and you're not my favorite singer." He nodded, understanding.

I continued. "Look, you sing damned well. You know that. Whether or not your singing is strong enough or good enough to make the kind of money you're used to is debatable. Maybe. Maybe not. Who knows? With a little luck . . ."

He shook his head dejectedly. "Naw. I like to sing, but singing isn't my thing."

It was late at night. Swing Street was nearly deserted. We heard music coming from one of the clubs, I forget which. We drifted in. The long, narrow little room was nearly empty. Allen Eager was playing a set onstage. Max Roach sat behind the drums. Buddy and I sat down at a table. He was despondent. Where was his life going?

Allen spotted Buddy. He announced to the few people in the place that the "world's greatest drummer" was among them. It seemed to me he said it with a touch of sarcasm, but I might have been wrong. He started to goad Buddy to "come up and sit in.".

Buddy shook his head and waved him off. Allen kept at it. The few customers there applauded. Max Roach gripped his sticks in his right hand and beckoned Buddy with them. Rich looked at me. Grimly. What could I say? What *should* I say? I was as worried about my friend's health as he was. I could tell he wanted to get up there behind Roach's drums.

Right or wrong, I said: "Go on, champ. Show 'em how it's done." That's all he needed. He mounted the tiny bandstand, accepted the sticks from Roach, and lowered himself onto the drummer's throne. Eager was in a naughty mood that night. He counted off "I Found a New Baby" faster than mortal man had ever played it before. The tempo was hopeless, but he had forgotten one thing: Buddy Rich was no mere mortal when it came to playing drums. I watched and worried as Buddy, playing four-to-the-bar on the bass drum, proceeded to fasten the little group together.

Then an astonishing thing happened. The club began to fill up. How the denizens of the night found out that Buddy was playing is something I will never figure out. Within three or four minutes of his having commenced "Baby," that club was full to overflowing! Allen Eager, caught up in this phenomenon (he had never, ever drawn half as many people into the place before), kept egging Rich on.

"Yeah! Yeah! Come on, B. Solo! Solo!"

And Buddy soloed. When he was finished nine minutes later, it was pure bedlam. Neither Bobby Thomson's famous home run for the New York Giants nor the Super Bowl champs nor the most frenetic rock stars ever received a greater tribute than Buddy Rich received that night from a near-hysterical crowd.

It was two in the morning when we walked back out into the cold, wet night. Buddy pulled his coat collar tighter around his throat, and we headed toward his apartment. I purposely kept quiet. When he finally spoke, there were no surprises.

"Fuck singing," he said. "I'm a drummer."

He was in such demand that the work came in hot and heavy. He put together several combinations of bands and played everything from the Steel Pier in Atlantic City to Birdland and the Café Bohemia in New York City, as well as appearances on TV, radio, and records, with the usual broad spectrum of musicians.

Into the 1960s he went, heading a fine quintet (or sextet or septet, depending on the dollars available) that featured a brilliant young vibraphonist named Mike Manieri. Buddy had previously worked with the peerless Terry Gibbs, and he loved the sound of the vibes. (He tried at one point to play them but soon gave that idea up.)

In late 1961 he took the sextet on a Far East tour; recorded once again for Norman Granz, together with Gene Krupa and a pickup band; scaled down to a quartet and played the Thunderbird in Vegas in 1963; and partnered with Louis Bellson on a jaunt to Tokyo in January of 1965.

In July of that year, he experienced what he described as his greatest triumph.

The scene was the Newport Jazz Festival. The "happening" was a confluence of drummers: Elvin Jones, Louis Bellson, Art Blakey, and Buddy. Needless to say, Rich played the final solo in this gathering of eagles. "That was the time," he told me. "That was THE time. When those other cats were all done, I sat down behind my drums and began. I'm telling you, I did things that day I didn't even know I was capable of playing. I mean, I actually astonished myself! When I was finished, I laid the sticks down on the large tom, stood up, and walked off. I had said it all, man. Like I had never said it before." Then he added, "Or since."

Observers of that performance seemed to agree with him. The noted writer/critic Dan Morgenstern wrote:

Then came Rich. He started with a roll and kept it going throughout his long solo, using his foot to keep a driving beat. The roll swelled and swelled, like a wave in a storm. Except for an occasional cymbal foray, during which he amazingly kept the roll up, he gradually brought it down to pianissimo, then raised it to a roar. It was a phenomenal performance, breathtaking in its so very difficult simplicity, void of grandstand effects, absolutely continuous and unrelenting, and though nearly superhuman in terms of technique, very much the work of a man and not at all mechanical in its perfection.

If nothing else of value had happened at Newport, to witness Rich would have made it all worthwhile. The audience's standing ovation seemed a modest tribute . . . . , without a doubt, the greatest drummer who has ever lived.

"Yeah," he admitted. "It was a killer. But I should have done it with a big band. My own big band, dig?"

I dug. The greatest big band drummer of all time rarely forgot what motivated him more than anything else: sitting within the warming confines of his own big band. Okay, so previous attempts to keep a large group of musicians had failed financially. But how about "one more time?" In 1966 "one more time" proved to be the charm.

◙ Chapter 25

"Buddy not only doesn't drink—he can't drink."
Johnny Carson

IN ADDITION TO his appearances with JATP, Buddy had been roaming in and out of the James band once again. If he were to begin once more with a new band of his own, it was necessary to squirrel away a lot of nuts for the winter of discontent that would surely come, as it always had, when he got big-band-mania. With the exception of Harry James and few other hardy leaders who were hanging in there, 1966 was not the heyday of the big band era.

Buddy chose a good baritone saxophone player named Steve Perlow to hold down that chair as well as function as the band's manager. Oliver Nelson began scoring new arrangements for Buddy; Rich was determined that this should *really* be a new band, with fresh charts for the public's ears. In April of '66 he hit his last cymbal and played his final rim shot for Harry James, took his new brood in tow, and headed for Las Vegas, where his agents had secured for him a long-term contract at the latest of the Vegas hotels, the Aladdin.

There were problems. Despite the presence of such top-drawer players as Jay Corre on tenor, John Bunch on piano, and Sam Most on flute, the Vegas audiences did not warm to this new edition of the Buddy Rich orchestra. It must be said, in all fairness, that Las Vegas has never been a town to appreciate jazz. Harry James had done well at the Flamingo hotel lounge, but James had been an established bandleader for many years, a "name" with a string of major hit records to his credit. Genius drummer or no, Buddy still had "sideman" stigma hung around his neck like an albatross. When the Aladdin management shrugged their collective shoulders and reduced the original deal with Rich by many weeks, he gritted his teeth, put the band on hiatus (not "notice"), and headed for the more receptive embrace of Newport, Rhode Island, and the jazz festival that once again awaited him. 1965 had been THE year, THE time, THE solo of all solos. From all reports, the '66 outing was nearly its equal.

Back he went to Vegas and the problems of re-forming and maintaining his own big band. Rounding up the players once again was difficult for many reasons. Many of them regarded this latest attempt as an exercise in futility. Rich lowered his head, like the stubborn bull-headed mule he was, and forged ahead. Luckily for him, Sammy Davis, Jr., was about to make an LP for Sinatra's new recording company, Reprise. He chose Buddy's new band to back him. The result, recorded live at the Sands Hotel in Vegas, is one of Buddy's (and Sammy's) best ever. They fit each other like a pair of rhythmic gloves, and it's easy to tell they inspired one another.

"I needed that," Buddy confessed. "I was beginning to have my doubts that I could ever get my new band off the ground. That record really helped establish us. The band was hot, and it would get even hotter when we went into the Chez."

The Chez, located on Santa Monica Boulevard in Hollywood, had formerly been a bastion of "rock" known as the Action. Apparently the "action" wasn't very rewarding for the owners, who abruptly changed the name of the club and its music policy. Buddy's band was the premier attraction at the renamed night club under its new jazz umbrella.

The word got around: Buddy Rich is fronting a new band over on Santa Monica Boulevard. Run, do not walk, over to the Chez to catch it. Sounds like one of those old Universal B pictures, where suddenly hordes of enthusiastic "hep cats" descend upon a "swing" joint, clapping their hands in time with the music, making the walls bulge, wide-eyed with excitement and enthusiasm. Well, sometimes life does imitate art, because that is exactly what happened. Buddy looked around one night at the jam-packed room, salted with celebrities from the movie and music world, grinned, and said to no one in particular: "I'll be goddammed! We're a hit!"

For the first time, it looked as though *this* band would make it. Affirming Buddy's expectations were a string of TV guest shots for himself and his men on some of the top-rated shows of the time, including "The Hollywood Palace," "The Ed Sullivan Show," and most significantly "The Tonight Show," starring Buddy's number one fan, Johnny Carson.

Carson, who incessantly taps a pair of pencils drumstickwise as Doc

Severinsen's band plays its way out of the commercials, had been an amateur drummer for many years and worshiped Buddy's work. Rich's fateful appearance in the waning days of '66 on Carson's show set up a relationship between these two men that was to have a direct impact on Buddy's future, not only as bandleader but as an identifiable personality in his own right, recognizable not only to the relatively small world of the music business or his cultish fans, but to the mass public, who instantly loved the give-and-take of quips, barbs, and laughs between Buddy and Johnny. Carson, who had always liked Buddy without really knowing him very well, now became one of Rich's closest friends. He ordered his producers to book Rich on "The Tonight Show" as often as possible.

As a result of these numerous guest shots, Buddy Rich became what he had been in his childhood—a genuine star in his own right. A grateful Rich presented Carson with a complete set of drums. Johnny treasures those drums to this day. Since they spent a great deal of social time together, Carson has a fund of anecdotes about his drummer friend.

Carson recalls one day when Buddy came over to his house late in the morning.

> We had been drinking wine all day. Buddy was a lousy drinker. About seven or eight o'clock that night, we went over to a place called Sneaky Pete's. We went in, sat down, ordered something to eat. By the time the salad came, I looked over at him and—zzzzzzz! When the waiter looked at Buddy, I said, "It's all right. He's just doing some religious thing. It's an old Jewish tradition or something. He's in deep prayer." The waiter went away. Finally I called a limo to get us both home. No way I was going to drive that night. I called him [Buddy] the next day and said, "How'd you enjoy the evening?" Silence on the other end.

When Carson and Rich were neighbors in Las Vegas, they spent considerable time together. Once when Johnny was visiting Buddy at his home, he looked around and asked: "Where are your drums?"

"What drums? I don't have any drums here."

"That struck me so funny," says Carson. "He never practiced. I asked him once, 'Why don't you practice?' and he said, 'Why? What's the point?' He didn't mean that to be cocky. He just sat down and played."

Johnny proudly showed me a pocket watch given to him by Buddy. It was inscribed: From Big G to Little G. "I once asked him who he thought the world's greatest drummer was. 'Me,' he answered. No hesitation. 'Well, if the title of World's *Second* Greatest Drummer isn't taken, I think I'll claim that.' 'Right on,' Buddy said, and one night, a bit later on, he slipped this watch into my hand and said, 'I'm Big G and you're Little G.' Generous guy."

When Carson booked Buddy's band to open for him at the Sahara Hotel in Las Vegas, the house bandleader, Jack Eglash, informed Johnny that there were complaints about the length of time Buddy was doing. "Would you talk to him, Johnny? Ask him to cut down a little? Last night he did nearly forty minutes before you came on."

Johnny mentioned this to Rich, who smiled and said, "No problem." Buddy went onstage for the very next performance and played for exactly eleven minutes. "Eleven minutes!" Carson laughs. "Then he walks into the wings where I'm standing, motions to the stage, and says: 'It's all yours.' Luckily I stood in the wings every show, watching him. I was always dressed, ready to go on, and I thanked God for it that night."

Carson also remembers an emotional evening at the Chez in Hollywood when over a dozen well-known drummers were in attendance to catch the Master. "I can't begin to describe how he played that night, but I will tell you this. When he finished, I looked around, and there were actually *tears* in the eyes of several of these guys. They were positively overcome by Buddy's playing."

The famous Carson grin is in full bloom as he recounts how Buddy was all thumbs when it came to setting up a drum kit. "He didn't know how! He had never set up his own drums. Once on my show when he tried to, Ed Shaughnessy [The Tonight Show drummer] had to point out to Buddy the fact that he had attached the hi-hat cymbals incorrectly to the hi-hat stand. Ed telling Buddy he had goofed! How about that!"

Johnny also related how, when Buddy was appearing in the south of France, Carson saw drummers Shelly Manne and Bobby Rosengarden standing way off to the side of the stage. "What're you guys doing, standing over here?" he wanted to know. Shelly looked at him and said, quite seriously, "We're watching Buddy's foot."

The initial engagement at the Chez was a breakthrough for Buddy in more ways than one. Arranger Bill Reddie had contributed a piece of work to the band's library that brought about a metamorphosis in Rich's playing. Reddie, who had written special arrangements for Vegas showroom production numbers, had been commissioned by Buddy to cook up something "special" for the new band. That "something" would prove to be of paramount importance to the Buddy Rich book, and it would change the public's perception of Buddy's drumming image.

Up to that point, every Buddy Rich band had made do with the usual "straight ahead" arrangements that were endemic to every other band of the same stripe. Fast-paced originals like "Desperate Desmond" characterized the first band. Tenor saxist Al Cohn wrote a more laid-back entry called "The Goof and I" for Rich band number two. But never before had anyone come up with anything like Bill Reddie's magnum opus on Leonard Bernstein's *West Side Story*.

A true concert piece, it boasted several changes in tempo and key signature, its finely paced programming alternating between swinging segments like "Something's Coming" to a beautiful-scored "Maria" featuring solo trombone. Surprisingly, considering its length, it lacked pretension. Intricate and innovative, the drum part would have boggled the minds and talents of the most schooled of percussionists. The thing is—there is no drum part. Rich's head and heart supplied the drum part.

The moment he heard "West Side" for the first time, he realized he was faced with a challenge as well as a rare opportunity to expand his horizons. He had the band play the arrangement once—just once—and already his amazing "radar" had gone to work. Almost eerily, his retentive mind transmitted the signals to his feet and hands, and there and then he had "West Side Story" nailed!

All ten minutes and forty-five seconds of it.

While there are several passages in which Buddy solos briefly, the featured drum spot comes late in the suite. It was always riveting, even though it was different every time Rich played it. The final solo bit took on a specific form that is worth noting. Just when you think the arrangement has reached its climax, everything stops and Buddy commences a single-stroke roll. This is accomplished by addressing the snare drum, one beat at a time, with hand-to-hand single strokes of the sticks. (A standard roll is managed by alternately bouncing the sticks in a two-stroke pattern. Drum teachers call this the "daddy mammy" method: left-left-right-right—"dad-dy-mam-my.")

Buddy used to harp on rolls. "Most drummers," he would say, "never learn how to make a good, even roll. The roll is the single most important part of a drummer's bag. Everything—EVERYTHING—stems from the roll." Difficult as a good roll is to master, it is always part of every drummer's repertoire, to greater or lesser degrees, depending on the player.

But the single-stroke roll!

To achieve evenness, symmetry, shading with the single-stroke is to invite paralysis of the wrists, for the single-stroke roll is a product of wristwork, pure and simple. There is an element of "bounce" to the application, of course, but pure control of the single-stroke comes from the wrists.

Buddy would begin the final phase of "West Side"—the single-stroke roll— with swift, even, clean playing, not too fast (but faster than anyone else could play); he would accelerate along the way, going from forte to pianissimo, bringing the sticks back to the rim of the snare drum head, tapping the drum with little-cat's-feet beats. Sometimes he would leave the snare drum entirely to continue the single-stroke roll on its metal rim. Occasionally, in a move worthy of the swiftest gunfighters of the Old West, the sticks would flash, faster than the eye could follow, to the pearl-encased drummer's throne upon which he sat, and the rapid stroke of the roll could be heard—tack-tack-tack-tack-tack-tack—resounding off the wooden seat. Then he would bring the single-stroke back where it belonged, to the waiting snare drum, and lead the band into the (almost) closing passage.

The "almost" had to do with one final burst from Buddy's sticks. And what a burst! This time he would play "choo-choo train." He would begin by starting, with ultra-slow deliberation, a single-stroke roll again. Slowly, slowly, almost boringly, the roll would begin to accelerate. Faster and faster it went, until it was up to the speed of the original single-stroke he had played in the previous extended solo. Suddenly he would kick in the afterburner, and this single-stroke roll became a totally different animal—a supersonic display of precision and speed that left even the most jaded watchers and listeners gaping in disbelief. It was impossible to differentiate between the left- and right-hand movements of the sticks. They were a total blur. The result was like listening to a perfectly tuned motor, its timing honed to perfection, the plugs new and firing in smooth concurrence, every cylinder pumping up and down without a single faltering movement—the entire engine turning revs in excess of the limit, the rev counter redlining beyond the capabilities of the power plant. That was Buddy Rich's final sally on "West Side Story." When the band made its dramatic end statement with five unison exclamation points, the audiences never failed to leap to their feet to shout, hoot, and clap their hands until they stung, which is exactly what you're supposed to do in the presence of genius.

"West Side Story" transformed Buddy Rich in the collective mind of the general public into a concert artist. No drummer before had enjoyed that distinction (or has since, or probably ever will again). Happily, his work on the suite did not detract from the fact that he was still the most swinging of drummers, nor did it push him into some kind of technical rut that would diminish his reputation as a jazz icon.

Buddy was on a "high," and that euphoric condition continued until later in the year when he and the band took the stand at New York's Basin Street East. Costarring on the bill was a popular singer named Dusty Springfield. She was an English girl who had made some noise with a few "pop" singles, and that year she had considerable "marquee value." With Buddy, it was hate at first sight.

Rich was a visceral reactor. People affected him chemically—and negatively—at times. Dusty Springfield was one of those unfortunate people. The drummer's pride in his new, exciting band, the string of successes that had ranged from the Chez engagement all across the country to Basin Street East, the fact that he was on his home turf, Manhattan, and that he was being upstaged by this ballsy girl singer, all contributed to a perpetual scowl on the face of the Man. At rehearsal, right from the git-go, they clashed. With Buddy within earshot, Miss Springfield asked the management: "How long is *the drummer* going to do?" Buddy countered with a rude remark. Dusty swung at him. Wrong move, lady. Buddy nearly tagged her. Needless to say, if he hadn't pulled the punch, he might have killed her. Pandemonium! Threats by managers on both sides. Warnings about going to the union, calling the police, suing for assault, and so forth.

Things calmed down, in a manner of speaking. The show went on that night, and business was brisk. The news had spread—Rich and Springfield are battling. New Yorkers like nothing better than a show-biz feud. They flocked to Basin Street East, but all they saw was Dusty Springfield, doing her best in front of a rather surly Buddy Rich orchestra, and the Genuis himself, playing his heart out on everything from the ballads to "West Side Story," which was the number two *piéce de resistance* of each evening. The number one kicker each night was Buddy's introduction of Dusty Springfield. Johnny Carson says: "I found myself going into Basin Street night after night just to hear B announce this woman. The things he said under his breath were perfectly audible. Audible, terrible, and very funny."

When the engagement was over, Rich never looked back. What the hell! 1967 was just around the corner, and it looked bright as a newly minted half dollar.

◧ *Chapter* **26**

> *"Win, lose, or draw, everybody has to pay taxes."*
> Mel Tormé to Buddy Rich, 1962

IN MANY WAYS 1967 was a banner year for Buddy. Once again the band went into the Chez in Hollywood for an extended run. This time there was a special added attraction: thirteen-year-old Cathy Rich supplied the vocals. The light of Buddy's life had grown into a winsome teenager who surprised no one by having talent. If she wasn't exactly competition for Ella Fitzgerald, she possessed a good sense of time (naturally!) and a bubbly personality, along with a voice not unlike many of the current pop singers. She was featured on Sonny and Cher's hit tune "The Beat Goes On," and she sang it creditably. Buddy's grin spread from ear to ear every time she stepped up to the mike.

Many of the band's current instrumentals had become great favorites with the Chez clientele: "Big Swing Face," the Beatles' "Norwegian Wood," a Peter Myers romper on "Love For Sale," and Bill Holman's imaginative rework of "Bugle Call Rag."

In April the band embarked on a European tour. Cathy Rich went along for the ride and the vocals, and it was a supremely happy time for her father. Triumphs in England, Switzerland, and Italy convinced Buddy he finally had found the combination for success with a big band. Now there was truly no looking back.

As if to confirm his expectations, his agents secured for him a summer-replacement television show. Since it was to fill in the slot of Jackie Gleason's show, no one was surprised when it was called "Away We Go." The show united Buddy with another Buddy—Greco. The two Buddys were perfect foils for each other. Greco, a fine singer, was also a good jazz pianist, having once played with Benny Goodman. The show ran through the summer. When it was over, it was over. Buddy was off and running again, on the road with his band.

First, though, he cut several sides with his current recording company affiliation, Pacific Jazz. The Newport Jazz Festival that year was graced by Rich's powerhouse organization. As he had mentioned during the 1965 Newport concert: "I should really be here with my own band." 1967 saw that wish come true.

In December he made his first tour of Japan. The Japanese, wildly enthusiastic jazz fans, feted Buddy and his troupe with unprecedented respect and fervor. When he and the boys returned to Vegas to do a taped segment for the Ed Sullivan show on New Year's Eve, he was relaxed and confident about his future as a bandleader. Unfortunately, his personal life and his financial status were far from rosy.

Try as they might, Marie and Buddy continued to battle. The fights were sporadic, but when they occurred they were tempestuous. In 1957 the Riches, with three-year-old Cathy in tow, had moved down to Miami, where they stayed with Robert Rich and his second wife, Louise. Back and forth they went, from New York to L.A., and then again to Florida, where they bought a house in Sky Lake Estates in North Miama Beach.

Buddy was hard-pressed to afford a house, even an unpretentious one like the Florida bungalow. His finances were strained, to say the least. His "I-work-hard-I'll-buy-what-I-want" credo had taken its toll on whatever money he had managed to put away. On top of which, the Internal Revenue Service was pressing him for unpaid back, as well as current, taxes.

When the government levied a lien on the Florida house, the Riches had pulled up stakes once more and moved to Las Vegas, in conjunction with Buddy's rejoining the James band in early 1962. At first James allowed Buddy and Marie to lease a house that belonged to him and his wife, Betty Grable. Shortly thereafter Buddy made a down payment on a house on Sombrero Road in a lovely section of town.

The salary Harry was paying Buddy did not do much to offset the burden of unpaid taxes or the ire of the IRS. They came down on him like a plague of locusts, dogging his steps, threatening him, trying to get him to meet his tax obligations. One evening when I was playing Vegas we had dinner together, and he filled me in on his tax problem. I had never seen him so distressed. He still wasn't feeling fit, and the IRS wasn't doing much to help his condition, physically or mentally. I knew it was dangerous to discuss this with him.

I tested the waters gingerly by saying, in a superquiet tone: "B, win, lose, or draw, everybody has to pay taxes. After all . . ." He became livid with anger.

He threw down his knife and fork and growled: "Why? Who the hell says so? Just because they order people to pay up—is that fair? You know how hard I work. I shouldn't have to come up with most of my bread to pay the government. Those . . ."

He launched into a diatribe that had other dinner patrons turning their heads in our direction. Marie kept perfectly still, not saying a word. She had been down this road before and had learned to keep quiet.

Aside from the hounding he was experiencing at the hands of the IRS, life went on. Professionally he could not have been happier. Having gotten his feet wet in the warm waters of Bill Reddie's "West Side Story" opus, he asked the arranger to come up with an alternate work—lengthy, diverse, and original. Reddie's answer to this request was something he called "The Channel One Suite." A long, interesting piece, it followed the pattern of the earlier "West Side Story," exhibiting tempo changes and wonderfully original melodic passages and affording Buddy yet another opportunity to stretch his seemingly limitless drumming talents. "Channel One" became the alter ego to the valuable workhorse "West Side," both showcases being among the most requested in Buddy's book.

Because of his immense power at the drums, Rich always sought out the hardest-blowing trumpet players he could find. The trumpet section naturally leads any band's ensemble figures, and Buddy's trumpets in particular were called upon to serve above and beyond the normal call of duty. In 1968 Rich secured the services of a man who was probably the finest lead trumpet player in the band business, Al Porcino.

Porcino did not merely play the notes; he phrased, he bent, he scooped, he pampered the little black dots that were put before him on manuscript paper in the form of first trumpet parts. In addition to his great strength and superb tone, Porcino possessed the one trait absolutely essential in a lead trumpet player: accuracy. His playing was as flawless as was Buddy's, and since he was a happy, funny, laid-back character to boot, he became a healthy addition to the band.

With his mind-boggling itinerary, it is amazing that Rich found time to be with Marie and Cathy, as well as his sisters and brother. He saw Pop Rich as often as he could, but those visits were limited to his occasional tours in the south, when he could hop into Florida and spend a few hours or days with the old man. Since he was raised in a family-oriented atmosphere, roots meant a great deal to him. He attempted to keep a balance between his road life and his home life. He wasn't always successful at it, but he tried.

In the spring of '68 his band appeared in support of Tony Bennett at the Palladium in London, as well as on the Mike Douglas TV show. In the summer of '68 Buddy appeared on "The Kraft Music Hall," an NBC-TV show, along with Bobby Darin.

August found the Buddy Rich band on tour with Frank Sinatra, the first of many such pairings. The band opened a four-day stand at Ronnie Scott's jazz club in London on September 30, 1968, Buddy's fifty-first birthday. Attendance records were shattered, and Buddy's band would return again and again to the English room in years to come.

The following year brought more of the same in the way of concerts, TV guest shots, and recordings. Al Porcino departed (Buddy's band through the years would always have an endless parade of new players); Buddy replaced him with Sal Marquez. The band was now recording for World Pacific. Buddy changed record companies almost as often as he changed band personnel.

He found himself booked into a club near Boston called Lennie's-on-the-Turnpike. Like the Chez and Ronnie Scott's, it was to become one of Buddy Rich's "homes"; he was given carte blanche by the owner to appear there whenever he wished. Lennie's was located near the Zildjian cymbal company. Armand Zildjian and general manager Lenny De Musio had become close friends of Buddy's, and the drum star spent many hours at the factory, selecting new cymbals and socializing with these two men.

In early November, the band once again flew to England for a tour that would entail many concert appearances around the UK as well as another stint at Ronnie Scott's and a BBC-TV special filmed at London's famous Talk of the Town night club. Shortly afterward Buddy and the band were to tour South Africa. It was an unfortunate way to end the year. Buddy was strongly opposed to apartheid, and he was stridently vocal about his feelings. When his black bassist was refused a visa, Rich canceled the tour.

As Buddy swung into the 1970s he began to play high school auditoriums, venues he enjoyed since he felt that jazz would only survive if the young could be initiated and exposed to it the way they were to "their" music, rock and roll. "Rock" was in full bloom. Radio stations playing jazz were almost nonexistent in 1970. Rich knew the only way America's young people would be able to hear jazz was to bring it to them and spoonfeed the young music fans. This he did, with mixed success. Naturally they reacted noisily to his protracted drum solos, but afterward there was not a perceptible rise in the sales of the band's records. Rock and roll had become too ingrained in the consciousness of the teenage record buyers. Undaunted, Buddy kept playing high schools and colleges, doggedly convinced he was making headway.

Thanks to the popularity of "West Side Story" and "Channel One Suite," Rich arranger Bill Holman put together a suite of music from the award-winning film *Midnight Cowboy*. Buddy reveled in this medley night after night and once mentioned that it was one of his favorite arrangements.

Buddy did a drum "duel" with Desi Arnaz, Jr., on a "Here's Lucy" episode during that series' 1970 season, then guested with his band on the popular sitcom "Happy Days." The band filmed and recorded enough material to span two of those "Happy Days" shows.

In mid-October Rich and company toured Italy, France, Germany, and Norway. The band was making money, and so was Buddy, more than he had in a long time. Expenses were high, but there was enough coming in to make Buddy secure and comfortable financially. The problem was, he kept spending as if there were no tomorrow.

On Buddy's behalf, he was generous to a fault with friends and relatives as well as business associates. He was particularly good about reciprocating kindnesses and favors. Back in 1969, having been a guest on innumerable occasions at the Playboy Mansion in Chicago, he surprised his close friend Hugh Hefner by furtively setting up his entire band in the mansion's great living room; when Hefner entered the room with some of his guests, Buddy and the band played a complete set for an awed and appreciative Hef.

That little adventure did not cost Buddy anything but time and effort, however. Gifts to acquaintances, the finest food in the most expensive restaurants, a succession of new cars, watches, tape recorders, cameras, and other assorted toys, boundless generosity to his family—all these kept his bank account at low ebb no matter how much cash flow there was.

Before he headed for his European tour in October 1970, Buddy, Cathy, and Marie moved from the house in Vegas to an attractive home on Mission Road in Palm Springs. Shortly after the move, Marie received a call from her former next-door neighbor in Vegas.

"Marie," the woman said, "just thought you ought to know, the government men came around this morning and stuck a sign on your front lawn here."

"A sign? What does it say?"

"It says: 'This house seized by the IRS for nonpayment of taxes.'"

Marie sighed.

Chapter 27

"You're sick, Osmonds!"
Buddy Rich in
Melody Maker, 1972

BUDDY SHRUGGED.

His tax worries were an old story. He recalled how, during the 1965 Newport Jazz Festival, he had been hauled into the Newport police station at the request of the "feds." The rap? Failure to file Nevada and federal income tax returns for 1961, 1962 and 1963. George Wein, entrepreneur of the Newport Festival, had come up with a thousand-dollar bond so that Buddy could be released and appear onstage. He always seemed to be one step ahead of the IRS, able to extricate himself from (or at least delay the prosecution of) his income tax situation. He had moved to Palm Springs just ahead of the government's takeover of the Vegas house. The fact that he had lost all his equity in the Sombrero Road home did not seem to faze him.

He had the utmost faith in his ability to make money. As long as his health held out, he could always swing a deal with a drum company that would generate a bonus for signing. Each time he guested on "The Tonight Show," his stock seemed to rise. More and more requests for his services came into the booking agency. He had become a genuine media star. His idiosyncrasies, his acerbic wit, his outspoken rantings against everything from bad music to bad speed limits to bad "pot" were widely quoted in newspapers and music magazines and on radio and television. In his mind, he was untouchable by his creditors (including the IRS). He regarded their efforts as flea bites. Problems? Stanley would take care of them.

Stanley Kay had become important in Buddy's professional life. A small, dapper man with street smarts, a wry sense of humor, and overwhelming admiration for Buddy, Kay joined the Rich organization in 1947 as alternate drummer for those occasions when Buddy either sang with the band or merely felt like standing in front of his orchestra waving his hands, bringing on the requisite girl singer, emceeing acts that appeared with him, or indicating his various instrumental soloists.

Kay, a better-than-average drummer, had a good deal more to offer Buddy than relief work at the drums. He was obsessed with the notion that Buddy's star should shine brighter than that of a mere bandleader. Carl Ritchie decided to hand over the managerial reins to Kay, and, in much the same way Norman Granz had guided the fortunes of Ella Fitzgerald and Oscar Peterson, Stanley set about making the whole world Buddy Rich–conscious. Kay was what every performer hopes for, dreams about, and seldom gets: an idolator, a runaway admirer of his client's talents, working in his client's behalf to the exclusion of all else.

Stanley was well aware of Buddy's tax problems. He also felt that an artist of Rich's magnitude should not have to deal with trauma of that sort. He set about putting Buddy in the hands of a good accountant. The theory was: get Rich to lay aside a part of his salary every week toward back and future taxes. It was a good theory, and it almost worked. Buddy was the monkey wrench in this otherwise well-oiled plan.

He would walk off the stage soaked to the skin, having exerted himself once again for his adoring followers. He was tired, aching, worried about his possible heart problems, his painful back discomfort, his troubled marriage, his little girl whom he saw sporadically at best, his imminent payroll, and a hundred and one other real or imagined things to bedevil him and ruin his sleep.

The one balm to his tortured mind and body was the pleasure he derived from spending his hard-earned dollars as he saw fit, government or no government. Buddy's running battle with the IRS was refereed by Stanley and the tax lawyer he had engaged on Rich's behalf. It was a no-win situation: the Rich faction's small guns against the Big Berthas of the Internal Revenue Service.

Stanley Kay was also concerned about Buddy's escalated use of "pot." Stanley, a nonsmoker (of anything), looked upon his hero's marijuana smoking as deleterious to his health as well as his playing. Rich laughed his objections aside.

"Hey! I've been smoking boo since I was sixteen years old. Never affected my playing one day of my life. Ever see me miss a beat? Drop a stick? Screw up an arrangement? No way! I like pot. I'm never gonna give it up."

Essentially clean-living and athletic, Buddy, to my knowledge, never fooled with hard drugs. There was once a rumor he had a cocaine problem. No one who knew him believes one word of it. Cocaine would have ruined his coordination, and he must have known that better than anyone. He had enough trouble handling pot. One night, while I was performing at his night club (Buddy's Place, Thirty-third near Seventh in Manhattan), I did see him falter, blow it, and then recoup the beat. When he came off, he looked at me, shook his head, and said: "Well, that's one in a row! I never lost it like that before." It bothered him enough that he cut his "pot" smoking drastically for the rest of that engagement.

His mood swings were sometimes terrible to see. He would be gregarious and expansive one moment, then, when he was on a "downer," his wrath could be a palpable, vengeful fit of fury. To say Rich was tough on his men would be a massive understatement. When we worked together, there were times when I actually feared for his life. His vitriol was so startling, he was so abusive, that I was afraid the band would rise in a body and beat him to death. As one of his departing musicians put it: "I came on this band to play music, not to join the Marines!" Yet another disaffected sideman, Bob Bowlby, was quoted as having said "Working for Buddy Rich is like walking through a mine field," although he added: "I achieved a level of self-respect and musicianship I might not have attained had I not played with a legend like Buddy Rich."

Buddy's famous outspokenness caused more than a mild stir in 1970 when he blasted English rock drummer Ginger Baker. In *Melody Maker,* the British equivalent of *Down Beat,* Buddy challenged Baker to play one set with Buddy's band at Ronnie Scott's. "If he refuses," Buddy remarked, "it'll show where he's at. If he's any man at all, he will do it." This was standard Rich operating procedure. Had Baker taken up the gauntlet, he would have been awash in the sea of complicated jazz arrangements, after which Buddy would have taken the stand and given Ginger a drum lesson.

Buddy's meat was "the challenge." He exhibited his propensity for head-to-head combat on that fateful evening when he had played Max Roach's drums after having been challenged by the taunting Allen Eager to do so. His double-bass-drum gambit at the Paramount had defied the world to deny his singular superiority over Louie Bellson's exploits with twin bass drums. His friends and fans recognized this facet of his character and somehow understood it. Yet even his hardiest supporters were nonplussed when, in yet another *Melody Maker* interview, he made scathing remarks about the harmless family act known as the Osmonds.

"You're sick, Osmonds!" he blurted. "I just don't understand the appeal of a 'midget' [Donny Osmond]. You have no talent, Osmonds. No talent!"

Actually the Osmond brothers, who had often sung in fine five-part harmony behind Andy Williams, had loads of talent in my opinion and that of many musicians and singers I admire. What set Buddy off is beyond comprehension. The *Melody Maker* headline read OSMONDS: SOUR GRAPES OR OLD AGE? Since Buddy was fifty-six at the time, I hardly think old age applied. It is possible that his harangue had to do with the changing musical scene in general.

Since he was deeply committed to jazz, it is easy to see why Buddy had nothing but contempt for teen singers and guitar-wielding, cymbal-bashing rockers with their vast storehouse of three-chord music. But trashing the Osmonds was uncharacteristic of Buddy. Later in life he commented on his Osmond remarks and seemed embarrassed about them.

His bluntness about drum teachers was more to the point. "There is not a teacher in the world today. What do they know? If they knew so much about drumming, they'd be out there, doing it. What could [drum teachers] show me? Mammy-daddy? I know my mammy and my daddy."

Rich went about his business, living the good life. He had taken an apartment in New York at One Lincoln Plaza. It was not a lavish pad, but it was comfortable, cozy, and, above all, in Buddy's beloved home state.

Marie hated it. "I was born and raised in California. I was always a warm-weather person. When we took the Manhattan apartment, I simply couldn't adjust. I never found anything warm enough to wear. I would stay indoors for weeks at a time. I just couldn't handle living there."

She went back to California and took an apartment in Marina Del Rey, a high-rise complex of condos overlooking the Pacific Ocean. She loved the place and soon began calling it "my place," just as Buddy looked upon the Lincoln Plaza apartment as "his." Now the Riches had *three* sets of living quarters, counting the Palm Springs home on Mission Road in Presidential Estates.

Quite a financial load to carry, "B"?

He put on his best Alfred E. Neuman grin and said: "What? Me worry?"

At that point in time, one could hardly blame him. Work was plentiful. He had become a god in Europe. Before he and the band boarded the plane that would take them overseas, their concerts in England, France, Italy, and Germany were presold to the roof. He had engaged a superior arranger, John LaBarbera, brother of Pat, who played in the Rich reed section. Lin Biviano, a lead trumpeter in the Porcino tradition, now spearheaded the brass section. And RCA Victor had signed Buddy to a long-term recording contract.

If it weren't for his nagging back pains, life would have been approaching perfection just then. Buddy tried to ignore the electric shocks he was feeling in his lower back nearly every time he straightened up or sat down. Once seated behind the drums, he functioned beautifully, but the wear and tear of traveling and the natural progression of age were taking their toll.

In January 1972 he went into a Philadelphia hospital to be operated on for his slipped disc problem. This was known as a fusion procedure, and, as bad as his back pains had been, many of his friends as well as some of his family members felt the operation was a mistake. The doctors pronounced it a success, but Buddy's back miseries were far from over.

Onward and upward went the Buddy Rich band. Rich himself fluctuated between being sweet-natured with his men and giving them stormy lectures about professionalism, sloppy playing, tardiness, and sloth.

Some of Rich's ire was directed at RCA Victor. He complained of a lack of interest and promotion on the company's part. He was absolutely right, although to expect a major label like RCA to devote much time, effort, and money to a jazz band in a rock-oriented recording world was the height of naiveté. Nevertheless, Buddy seethed over RCA's obvious apathy. He left the company in a huff, determined to affiliate with a lesser outfit that would at least exhibit enthusiasm for his brand of music.

1973 was full of what Buddy's friend Jerry Lewis liked to call "good stuff." In the offing were a television special called "Rich at the Top," filmed at the Top of the Plaza in Rochester, New York, as well as a funny Miller Lite beer commercial. Buddy also signed with a New York–based independent record company called Groove Merchant International. He engaged heavyweights like Don Menza and Manny Albam to contribute to his library.

No year, however, is perfect, and 1973 was not an exception. Gene Krupa died of leukemia on October 16. Buddy took his passing hard. Gene, after all, had made "drums" a household word, and no one knew or appreciated that fact more than Buddy Rich.

Gene's passing also hurt me deeply. The last time I ever saw him was during the shooting of a 1971 TV special in Toronto called "One Night Stand." I had hosted the show, which wound up with a four-way drum challenge featuring Gene, Buddy, Lionel Hampton, and myself. Gene was his usual gentlemanly self: warm, friendly, and effusive. And Buddy seemed to look upon him as something of a father figure, even though Krupa wasn't that much older than Rich.

Gene's death wasn't the only thing that laid Buddy low in 1973. In late autumn the band took an interminable jet ride to Australia. After his great successes in Europe, Buddy was bored with the beer-guzzling, noisy Aussies. It seemed as though they could not have cared less whether Buddy Rich was the greatest drummer they had ever heard or seen, or that the band was wonderfully exciting. And then came the "bust."

A small quantity of marijuana was discovered in Buddy's room by Australian police. Beneath a picture of Buddy, a newspaper caption read: "SAD NOTES: Band Leader Buddy Rich was ordered by an Australian court yesterday to appear February 18 [1974], on a charge of possessing marijuana."

Nothing came of this charge, and when the band flew home to the States, their leader was comfortably seated in first class, listening to his onboard stereo phones and enjoying a glass of champagne.

Early 1974 found the drummer weary not only physically but mentally, from that old devil, money problems. Year by year the "road" had become more costly, and musicians, wanting to keep pace with the national standard of living, were demanding higher salaries. Rich felt it was time to make a change.

In mid-March of that year, he once again disbanded. This time, though, there was a method to his not-so-madness. He had nurtured a dream for a long time, his own magnificent obsession. It came in two parts: his own sextet—in his own club.

◩　*Chapter* **28**

> *"It's my club. I do what I want here."*
> Buddy Rich, 1974

BUDDY'S PLACE WAS located at Sixty-fourth Street and Second Avenue on Manhattan's East Side. It was an upstairs club, the lower half of the building being occupied by a cocktail lounge known as Sam's. It had died as the Rat Fink Room, which comic Jackie Kannon had operated as host and resident clown. Buddy's tenancy promised to be far more fruitful.

Stanley Kay oversaw the operation. The idea was that Buddy and his new sextet, which featured two excellent saxophone players, Sal Nistico and Kenny Fortune, and a full rhythm section, would be in residence several times a year. When the new combo hit the road, Stanley planned to book other groups into the club.

The grand opening, on April 10, 1974, was celebrity studded, an event. Buddy was delighted. His own club! Where the funding for this venture came from is anybody's guess. Certainly not from Rich's own strained coffers. The main thing was: it happened. Buddy's Place was a fact of New York life. Soon it became the "silly season." In Whitney Balliett's "Journal of Jazz in the Seventies," the noted critic wrote:

> Buddy Rich, wearing his Superman costume . . . has dumped his big band. Buddy's Place at Second Avenue [is decorated] with pictures of himself and stocked with a seven piece group. [By April 30 he had added a conga drummer.] The band is sleek, musicianly, driving and apparently at Rich's behest, very loud.

Buddy ran a tight ship where his customers were concerned. "No loud talking while I'm performing" was the house rule, and Rich saw that it was strictly enforced. Several times he ordered an individual or a clump of patrons out of the place for what he felt was conduct unbecoming a Buddy Rich fan. Stanley Kay tore his hair over these incidents. "B," he would implore, "you can't do that. It's a night club. People are going to talk."

"It's my night club," Buddy would correct him. "I do what I want here. I run it my way."

Even though he had not invested one red cent in Buddy's Place, his name was the main attraction of the venue. "When people come in here, they want to hear me and my group, not some loudmouthed son-of-a-bitch ruining their enjoyment of the music. If somebody wants to talk loud or behave like an animal, let him do it out in the street, not in here!"

Stanley Kay backed away from that argument, because he knew Buddy was absolutely right. Rich had earned respectful behavior on the part of his audiences. He seemed more agitated over noisiness from the crowd when one of his musicians was soloing than when he himself was center stage. That trait endeared him to his sidemen. Despite his reputation for being rigid and uncompromising, jazz musicians wanted to work for Buddy Rich.

Although he hopped over to Philadelphia a few times to appear on the Mike Douglas TV show, Buddy and his septet held forth at Buddy's Place until July 20 before taking to the road. It was a healthy time in the drummer's life. Marie and Cathy spent much of the early summer in New York with him. He was enjoying his newly minted celebrity as a saloonkeeper (even if he didn't really own the club that bore his name). The septet was making fine records for Groove Merchant and appearing (as a quartet) on the "Today" show as well as Sid Mark's "Mark of Jazz," a syndicated PBS-TV show.

When the septet went on the road in July, the club did not fare nearly as well as when Buddy and his group had been the magnet for the jazz-loving New York audiences. Rich also had his occasional difficulties away from the warm ambience of Buddy's Place. A week-long run in Chicago at a popular club called

Mister Kelly's gave the group the impression they were working in a meat locker. It wasn't the temperature in the room; it was the audiences. Apathetic and indifferent, they greeted the septet with minimal applause and faltering attention.

"This is one of the finest morgues I have ever played," Buddy quipped one night. The audience was not amused.

Rich smiled happily when he returned, late in the summer, to his own club. The contrast in audience reaction was pronounced. In Manhattan he was king of jazz, and the crowds let him know it. Turnaway business greeted his six-week stand at Buddy's Place.

He accepted a brief tour of England and Italy in the middle of October, then returned once again to Sixty-fourth and Second Avenue with a newly formed sextet that featured the gutty tenor sax work of Illinois Jacquet. Nightly the customers howled for more. Successful as it appeared to be, this first edition of Buddy's Place was doomed. Expenses exceeded profits, due to the limited seating capacity. Late in November of 1974, the club closed its doors.

Rich wasn't at all dismayed by this turn of events. "Relocate," he commanded Stanley. "We'll relocate!"

Kay was way ahead of him. Before Buddy's Place went under, he had been in negotiation with a savvy young New Yorker named Marty Ross, who owned a roomy downstairs establishment called Marty's Bum Steer. It was located on Thirty-third Street near the old Pennsylvania Hotel, where Artie Shaw had walked away from his great 1939 band.

The "steer" was anything but "bum" in Marty's restaurant. It was generally conceded that Ross served the finest cut of roast beef to be found in New York. Or the tri-state area, for that matter. Marty himself was a good-looking young man-about-Manhattan. Of medium height, curly-haired, with an engaging smile, he made the perfect restaurant owner-host. He liked the ladies, and the ladies liked him. He was envied for his long-standing relationship with a lovely actress named Erin Gray.

One more thing: he loved music, especially jazz. Stanley Kay convinced him to convert his Bum Steer operation into a second edition of Buddy's Place. He didn't need a lot of convincing. By late April of 1975 Buddy's Place II was a reality. Compared with the previous operation, the second edition looked like Grand Central Station. All chrome and mirrors, it had a right-now, modern feeling that was attractive yet functional. The bandstand, set at the far end of the large dining room, was big enough to accommodate a sixteen-piece band, which was exactly what Buddy had in mind in conjunction with the April 28 premiere.

He had dabbled in small groups for over a year. The septet had sometimes become a quartet, a quintet, and a sextet. Great fun and economically sensible.

However, the world's greatest big band drummer once again longed for seven brass and five saxes. Lloyd Michels put together a new big band for Buddy. The general opinion was that it lacked the precision, the cleanliness, that had marked previous Rich orchestras.

It sported some fine soloists, headed by the loyal Steve Marcus on tenor sax, and some innovative arrangements were being exposed nightly. "Three Day Sucker," a Bruce Lofgren original, had been buried in the Rich book for months. At Buddy's Place II it saw the light of day. It was a rock excursion that dazzled the paying customers and proved to perceptive ears that Buddy Rich was not only the greatest jazz drummer alive; he was also the greatest "rock" drummer in the world. Arranger Mike Longo expanded the R and R idiom in the Rich book, penning a bravura medley from the rock opera "Tommy." This was yet another adjunct to the "concert piece" portfolio of the library, scintillating and contemporary.

Buddy's guest artists for the April engagement were Carmen McRae and Nipsey Russell. The opening night capacity crowd lapped up the evening, but the consensus was that the band had been poorly rehearsed and was sloppy. Buddy, a fashion plate for so many years, had taken to wearing sweaters, sweatshirts, and on occasion, T-shirts during this engagement. All very "in" at the moment, but not the stylish image he had always maintained. Perhaps he felt his new mode of dress was concomitant with the New Wave name he had bestowed upon his young crew: "Buddy Rich and the Big Band Machine."

On May 24, thanks to Stanley Kay's repeated invitations to play the club, I opened for a two-week stand with Buddy's band. I approached the date with some trepidation. Buddy and I had been on one of our foolish on-again-off-again kicks. He did not need unpleasantness in his life at that stage of the game. Neither did I. Still, the lure of working with him, watching him play every night, was irresistible, and so I headed east.

A steady rain pelts me as I get out of the taxi in front of Buddy's Place. My drummer and I enter the club and descend into the chrome and leather environs of the new establishment, wondering why such elegance reposes in so strange a neighborhood. One half block away sits Madison Square Garden. Across the street the old Hotel Pennsylvania—onetime harborer of the Cafe Rouge, which boasted a name band policy in the late thirties and early forties—is now disguised and decorated in Early Salesman, operating under the name of the Statler Hilton. Thirty-third Street itself is a handful of bars, cheap eating joints, and Chinese laundries.

Yet here, two stories below ground level in what used to be a great steak house called Gallagher's before it was Marty's Bum Steer, is the brand-new home of the Buddy Rich band, Buddy's Place, transported from the fashionable east Sixties to the nitty-gritty west Thirties; modern, shiny, and attractive, much larger than its predecessor, with comfortable listening and looking areas for the swarms of patrons the management hopes will flock to this new watering place.

I meet Marty Ross, who shakes my hand effusively and says how happy he is to have me here, and I respond in kind. I have in the past played the big theaters in New York—the Paramount and the Roxy—and the cafés and hotels—the Commodore, the Copa, the Round Table, the Maisonette of the St. Regis, and the Royal Box of the Americana. This engagement is different, a labor of love, a gesture of friendship for "B."

My drummer, Donny Osborne, begins doling out the music books to the members of the band now filtering up onto the stand. They look weary, as do all musicians who have only just returned the previous night from a one-nighter a few hundred miles away, sleep-poor, bone-tired. I test the microphone and check the monitor speakers as a tentative warming up, tuning up begins. Rich is nowhere in sight. Marty Ross considerately brings a hot cup of tea. I down it gratefully, and the rehearsal begins.

The band is ragged, which is a surprise. Buddy is the best, and he insists on the best, so the quality of musicianship I am being treated to is not par for the course.

We take a ten-minute break after fifty minutes of rehearsing, and I socialize with the guys. They are friendly, complimentary about my arrangements, and I'm feeling hopeful.

We begin again. In the middle of the next tune, there is a commotion behind me. Someone is yelling, "Hold it, hold it." The band stops playing. I turn to find the leader standing there, waving his arms. Buddy Rich is dressed in expensive slacks by Cardin and, somewhat incongruously, a thick, gray sweatshirt. Around his neck hangs a gold rope-chain, dangling from which is a gold dog tag. He is lean and hard-looking, and even close scrutiny will not disclose his age. He looks about forty. I know better.

He gives me his steely stare, stolen from Benny Goodman's "death ray" days, and in his best and favorite imitation of Clark Gable barks: "Hey, what the fuck are you doing? My band's tired. You've rehearsed enough, Tormé. I don't want you to wear the guys out." We have rehearsed fifty-five minutes. Four numbers.

I play the game.

"What the hell are you doing here?" I inquire. "Old people need their sleep."

He makes fists and beats them against his chest like a gorilla in heat. "Hey, dummy. You're working for me now. I don't take that kind of shit from employees. How'd you like a broken arm?"

"Why don't you go out and play in the traffic, little girl? I've got business with these gentlemen."

"You've got business with my fist, motherfucker. Okay, you guys. That's it. Rehearsal's over. See you tonight."

I grin at him. "Fine with me, Kong. I'll do my four tunes tonight and get back to the hotel in time for 'Monday Night at the Movies.'"

"Perfect. Four tunes is about all the patrons can stand, anyway."

"I just hope to God they can hear them after you finish puncturing their eardrums with that noise you call drumming."

He smiles his big-toothed smile and shakes his head. "One of these days, Tormé. One of these days," he says, holding up a threatening fist.

"Yeah, yeah, sure," I answer. It is ritual, this silly badinage between us. It has been going on for years. He bear-hugs me. He thanks me for coming. I assure him the pleasure is all mine. The rehearsal resumes.

It's going to be fine.

◻ *Chapter* 29

"Straight ahead."
Buddy Rich

AFTER THAT ENGAGEMENT Buddy gave me a gold dog tag inscribed "MEL— FRIENDS—BUDDY." I wore it with pride. Right after Labor Day, I once again went into Buddy's Place for a two-week run. The band was considerably better by then—tighter, cleaner—and they played my arrangements with far more accuracy than they had on the previous outing.

On September 13 I celebrated my fiftieth birthday there. When Marie Rich found that Buddy had forgotten to buy me a birthday present, she ordered him to take his gold identification bracelet off his wrist and put it on mine. This he did without a word of protest. I was deeply flattered, since Marie had given him that bracelet, with his name and the date engraved upon it.

Buddy was in a prankish mood in those days, and he pulled not one but three of them on me during that engagement. But more about that later.

Stanley Kay had been working on a special project for some time. On January 11, 1976, Buddy, along with a carefully selected trio consisting of Ross Konikoff on trumpet, Chicagoan Larry Novak on piano, and Ben Brown playing fender bass, appeared at Uihlein Hall in Milwaukee, Wisconsin, with the Milwaukee Symphony Orchestra.

It was a dream come true for Stanley, whose aspirations for Buddy knew no bounds, and for Buddy himself, who thrilled to the sound of eighty-five musicians accompanying him on "West Side Story"—not the Bill Reddie big band chart, but an entirely new version arranged by "Tonight Show" musician/arranger Tommy Newsom. This was "West Side" in its fullest glory, and Buddy played what can only be described as an inspired solo that not only brought down the house but had the normally staid symphony musicians cheering loudly. It was the first of several symphony dates Rich would play.

Having "done" Europe for the past few years, Buddy chose to remain "domestic" in 1976. He played the usual high school/college dates, recorded the band, appeared on radio and television shows, gave his nephew Josh (Mickey's son) a crack at the guitar book in the band, and in general kept his head above water financially, although the tax hassles were ever-present.

His macho image became notorious thanks to his repeated visits to "The Tonight Show." Therefore, no one was surprised when he coined yet another new name for his band. Henceforth it would be known and billed as "Buddy Rich and the Killer Force." He loved it. It went right along with his tough-guy persona, like expounding on the joys of karate and his murderous approach to big band drumming. Not that he had lost any of the subtlety of gentler drumming when the occasion called for it. His ballad work with brushes could be hushed and whispery, in perfect concert with the pretty charts created by his arranging staff. When the band was in its "Killer Force" mode, though, he was really in his element, hard-driving and almost brutal behind the drums.

We had been on extremely good terms for a long time. There were phone calls back and forth from all over the country. I was always pleasantly surprised to pick up the phone and hear his gruff tones on the other end. "Hey, Tormé, you dumb bastard, I miss you!"

"B? Where the hell are you?"

"We're playing a high school in Arlington Heights, Illinois."

"Gee! Your agents are booking you into all the big towns, huh?"

"How's this for an ad lib: Go fuck yourself!"

"My God, what a quick, inventive mind you've got!"

"I'd like to invent a cure for you. How about a forty-foot drop off a cliff?"

I laughed, and we talked. I asked him how he felt. He sounded tired during that particular call, but he didn't complain. He loved being on the road with the band. He told me he missed Marie and Cathy very much, but the band was "cooking" and generally things were all right.

"When am I going to see you?" I asked him.

"Well, we're doing Stamford, Connecticut, and the Waldorf together, aren't we?"

"Yeah, that's right. Right around Memorial Day."

"All right, ma man. I'll catch you then."

"You got it! Hey, thanks for the call, B."

"Straight ahead."

In early June we played the Hartman in Stamford, Connecticut. Business wasn't bad; it was horrendous. Opening night we drew 104 people. The theater's capacity was two thousand, as I recall. The second night was even worse. Buddy and I began to laugh. It was so unbelievable, we couldn't contain ourselves. It brought back memories of our Paramount engagement together back in 1949.

We would stand on the stage of that huge New York theater and break each other up. Several times, as the band lowered into the pit to make way for the movie, B and I were giggling uncontrollably. Bob Weitman, managing director of the Paramount, came back into our dressing rooms and scolded the hell out of us—rightfully so.

Now here we were, twenty-seven years later, once again sharing the stage of a theater, acting like a couple of schoolkids who had planted firecrackers under the teacher's chair and couldn't stop laughing about it. I don't think even Bob Weitman would have blamed us in this situation. Buddy and I had both been doing great business, following our respective stars. The theory was that together we would jam-pack the Hartman.

Saturday night proved to be the loneliest night of the week. Two hundred hearty souls braved the perfect weather to come and watch us make complete fools of ourselves. We could never figure out why the Hartman date was such a disaster. Neither could anyone else. We moved directly from Connecticut to Manhattan and the Empire Room of the Waldorf. That was more like it. Business was excellent, and the reviews were more than kind to both Buddy and me.

Following the week we spent there, he went back on the road, and I headed for England with my wife and our kids for a stay at the Talk of the Town in London. Buddy and I said our goodbyes. We both looked forward to our next stint together—over the Labor Day weekend in Concord, California, at the Concord Jazz Festival.

Something unexpected happened. My wife of ten years broke up our marriage. It came as a complete surprise, and I was devastated. From the day of the breakup in early August until I played the Concord date in early September, I lost eighteen pounds. I simply could not keep food down. I looked forward to seeing my friend. I needed help, and I knew that Buddy had heard the news and would be sympathetic and caring.

When I got to the Concord Pavilion, Buddy and the boys were onstage performing. My hired conductor had rehearsed B's band for me. After Rich had played "West Side Story" and received his usual standing ovation, it was my turn. I felt about as much like singing that night as I felt like stabbing myself in the eye with a sharp stick. As a matter of fact, in the state of mental torture I found myself in, I could have poked my eye out without even thinking about it.

I wanted to see Buddy before I went on. I had to see him, to feel his commiseration, to receive his friendly embrace and a pat on the back or a good, strong, understanding handshake. He came toward me backstage. I tried to smile and failed. I felt rotten. He walked up to me. He was smoking a cigarette. He looked at me and said: "How you doing?"

I shook my head. "How do you think?"

He nodded once, said, "Well, hang in there," walked by me, got into a car, and drove away.

On November 12, just a few weeks shy of his ninety-second birthday, Robert Rich died at his home on Ocean Parkway in Brooklyn, to which he had returned after having resided in Florida for several years. His second wife, Louise, an attractive Frenchwoman, was by his side when he died. Buddy was on the road with the band. He took the news badly. Sister Marge says:

> He was riddled with guilt, why I don't know. When my mother died, Brother kept insisting it was his fault. I told him he was crazy. How could her dying of cancer be his fault? He wouldn't listen.
>
> The same thing happened when Pop passed away. Despite everything that had gone on when he was a kid—the whippings and such—Brother loved Dad, and he kept telling himself that he could have done more for him, that he could have kept him alive longer somehow. Pop's passing hurt my brother for a long time.

When Robert died, I found out where Buddy was appearing and sent him a wire of condolence. I never knew whether he received it or not.

Nearly a year passed before I saw Buddy again. I was busy trying to sort out my life, coping with my broken marriage. He was perpetually on the road or in Europe with the Killer Force. My agents called. There were some concert dates being offered in Ohio, as well as a week at the newly restored Palace in Cleveland. The other element on these dates was to be the Buddy Rich band.

Did I want them? It wasn't a matter of "want." I needed them to pay lawyers' fees, temporary alimony, and the like.

I hadn't seen Buddy for months, not since the Concord concert when he had driven off into the night, apparently unconcerned over my pain. What would our next meeting be like?

I took the dates. Our "next meeting" was just fine, as though we had just had lunch together the day before. No mention of the night at Concord. Straight ahead.

That was Buddy for you.

◧ *Chapter* 30

"Together Again for the First Time"
Buddy and Mel,
direct-to-disc, 1978

BY LATE JANUARY of 1978 I was sufficiently recovered from my marital mess to write some new arrangements for an album I was to make with Buddy. People had insisted for years that they loved the LP we had made together. I would advise them they were incorrect; Buddy and I had never recorded together. No, no, they would argue. You're wrong. We have that album. It's terrific. Buddy experienced the same kind of obduracy when he tried to explain that we had never made a record in partnership. Norman Schwartz, a friend and admirer as well as a producer of tasteful records, made a deal to have Buddy and me cut a direct-to-disc LP.

When we walked away from the studio after completing the project, we agreed it had been among our best work ever. Norman came up with a kicky title: "Together Again for the First Time." After the initial release, Schwartz re-pressed it on his own Gryphon label. For nostalgia's sake, on the back of the album we had him print a picture of us taken one night in 1947, when we drove our brand new MG-TC midget sports cars across the George Washington bridge to see Nat King Cole at the Meadowbrook.

Once again Buddy got back on his bus or on a succession of airplanes and dragged the band from pillar to post. In July the Killer Force reverted to "Buddy Rich and his Orchestra." At the same time, Rich became disaffected with his longtime admirer/manager Stanley Kay. The why of that fracture remains a secret to this day. Buddy would never reveal it; neither would Stanley. They parted company, never to speak to each other again. Rich engaged Steve Peck, an amiable young man with a sunny personality, to oversee the daily details of life on the road that a manager normally deals with. The relationship lasted until the end of Buddy's life.

Late in September Cathy, Buddy, and I found ourselves appearing on the Merv Griffin show together. It was fun, and I was reminded that B's sixty-second birthday was coming up. I cooked up a birthday prank with our mutual friend Marty Mills. Marty was the son of music publishing magnate Jack Mills, and one funny guy. Buddy, Marty, and I had spent some riotous times together.

Buddy, in his wacky mode, would walk down Broadway with Marty and me and suddenly point at me and shout to the passers-by: "Look! It's Mel Tormé! My God! Mel Tormé, walking right here on Broadway, like a normal person!" Marty would throw a huge arm around my shoulder, beam at the gawkers, and echo: "That's right, folks. Mel Tormé. In person! Come over and shake his hand. Get his autograph. He wants to meet you." Buddy would stand in the middle of the sidewalk like a hawker, cupping his hands to his mouth and yelling at the top of his lungs: "Hurrr-y, hurrr-y, hurrr-y! Meet Mel Tormé. In person. Last chance to say hello to a man who's a legend in his own mind!"

I would be looking around for a convenient manhole cover to slide under and disappear.

With Buddy's sixty-second days away, Marty and I cooked up a gag that was nicely retributive. We all made a date to meet for lunch at Nate 'N' Al's, Beverly Hills' finest deli, on B's birthday, September 30. No sooner had we seated ourselves in a booth than Marty rose up in his place and advised the crowded restaurant: "Attention! Attention, K-Mart shoppers! We've got Buddy Rich, the world's greatest drummer, here in this booth. He is honoring Nate 'N' Al's with his presence today."

I stood up and continued, "That's right, ladies and gentlemen. It's Mr. Rich's eighty-second birthday today. This man is a legend in his own lunchtime, and I think we should give him the round of applause that all senior citizens of his ilk so richly deserve."

The Nate 'N' Al's patrons laughed and applauded. For once, Buddy flushed with embarrassment. His discomfort was not lost on Marty and me. We loved it—turnabout and all that jazz. After lunch I placed a little gift-wrapped package on the table.

"B," I said, "you once gave me one of these. I never forgot it. I wanted to return the compliment, so—happy birthday."

He seemed genuinely touched. He tore away the paper and opened the box. In it was a silver identification bracelet. It was the large, clunky kind popular with servicemen during World War II. It was also scratched, rusted, and falling apart. He looked at me and Marty with murder in his eyes. We laughed.

"Okay, okay. Joke over," Marty said. He pulled a similarly wrapped package out of his pocket and laid it on the table. "We love ya, B. Happy birthday and many more."

Buddy grinned at us. What a pair of nuts his pals were. Now for his present. He opened the box. Inside was a grungier, rustier, more disreputable ID bracelet than the previous one. Now he did laugh, hard and long. We all broke up for a few minutes. Then I reached under the table and placed a much larger box before him. He looked at us and shook his fist in warning.

"If this is another . . ."

He opened the box. In it was a Nikon F 35mm camera, something we knew he had been wanting. His eyes misted over. It was a good lunch date. Marty had an appointment, so he took his leave as Buddy and I walked up Beverly Drive to where he had parked his 450 Mercedes convertible. He seemed suddenly glum. I punched him playfully on the shoulder. "What's the matter, birthday boy?"

He had shifted into a serious mood. "Yeah, that's just it, Melvin. Sixty-two. Jesus! What am I accomplishing? Running around the world night after night, beating the shit out of a set of drums. My home life stinks. I've proved everything I want to prove as a drummer. It's just the same thing, over and over and over again. It's—endless."

He was rarely in so introspective a mood. He seemed to need some understanding, a bit of commiseration, but I withheld any comment. Perhaps it was selfish of me, but I remembered how insensitive he had been to my feelings back in Concord, and I simply could not bring myself to pat him on the head and assure him that his life and his work were not in vain. In retrospect, I wish I had not been so cool to his mood of the moment, particularly on his birthday, but I'm as human as the next guy and I couldn't shake off the disappointment I had felt when he had had nothing to offer me but a brief hello and goodbye months before.

In January of 1980 we appeared together at a club called Park West in Chicago. It was a hangout for the young, who were used to seeing rock acts there. I did poorly with the sparse crowd that did attend. Buddy fared much better, but it was not our finest hour.

The band went to England once again to do concerts, and Buddy appeared on "The Muppet Show," which was taped in Birmingham at the ATV studios.

He reverted to his childhood career by playing on anything in sight with a pair of drumsticks, including the walls of the set, the chairs, the tables—everything. As a finale, Buddy engaged in a drum duel with that rugged little Muppet known as "Animal," to the delight of everyone present. Animal's offstage drumming was done by ex–Ted Heath drummer Ronnie Verrell. That segment has been shown innumerable times on American TV. It is still one of the most entertaining half-hours ever filmed.

In October of that year Buddy, the band, and I did four one-nighters in the midwest. October 3 found us in Muncie, Indiana, followed quickly by Fort Wayne, Kalamazoo, Michigan, and Michigan State University in Lansing. Just prior to going onstage in Kalamazoo, Buddy sent Steve Peck to find me. I boarded the band bus to find Rich doubled over in pain.

"My back," he groaned. "It's my back. It hurts like hell." He looked up at me. His face was strained and white with discomfort. "Donny may have to play for me tonight. I just don't know if I can make it."

He must really be hurting, I thought, if he says he might not go on. "Going on" was his whole life. My drummer, Donny Osborne, Jr., was a kind of protégé of Buddy's and knew every arrangement in the Rich book. But the capacity crowd out there would be terribly disappointed if Buddy didn't appear.

"Steve," Buddy called to his majordomo. "Tell you what. Help me get dressed, and we'll see." Peck hastened to assist him as he rose from his seat in increments. His face was contorted in agony as he finally pulled himself up to his full height, struggling to place his arms in his shirt, his legs into his pants. That night on the bus he looked 108 years old.

With great difficulty he hobbled up the stairs to the stage door and made his way to the drums. What happened then can only be termed a miracle. The band began to play. So did Buddy. Magnificently. He seemed transformed into a totally different man, seated behind the Slingerlands. Not a trace of the back problem was in evidence. He played vociferously, thunderously. His solo effort on "West Side Story" was one of his best ever.

After the concert, with fans and admirers rushing backstage to shake his hand, get an autograph, praise him for the great musical experience they had enjoyed, we got back on the bus. He slumped into his customary seat, directly behind the driver. In front and above him sat a 19" TV monitor, under which there was a VCR. Steve Peck opened an ice hamper that sat across the aisle from Buddy. In addition to cans of beer and soft drinks, there were dozens of Milky Way, Snickers, Three Musketeers, and Hershey bars, as well as a large quantity of Ding Dongs, Twinkies, and chocolate cupcakes. Years later, when, after shooting San Francisco mayor George Mosconi and Supervisor Harvey Milk, Dan White pleaded "not guilty" by invoking what became known as the

Twinkie defense, I remembered that night on the bus and wondered whether Rich's mood swings were caused not only by his continual pot smoking but also by his compulsive junk-food habit.

On the morning following the Kalamazoo concert, Donny and I were to see one of those abrupt mood swings in action. Buddy always stayed at Howard Johnson hotels, since he felt the quality of the rooms as well as the food was uniformly good. We went over to have breakfast with him. He ordered eggs. He was in a chipper frame of mind, joking and mellow. The eggs came. They were not done to his liking. Without warning, he viciously lashed out at the waitress. Donny and I were shocked by his behavior. It had been so unexpected, so sudden. Delayed junk-food reaction? Possibly.

In Lansing, when his long drum solo was illuminated by a large "traveler" spotlight, he stopped playing and loudly excoriated the spotlight operator, calling him, among other things, a stupid son-of-a-bitch. The dean of Michigan State was outraged. He swore Buddy Rich would never again be welcome in Lansing. He was wrong. A few years later Buddy played the university auditorium again, drawing a huge crowd of Michigan State fans. The dean was nowhere in sight that evening.

◨   Chapter *31*

*"I'm going no place—like I'm on a treadmill—I've
been thinking about how . . . pointless it all is."*
Buddy Rich, 1980

I COULDN'T PUT the four concerts we had done together in Michigan and Indiana out of my mind. For the first time, Buddy had looked, well, old. For that matter, considering his profession, he *was* old. I had always thought of him as an athlete/musician. He had stayed trim and in shape for so many years, just like a good lightweight boxer. Now, thanks to the long bus trips, the increasingly irregular hours, and his obvious addiction to sweets, he had developed a mild paunch. On top of which—how many sixty-two year old boxers were still plying their trade?

"Age is just a number," Rich was fond of crowing. For years, that saying was applicable to him. Yet one night during those midwestern concerts we had done, something new had surfaced, a Buddy I had seen only once before, in Beverly Hills on his sixty-second birthday. When he had boarded the bus after the Lansing concert and dropped into his seat, I sat down alongside him. Even though he had dried his face with a fluffy towel, a fine layer of perspiration still clung to his forehead. He slowly shook his head from side to side. "What's it all about, Alfie?" he asked me.

"It's about fame, money, the pursuit of your craft, the roar of the crowd, personal pride . . ."

"Whoa! Hold it! Sorry I asked."

I laughed and looked closely at him. I could tell he had modulated into one of his philosophical moods. I could have made money betting on just what he would say next.

"Yeah, but what does it all mean? [Bingo!] So I go out there, night after night, and I play, and they stand up and cheer. Then I get in the bus and we do it again. The next night and the next and so on. It's like—I'm going noplace. Like I'm on a treadmill. Like one of those . . . what do they call those little animals that run inside a sort of wire basket?"

"Hamsters."

"Yeah, yeah. Hamsters. Well, that's how I feel on nights like this. Like I'm running and getting nowhere."

"Ah, you're just tired. Beat."

"I'm tired, sure. But lately, more and more, I've been thinking about how— I don't know—how *pointless* all of this is, you know?"

I knew. I had often suffered self-doubt, indecision, depression, and aimlessness during my own career. Was B looking for corroboration, advice, empathy, or all three? Or none of the above? Was he merely "ventilating," getting it out, off his chest, as a kind of purgative? The tack I took was the one I thought least likely to sound pontifical or patronizing.

"Are you saying you're tired of playing drums?"

"Hell, no. I live for that. I look forward to playing every night. It's just all the other shit I have to put up with."

"Like?"

"Oh, you know. The long jumps in the bus, bad food on the road, lousy hotels, wiseasses in the band, guys that don't do their jobs right . . ."

"Uh-huh. In other words, everything you've been putting up with since you were a baby in vaudeville."

"Well . . . yeah. Right on. I guess I've just been putting up with all of it for too long."

"Can you quit? Do you want to quit?"

He thought about it. "No, I can't. Too many responsibilities. And I don't really want to. What would I do with myself? Sit by the pool and listen to records for the rest of my life?"

"Well, then, what are we talking about?"

"Jesus, you dumb fuck!" [Ah! Now there was the Buddy we had all come to know and love.] "I'm just saying . . ."

"You're just saying, 'Is this all there is?' Correct?"

"In a way, yeah. Don't you ever feel like this?"

"Only every other day, B. But Christ Almighty, it's a good living. A *great* living. And I'm getting paid to do what I like to do. Think of all the poor bastards out there who get up in the morning gritting their teeth, hating where they work, what they're doing. Maybe I'm nuts, but I think we're so goddam lucky . . . wait a minute. Let me step down off this soapbox."

I thought he would put me down for my tiny outburst. Instead, he remained serious. My God, I thought. We're having a heart-to-heart.

He carried on in the same vein for a while. What brought on his ruminations? I had no idea. An earlier beef with his agents? An argument with Marie? His aching back? Take your pick.

I didn't see him after that for several months. Of course, I watched him on his frequent "Tonight Show" guest shots. He always seemed happy around his friend Johnny Carson. I did notice something different about his playing on these occasions.

Buddy seemed to have settled into a set bag of tricks. He would leave his "Tonight Show" chair and sit down behind a set of borrowed drums directly in front of Doc Severinsen's band. After a brief band intro, Rich would play the obligatory solo, replete with crossovers from the snare drum to the tom-toms, as well as the under-over cymbal tapping he had pioneered.

These solos began to take on a flavor of sameness. Highly technical, full of speed, hugely crowd-pleasing. Yet it seemed as though Buddy had begun to repeat himself, a habit he had never fallen prey to earlier on in his career. A drummer friend of Buddy's commented to me during this period that it seemed as if Buddy was playing some of these solos by rote, indulging in the crossover pyrotechnics because it was expected of him. Perhaps.

Maybe he did give up a bit of his *swinging* abilities for the showier aspects of his vast talent. The more I watched him in the early eighties, the more convinced I became that there was some truth in what Buddy's friend had said. And the more I watched him on the Carson show, the more I thought: so what? Who in the world could move around a set of drums with B's lightning speed? Who could accomplish the demanding single-stroke roll with such total perfection?

Who could approach Rich's flawless crossovers, with nary a single miscue of an errant stick clattering against a chrome rim?

And what was wrong with pleasing the studio audience visually as well as aurally? How many listener/viewers understood or appreciated the fine points of the man's playing?

I stopped listening to critiques on Buddy and deleted my own from my mind. As I said, I saw him only occasionally for the next several months, although he surprised me a few times by calling me while we were both on the road, sometimes at the opposite extremes of America. He would find out where I was appearing and telephone to ask how I was, what I was doing, and, more than once, "Where is my frigging copy of 'Bluesette'?"

He had particularly liked the chart I had written on the fetching Toots Theilmans jazz waltz when we had recorded it on our "Together Again" LP. He wanted a copy of the arrangement to use as an instrumental showpiece, with Steve Marcus doing all the solo work in place of my vocal.

I found myself at home in L.A. during a time when Buddy's band was appearing at the Comedy Store, a popular Sunset Boulevard night spot which had seen an earlier life as Ciro's. Rich called and asked me to come in one night as his guest. He had not mentioned "Bluesette" for some time, and I decided to surprise him.

I raced over to my copyist's office and had the arrangement photocopied. That evening I showed up at the Comedy Store, careful to secrete "Bluesette" under the table of the booth I occupied. Late in the second set, Buddy introduced me and invited me to come up and sing one. I waved my hands in the air and shook my head. He insisted. The audience applauded. Johnny Carson, sitting in the next booth, nodded at me: go on, get up there. With seeming reluctance, I rose slowly and yelled up to Buddy: "Well, if you insist. Strangely enough"—I raised the arrangement high above my head—"I've come totally prepared!"

Everyone laughed and clapped. Buddy, sensing what I had brought, seemed very pleased as I stepped onto the stage and began handing out the parts. Now Rich's Machiavellian sense of humor surfaced. "Hey, folks!" he announced. "We've got another great singer in the house tonight. Let's hear it for Jack Jones!" Again wild applause, as Jack, who had been sitting directly behind me, stood and accepted the cheers of the patrons. "Come on up here with Mel, Bones [Buddy's favorite nickname for Jack]. You can both sing this thing."

I turned to Buddy and said, *sotto voce,* "Hey, B. Jack doesn't know this chart. Let's just do the blues or . . ."

"Naw, man. He'll be able to dig it."

Uh-oh, I thought. Another one of Rich's childish delights: make the singers look stupid. I was right. Jack Jones, one of the finest singers in the world and a close friend of Buddy's and mine, struggled uncomfortably through that convoluted, unfamiliar arrangement as best he could but still came out looking foolish, through no fault of his own. Both Jack and I could have shot Peck's-bad-boy-Buddy that night.

I called Jack repeatedly after I got home until I finally reached him and apologized for what had happened. Class act that he is, Jack remarked: "Why are you apologizing? That was our buddy Buddy, doing a number on us."

"You're right. He's going to be five on his next birthday."

"Played the crap out of the drums, though, didn't he?"

"Business as usual."

When Rich pulled devious, childish stunts like that, I really wondered whether there was any depth of feeling within him. Was he strictly a jokester? Did anything ever really touch him?

One day in 1982 he called me and said: "Quick! Get in your car, come out to MGM, and meet me in Projection Room One."

"What . . ."

"Don't ask. Just do it."

I hightailed it out to Metro, parked the car and walked down to Projection One, located in the Irving Thalberg building. Buddy greeted me excitedly. "Wait till you see this," he cried enthusiastically. "When I was twelve, I saw this movie at the Capitol in New York. I stayed for all four showings that day. It's, like, my favorite movie of all time, with my favorite movie star."

We sat down in the deep leather seats as the lights dimmed and the projectionist began running the only extant print of a 1932 MGM film called *Smilin' Through*. The stars were Fredric March, Leslie Howard, and Buddy's favorite, Norma Shearer. I hadn't seen the movie since I was a kid. It was sentimental, bittersweet, and, although dated, extremely touching. By the time it was over and the lights came up, Buddy and I had gone through a large, economy-size box of Kleenex. We had to go to the men's room and wash our faces before we dared make our way out into the sunlight and the realities of 1982.

B kept shaking his head. "Norma Shearer. Now there was an actress, man. That's what I call a movie star. I'm telling you, Tormé, I was in love with her when I saw that movie. I still am. She was great. Boy, I wish I had a cassette of that movie to run on the bus." I thought: he *is* capable of deep feelings. The practical joker, the wisecracking Brooklynite, is one side of the man. I had seen the other side in MGM Projection Room One. It comforted me to know there was a balance of sorts within the complex individual known as Buddy Rich.

◨   *Chapter* **32**

"Fuck the doctors."
Buddy Rich just after
his quadruple bypass

ON JANUARY 23, 1983, Buddy and the band prepared to play a concert at the University of Michigan in Ann Arbor. Rich had been tired, more so than usual, for the past several days. Suddenly, without warning, a flood of pain enveloped the entire length of his left arm. At the same time, he felt as though someone had slammed him in the back with a two-by-four.

He was quickly taken to the university hospital. Luckily for him, it was not only one of the finest medical facilities of its kind; it was also a teaching institution with some of the top-rated doctors in the country on hand.

He had had a serious heart attack. The recommendation was instant bypass surgery. He refused to be operated on until his family could be there with him. Hurried calls were made to California. Marie, Cathy, Jo, Marge, and Mickey raced to Los Angeles International and caught the first flight to Detroit. They scrambled out of the plane the minute the door opened and sprinted toward a waiting limousine, which sped to the college hospital in record time.

Buddy was greatly relieved when he saw them pour into his room, but they had barely had time to say hello when two attendants wheeled in a rolling gurney and lifted Rich onto it. They cannonballed down the corridor to the operating room. So life-threatening was Buddy's condition that a woman in the OR who had already been prepped and sedated for surgery was wheeled out to make room for the dangerously ill drummer.

Several hours later, Buddy was moved into the intensive care unit, having undergone a successful quadruple bypass. His friend Jerry Lewis quipped: "Sure. He had to top me. I only had a triple."

The band was left in a holding pattern while Buddy was flown back to Palm

Springs to recuperate. Two weeks after the operation, Marie called me from the Springs and said B wanted to meet me for lunch at the Ginger Man in Beverly Hills.

"What is this, a gag, Marie? He's coming into L.A.? Now? After only two weeks of recuperating?"

"Oh, sure. That's the way they do it now. Heart patients are encouraged to get up and move around. Also, we have to see his doctor and have him checked over."

He walked into the Ginger Man with a lighted cigarette dangling from his mouth. His complexion was sallow. He sat down slowly at the table. The real shocker was his voice. Those normally gruff tones had been reduced, thanks to surgery, to high-pitched wheezing exhalations.

He put out the cigarette and said haltingly: "Hey, Tormé. [breath] What's happening? [breath] Good to see you. [breathy, rasping laugh] What am I saying? [breath] It's good to see *anyone!*" His voice sounded like an Andy Devine replay, only fainter.

"Are these aging eyeballs deceiving me, B? You're . . . *smoking?*"

As if in defiance, he produced a pack of cigarettes and lit another one. "Of course, ma man. I'm doing everything I did before, only I'm much healthier now." He showed me an outturned palm, honor-bright fashion. "Straight life. I'm actually in better physical shape because of the bypass."

He breathed laboriously between almost every word and coughed twice while inhaling the cigarette. I asked him: "You mean the doctors told you you could smoke after what you've just been through?"

He smiled imperiously, raised the cigarette to his lips, took a deliberate, deep drag on it, and blithely blew a cloud of smoke toward the restaurant ceiling. "Fuck the doctors," he wheezed. "Fuck 'em."

We had lunch.

"What time are you going for your checkup?" I asked over coffee.

"Marie's picking me up in"—he looked at his watch—"ten minutes. I'll go see the doc, and then I'm heading over to Bob Yeager's."

That got my attention. Bob Yeager was the proprietor of Hollywood's leading percussion hangout, the Professional Drum Shop.

"What's playing there?" I asked.

"I'm playing there. Hopefully."

"What are you saying?" I inquired, not quite believing what I had just heard.

"Yeah. He set up some drums for me. I gotta go see if I can play. Check on my strength, you know?"

With his breathing difficulties, his slightly sagging shoulders, and that high, scratchy voice, he sounded like Laurence Olivier, playing one of those old, feeble types he impersonated in some of his final films.

"B, for the love of God! There's plenty of time to . . ."

"No, there isn't. I'm due to go to Europe in a couple of weeks. Supposed to play England at Ronnie's [Scott's] and do some other dates over there. It's a good tour. Plus my band is waiting for me."

Knowing Buddy's reputation for never "dogging it," for always delivering a demanding, fatiguing performance, I had a terrible mental picture of him dropping dead behind his drums as he played the final rim shot of "West Side Story" to an enthralled opening night audience at Ronnie Scott's. I was about to comment on this suicidal plan of his but thought better of it and shut my mouth. What was the point?

He sat there, incautiously smoking a cigarette, pale, slightly wasted-looking, yet exuding supreme confidence in his ability to bounce back and carry on.

Oh well, I thought. Wait till he gets to Bob Yeager's. Then he'll realize he can't push himself like this. Two minutes behind a set of drums, and he'll long for bed. On top of which, the family—Marie, Cathy and his sisters—will never let him go to Europe so soon after the operation. I mean, this is no young kid we're talking about here. This is a heart patient in his sixties. No, no, they'll stop this foolishness. I'm right about this.

I was wrong. Rich went over to the Pro Drum Shop and played hard for the best part of an hour. The customers hurrahed. Bob Yeager stomped his feet. Two weeks later the Buddy Rich band, with its leader in tow, landed in England. The Ronnie Scott engagement was a sensation. Buddy cut loose on opening night with a solo that had his English admirers screaming themselves hoarse.

He did not die behind his drums that night, but his days were numbered. He had a little over four years to live.

Chapter 33

"Who is this?"
Buddy Rich,
1983

THROUGH THE YEARS, Buddy and I gave each other an assortment of toys for men: cuff links, cameras, guns, books, drums, gold ID dog tags and bracelets, and other things. The point is that's precisely what they were—"things." I couldn't get our meeting at the Ginger Man out of my mind. He had seemed so frail, so tired. Nothing like the Buddy Rich I had known all those decades. He had been through a lot. Back problems, leg pains, a quadruple bypass. I thought about the nights on the bus. Four- to six-hundred-mile journeys through lousy weather, stop and go jerkiness, sleepless conditions. Wifeless, childless on these wrenching trips with nothing but his bandsmen and his VCR to keep him company.

His VCR.

I suddenly got a great notion, which soon turned into a grand illusion. His reaction to *Smilin' Through* when we screened it at MGM had surprised and touched me. I had rarely, if ever, seen him so emotionally overcome. I decided to get that movie transferred onto a VHS videotape and give it to him. I could just picture him, night after night, sitting back after an exhausting performance and running it on his nineteen-inch TV monitor on the bus. This would be no mere present, not just another "thing." It would become one of his prized possessions. The prospect of gift-wrapping the cassette and handing it to him excited me.

My excitement proved to be premature. The 35mm print we had seen in the Metro projection room was the only existing copy of *Smilin' Through*. When MGM had remade the film with Jeanette MacDonald and Brian Aherne in 1941, the Norma Shearer–Leslie Howard original had been withdrawn from release, and all prints save the one we had seen had been destroyed. Damn!

I won't bore you with the details, but after a couple of months of pleading and promising, I obtained, with the help of certain MGM and TV station executives, a VHS copy of Buddy's favorite movie. I wanted to make giving it to him a special occasion. We hadn't seen each other since the Ginger Man luncheon. I checked with his agents and discovered that he would be playing the Great America amusement park in Santa Clara, California, at the same time I would be fulfilling my yearly obligation at the Paul Masson winery, a five-day stand George Shearing and I look forward to each Labor Day weekend.

I found some festive paper, wrapped the precious cassette, and took it north with me. I had booked into the same hotel where I knew Buddy and the band would be staying, right across the street from Great America. The moment I registered for myself, my two youngest kids, and my fiancee, Ali Severson, I asked whether Buddy had arrived. "Not yet," came the reply. Good, I thought. Gives me a little more time to savor the thought of that moment when he opens the package. I had purposely camouflaged the VHS cartridge in a much larger box. Can't wait to see his face!

After a few more attempts, I finally got him on the phone.

"B?"

"Who is this?"

"Well, sometimes you refer to me as your favorite singer."

"Who is this?"

"Very funny. Okay. Enough of this small talk. How are you feeling? Haven't seen you since—"

What he said to me then is not worth printing. I stammered through a few more sentences and gently laid the phone in its cradle. I walked over to the mirror on the dresser, looked myself in the face, and said: "Let's face it, Melvin. This man doesn't like you." My daughter Daisy looked stricken. She put her arms around me and started to cry.

"What did he say, Dad?" she asked me.

"Not important, honey."

"But, Daddy, you're always saying that he and you are best friends."

"I know, Daze. I was wrong."

Why Buddy chose that moment to lash out at me with one of the most insulting, demeaning remarks imaginable is something I still cannot fathom. I thought about Stanley Kay, Rich's erstwhile devoted friend and manager. Since their splitup, Stanley would not even mention Buddy's name. He came within an inch of becoming downright violent if you pressed the issue of his breakup with Buddy. Now I thought: perhaps Buddy had vilified Stanley in the same way he had verbally abused me. Sadly, I wrote off my friendship with Rich.

Too bad, Buddy, I thought, with a rueful inward smile. You should have waited to be abusive until after I had given you *Smilin' Through*. I threw the gift-wrapped cassette into my suitcase and forgot about it.

Time passed.

In 1984 I found myself performing at the ill-conceived New Orleans World's Fair with the Buddy Rich band. Steve Marcus and Steve Peck greeted me warmly and almost immediately asked what was wrong between me and the Old Man. I dodged answering their questions.

Steve Marcus wanted to fill me in on what was going on in Buddy's life.

"Sorry, Steve. I'm not interested."

"But, Mel, he's gotten so mellow. Honest to God, he's been a pussycat ever since Nicholas was born." Nicholas was Buddy's new grandson. Cathy Rich had grown into a good-looking young woman and had married. She had given birth to Nicholas, on September 21, 1984, and by all accounts Buddy was besotted with the kid.

I said, "That's great," and I meant it. Someone once told me that you can't like anyone until you can start liking yourself. Maybe that had been Buddy's problem all along—a lack of personal self-worth despite his undeniable greatness as a musician. If the birth of a grandson had made him easier to be around, mellower to socialize with, gentler on his employees, why, fine and dandy. However, I was merely guessing. I hadn't seen or talked to Buddy in months. Better this way, I decided. Steve Peck chimed in with "He really misses you, Mel. I know he does."

"Well, for what it's worth, Steve, offer him my congratulations with regard to his grandson, and be sure to give my best to Cathy and Marie."

I was feeling ambivalent about my broken friendship with Buddy. I missed him. At the same time, I had a strange feeling of relief. I would never have to worry about his abrasive tongue again. I need no longer wonder about the condition of our long-term friendship. Was it on? Off? How would he act the next time we saw each other? Better this way. Enjoy his records, the videos of his concerts. He was still my drumming idol; he was merely no longer my friend.

More time passed.

One day the phone rang. It was Marie Rich.

"Mel, I'm calling from the Springs. We miss you. What happened between you and Buddy?"

"Marie, I honestly don't see any value in dredging up the past. Let's just say we can't get along anymore and leave it at that. By the way, how's his health?"

"Great, just great. He seems relaxed and happy. But he misses you."

"Come on, Marie."

"No, I swear to God, it's true. He talks about you a lot. He doesn't know what happened."

"Marie, forgive me, but we've known each other long enough for me to say 'bullshit.'"

"Melvin, what did happen?"

"Nothing that's important enough to worry about. Hey! I'm still the number one Buddy Rich fan on the planet. That'll never change. I'm just taking a pass where the friendship is concerned, and for the record, I miss you guys too. All of you."

"This is terrible. I mean, you're family. We've always thought of you as family. Can't we fix this?"

"Look, I don't want to come on like some aloof, unmovable jerk, but what's the point? I simply don't want to let myself in for future grief from B. This is an exercise in self-defense."

She said goodbye, sounding confused and disappointed. Three days later, she called again:

"Buddy wants to meet you for lunch at the Ginger Man."

"Not a good idea, Marie."

"I think it is. So does Buddy."

"Well . . ."

"We gotta get you two idiots together. Don't make me beg you, Melvin."

"No, it's not that. It's just . . ."

"All right, stubborn mule. Please!"

Two days later I showed up at the Ginger Man with misgivings and no small sense of futility. Rich walked in, wearing a cardigan and freshly pressed slacks. He looks like the Buddy of old, I thought, noticing the deep tan and the springy walk. He walked up to me, showed me a broad expanse of well-tended teeth, and hugged me. We sat. I wasn't exactly Mr. Warmth at that moment.

He gave me a sidelong glance and demanded, "What the hell has been the matter with you?"

I took a deep breath and told him. He shook his head. "Tormé, you dumb bastard, you know I love you. So I said those things to you in Santa Clara. So what? That's me. You know I didn't mean them. When the fuck are you going to grow up?"

I remembered Marge Rich Ritchie once telling me, "Buddy has never, ever said 'I'm sorry.' He just never learned how."

I sighed a deep mental sigh. I guess, I told myself, that I just got what amounts to an apology from Buddy. In that milisecond, I realized I would have to be content with it if I wanted the relationship to resume. And deep down, I did. I had missed the man. Looking at him there in the Ginger Man, I knew we weren't getting any younger and that I would need to finally accept Buddy Rich as he was. I had brought an attaché case to the Ginger Man. I opened it, took out a brown-paper-wrapped box, and shoved it across the table toward him.

"Here you go, Mr. Wonderful. You could have had this months ago if you hadn't opened your big mouth."

He opened the package, read the label on the cassette. He looked at me with genuine surprise and delight. *"Smilin' Through?* No kidding?"

"No kidding, Kong."

"When did you . . ."

"I had it with me in Santa Clara. I brought it there to give to you, but . . ."

He took out a handkerchief and wiped his eyes. "That'll teach me to keep my mouth shut."

"Amen to that."

We had lunch, and it was like old times. On the way out he paused, embraced me, and, holding up the videocassette, said: "Thanks, Melvin."

"Aw, shucks. 'Tweren't nothin'."

"Like hell. I'm sorry about . . . well, you know."

Now it was my turn to be surprised. He had said "I'm sorry."

A moment to remember. We were back on track.

◉ *Chapter* 34

"He has *mellowed."*
Observation at
Sam Nase's party
for Buddy, 1986

IN THE NEXT few years, we stayed in touch with each other more or less regularly. While the opportunity to work together did not present itself during this period, I followed his activities closely in the music magazines as well as the newspapers. All seemed to be well with him, and judging from the tone of his voice in our telephone calls he was reasonably content with his lot.

Buddy had lost much of his hair during his late thirties and early forties. He had tried several styles of hairpieces and, I believe, at one time had investigated the possibility of implant and/or weaving. I never knew whether he would turn up wearing a short, GI-style "cut" or go with the flow when, for instance, the Beatles Prince Valiant–like do was in vogue.

When I finally saw him in December of 1986, he was wearing a silver-gray hairpiece that was very becoming. The occasion was a party at Sam Nassi's home in West Los Angeles. It was actually a belated celebration of Rich's sixty-ninth birthday, which had occurred on the previous September 30. It was a wild, festive evening with beautifully catered food, a huge complement of Buddy's friends and relatives, and Greg Fields's big band to supply the music.

At one point Annie Ross, Jack Jones, and I got up and did a scat challenge. Fields, a fine young drummer himself, coaxed Buddy onto the stand and into the drum chair. Fields had put together a group of heavyweights for the evening's entertainment. I particularly remember ex–Jimmie Lunceford trumpeter Snooky Young's electric presence. Rich set a tempo with the hi-hats, and away they went with a rousing finger-snapper. Naturally, Rich favored us with an extended solo. I had heard someone remark in recent weeks that Buddy was "slowing down, showing his age." Utter nonsense. That night he played with such gusto, flair, and humor that it was like going back in time to his so-called prime with Shaw, Dorsey, and the Buddy Rich band of 1946.

It was an affectionate evening with sentimental speeches, toasts to the birthday honoree, and much hugging and kissing. Marie and Cathy looked radiant and relaxed. Buddy and I talked for a long time. We were both pleased about a PBS special we would be doing in mid-January of the new year. We had not appeared together for some time, and we were looking forward to being on the same stage during the Public Broadcasting project.

As we talked, I looked closely at him. He was having an especially good time. He was being feted by admiring people, honored by some of his peers, respected for his longevity in the music business by all those present. Hey, I thought. The man is happy! He is a legend. He knows it; we know it; and he's reveling in it. His face seemed young and unlined. He was especially sweet-natured that night, and I came away from the Nassi party thinking it was the single nicest evening I had ever spent with him.

On January 12 we began rehearsing the PBS special. It was to be a ninety-minute presentation called "Sentimental Swing: The Music of Tommy Dorsey." The guests would be Jack Jones, Maureen McGovern, the L.A. Voices, the then-current road edition of the Tommy Dorsey orchestra led by trombonist Buddy Morrow, and special guest star Buddy Rich. I was to host the show and sing a few tunes.

The fact that the show was being done from the Hollywood Palladium tickled me. Buddy and I began our friendship in that enclosure and now, nearly forty-five years later, here we were again, back in the old big band stomping ground, celebrating that golden era and saluting Rich's old trombone-playing boss.

I thought B might become a little fractious regarding this Dorsey tribute. At one point in his life, he had absolutely detested Tommy, and by all accounts the feeling was mutual. Instead, he seemed to rise to the occasion. I had never seen him more cooperative, more enthusiastic than on that first rehearsal day. He was friendliness personified toward everyone connected with the show. In short, an absolute joy to be around. He *has* mellowed, I realized, remembering Steve Marcus's comment to me at the New Orleans World's Fair.

During a break in the rehearsal, he dragged me over to the piano and asked me to sing the song I had written about his daughter Cathy years before. When I began to sing:

> If anybody
> Can remind you the world's not so bad
> When the fates have dissolved
> Every sensible plan
> Cathy can

he began to weep. Stagehands, musicians, and performers saw him crying and were astounded. Buddy the macho? Buddy the tough guy? Crying? They didn't know him like I did. I had seen him react this way before, to a song, an orchestration, and particularly anything that had to do with the light of his life, Cathy. At that moment, I think I felt better about him and our friendship than I ever had before.

On the night of the taping, January 15, the Palladium was packed with celebrities, dignitaries, and a general mix of music fans, socialites, and related show business mucky-mucks. Everyone sensed it would be a special night, and it was, thanks in no small part to Buddy's stellar contribution. To say he was "up" for the evening would be to vastly understate the case.

Watching him, I thought about the memories bouncing off the venerable old walls of the ballroom and lodging in Buddy Rich's head. The premiere opening night with the Dorsey band, back in the days of prewar Hollywood; the exhilarating sets, backing the likes of Ziggy Elman and Don Lodice, meshing the gears of the perky Sy Oliver charts; the tension between the drummer and the band's great male singer; Lana standing in front of the bandstand, her beauty shining like a beacon, smiling her dimpled smile at the kid from Brooklyn. He's got to be thinking about all of it tonight, I told myself. It has to be affecting him.

It was.

He drummed his brains out on that show. He sang, joked, and brought everyone in the place to their feet with a stirring performance of "Hawaiian War Chant." The din at the close of that arrangement was something to hear. Buddy came out in front of the band. He was perspiring profusely. He mopped his face with a handkerchief, then comically put his hand inside his coat and mock-pumped it back and forth, as though his heart were bursting out of his chest. The audience laughed to see such sport, and the dish ran away with the spoon.

Had we known what fate had in store for Buddy in the immediate future, the laughter would have choked in our throats and died. Without realizing it, we had all witnessed Buddy Rich's final public performance.

□   *Chapter* 35

> *"What's wrong with me?"*
> Buddy to Marie,
> January 29, 1987

IT WAS A little over a week since we had taped "Sentimental Swing." The phone rang. Jack Jones's wife, Kim, a lovely young blond, was calling from New York. She could barely get the words out because she was crying.

"Mel. Oh, God, Mel. Have you heard about Buddy?"

"Buddy. No. What about him? What's wrong, Kim?"

Sobbing, she told me that Buddy had been out walking when suddenly his left arm began to "windmill." It kept going round and round, describing a 360° arc reminiscent of Joe E. Brown's comic windup when he played a baseball pitcher in *Elmer the Great*. Except there was nothing funny about Buddy's "windup." He regarded his flailing arm in stunned surprise and fright. He clamped his strong right hand over his left wrist in an effort to stop the involuntary action. He could not stop it. It was as though his left arm from the shoulder down had a life of its own.

Genuinely frightened, he fought for self-control, and to his surprise and relief the windmilling suddenly ceased, although his whole left side tingled with that sensation that one gets when your hand or foot falls asleep.

He went about his business all day with no recurrence of this aberration. That night, however, as he lay in bed in his Lincoln Center apartment, the nightmarish movement of his arm started all over again. Wet with fear, he called one of his closest friends, drummer Freddy Gruber, as well as Jack Jones, who, luckily for Buddy, was in New York for a few days before returning to his home in Los Angeles. Fred Gruber quickly went to Buddy's apartment and brought him to Mount Sinai Hospital.

Preliminary tests were done, and the results were inconclusive. The doctors' best guess was that Rich had a brain tumor. They wanted to do more testing, but Buddy, who had never experienced anything of this kind during his long history of health problems, insisted on getting out of there and going to Los Angeles. Kim and Jack, two of Rich's closest friends, went to Mount Sinai at three in the morning on January 29.

To their dismay they found Buddy on the floor of his hospital room, pincushioned with IVs. At his request they pulled the needles out of his arm, got him into pants and a T-shirt, the only clothing of his they could find, made their way out of the seemingly deserted hospital, drove to Kennedy airport, and boarded a westbound plane with him. They had planned a longer stay in Manhattan but would not even think of allowing Buddy to make the crosscountry trip alone in his current condition. Also accompanying Buddy and the Joneses on that flight was Casey Conrad, a friend of Buddy's and son of Hal Conrad, a well-known writer/producer.

Rich nearly had another seizure on the plane, and they were glad they had decided to get Buddy to UCLA Medical Center directly from Los Angeles airport. Marie, arriving in Sam Nassi's personal limousine, met them when they disembarked. They rushed toward West Los Angeles. On the way Buddy had yet another uncontollable spasm. Kim and Jack looked at each other, then at Buddy, with great apprehension.

At the hospital Rich was speedily admitted and taken in a wheelchair to a private room. He held Marie's hand on the way up, shook his head, and poignantly asked: "What's the matter with me?"

Dr. Donald Becker, a young brain specialist, began to examine the stricken drummer. Becker had his suspicions but refrained from making any judgment or offering a diagnosis until he could be sure. He did not believe that Rich had suffered a stroke. He thought initially that the cause of the trouble might be viral. Yet anything was pure conjecture until he could complete a thorough examination and make exhaustive tests.

Meanwhile, Rich's room was the scene of a constant parade of visiting friends and admirers. Johnny Carson was among the first to show up at UCLA Medical. When Rich told him, "They're taking me in for tests tomorrow," Carson quipped, "You just better be thankful it's not an intelligence test." Buddy laughed his first laugh in several days. To compound Rich's depression was the sad fact that directly down the hall from his room lay his younger brother Mickey, fighting cancer.

Naturally Buddy wondered whether his own affliction had anything to do with cancer. Was it hereditary? Mickey had been suffering with it for some time, in and out of the hospital. Buddy thought about it and decided in his own mind that he had simply had a stroke of some sort or was suffering from a viral infection. It would pass, he was sure. This was temporary. He had always had the constitution of a horse. If a spinal fusion and a quadruple bypass hadn't put him out of action, nothing would. Nothing. The only thing was—his entire left side was now tingling constantly. Still, he was absolutely certain that this condition would pass and he would be able to "get on with it."

His left hand was numb. His right hand was fine, perfectly normal, and he used it to make innumerable phone calls to his agents ("I'll be out of here soon. Of *course* book those dates. I'm going to play them!"); to his accountant, Joan Resnick, who informed the press that Rich was in good spirits and waiting for the test results; to his friends and band members, complaining that the hospital food "sucks" and informing all who would listen that he would be back behind the drums just as soon as he could "blow this pop stand." The way he held court in his private room you would have thought he was a royal personage, some foreign potentate, the Shah of Iran, receiving well-wishers at bedside. They all came, everyone you would expect and more: Carson and Sinatra and Jack Jones and Freddy Gruber (who literally took up residence in Buddy's room), Phil Collins, Ed Shaughnessy, Joanne Carson, Johnny's second wife, who became a strong shoulder for a gravely concerned Marie to lean upon, and, of course, the family—Jo and Marge and Cathy and her husband and even little grandson Nicky. If ever Buddy wondered about his place in the hearts and minds of his friends and fans, that first hospital stay must have convinced him that there were hundreds of people who cared for him on a personal level and thousands more, judging from the "get well" mail he received, who were pulling for him to "beat this thing."

What was "this thing?"

Buddy was discharged from UCLA after a two-week stay and was told to go home and wait for the test results. Sam Nassi insisted Buddy move into his spacious home on Moraga in West L.A. Sam had several household employees who could look after Rich. Buddy and Marie accepted his gracious offer.

In Nassi's mansion, the flow of friends continued. Rich wasn't in any kind of serious pain at that time, although he was receiving medication. Joanne Carson, Marie, and Cathy bustled about the house, feeding guests and seeing to Buddy's needs.

At UCLA Dr. Becker was trying to evaluate the results of the tests. The fact that Buddy had continued having seizures, not only during his hospital stay but currently at the Nassi residence, disturbed Becker greatly. There was so much edema, such a large amount of swelling in the brain, that he could not at first get a true picture of what the problem was.

Buddy had been working with a physical therapist at Nassi's house. He was hobbling around, forcing himself to be mobile. Late in February, without warning, he suffered nine seizures in a single day. The final jolt left him completely paralyzed on his left side. A badly shaken Marie called Dr. Becker. When he heard the news he advised: "Let's get Buddy in here right away for a biopsy."

Chapter 36

"Is this what you want for me?"
Buddy to Marie, March 1987

ON MARCH 1, 1987, Dr. Becker performed a biopsy on Buddy. As soon as the results were in, he called Marie and Cathy into his office and broke the news to them. *Time* magazine informed the world about Rich's dilemma by stating that "Buddy Rich, 69, artful and acclaimed jazz drummer . . . [has] an inoperable brain tumor. . . . He is undergoing chemotherapy."

In fact, Rich did not merely have a single tumor; three were growing inside his brain and "grapevining," spreading tentacles into his body. Buddy was informed of his illness, but the word "malignancy" was carefully avoided.

Those who went to see him at UCLA right after the biopsy procedure found a disturbed, depressed, and frightened individual but not a self-pitying one. He was restless and annoyed over the "inconvenience" his malady was causing. "I want to get the hell out of here and back on the road with my band" was his constant complaint.

His one-time flame Martha Raye came to see him. So did countless others. Bill Cosby, hamstrung with his TV shooting schedule, called Buddy every single day, as did Sinatra. Milton Berle was on the road, but his wife, Ruth, herself destined to die within months, was a frequent visitor. Of course, the family was ever-present. Jo and Marge practically camped at UCLA Medical, and their visits were terribly melancholy, moving between Buddy's and Mickey's rooms. It tore their hearts to see both brothers incapacitated, their futures uncertain. Luckily, the Rich family is made of tempered steel, and the sisters managed to smile, joke, and create a lighthearted atmosphere in both sickrooms. Mickey and Buddy benefited greatly from their sisters' combined strengths.

The mental anguish Marie and Cathy were suffering was not measurable. They knew how important it was to keep Buddy's hope alive and his spirits up, but they were living with the news that Dr. Becker had imparted to them: Marie's husband, Cathy's father, Nicholas's grandpa was terminal. There was nothing to be done. Dr. Becker answered their question regarding the feasibility of an operation: No. He recommended cobalt treatments. An operation, he felt, would only put the stricken drummer through unnecessary pain and trauma.

Yes, Marie persisted, but what if Buddy wanted the operation? Becker explained that three things could happen; Buddy could improve slightly, be exactly the same, or, he warned Marie and Cathy, die on the operating table. Buddy was then given the facts and offered the options. He decided to think about them for a week or so.

Meanwhile, he was rarely alone in his room. If the family wasn't there, Freddy Gruber was on hand. Jack Jones and his Kim were near-daily visitors. Seemingly every drummer in town made his way to Rich's private room to pay his respects. As Cathy put it, "You'd have thought Dad was the well one and all the visitors were the patients. He spent his days trying to see that everyone who came to see him was comfortable, fed, and not wanting for a drink." Jo and Marge, Marie and Cathy took turns at playing den mother, with Joanne Carson filling in when they weren't there.

Johnny Carson continued his frequent visits. On one occasion the talk-show-host-cum-onetime drummer gently needled Rich, "Well, now I have a better left hand than you!" Buddy laughed but soon fell into a deep depression and threatened to jump out of a window. Carson handled the situation perfectly. He walked over to the sickroom window, opened it, and said, "Go ahead! I'll hold it open for you!" Just that, nothing more. No speeches on how every minute of life is precious, no admonitions, no sermons about how devastating his suicide would be for his family. Just the simple expedient of an offer to help him do away with himself. Buddy got the message and changed the subject.

Paul Werth, an old friend of Rich's and a sometime producer/writer, was an alter ego spokesman for accountant Joan Resnick, on hand a great deal to field the inquiries of the press, friends, and fans. Despite Dr. Becker's determination not to put Buddy through dangerous (and in his judgment hopeless) brain surgery, Rich had gathered strength and courage with regard to an operation. Maybe it was the encouragement he was getting from friends like Gruber and Werth to try anything that might help. Maybe it was his natural obstinacy. When a concerned Marie questioned the sense of undergoing the procedure, he looked at her, set his jaw, and said, looking down at his inert left side: "Is this what you want for me?" Buddy must have known he had nothing to lose at that point. Any ray of hope, even a tiny glimmer . . .

That first week in March I was doing a guest shot on the NBC comedy show "Night Court." On the first day of rehearsal Sinatra phoned me on the set. He had recently been through surgery and was in considerable postoperative discomfort, but his first words to me were not about himself or his health problems.

"Hey, how about Buddy? The poor bastard!"

We spoke about Rich's condition for several minutes, and after he said goodbye, I made up my mind to visit B at UCLA that evening. (I had been on the road when he had suffered the nine seizures that had left him paralyzed on his left side, had come home to L.A. late Sunday night, and gone to work early Monday on "Night Court.")

He was on the phone as I walked into his room, talking to his agent. "Hey, man," he said, almost his old brusque self. "You heard me. I'm going to be out of here in a few days. Book the European tour. Book it! I've still got one good hand and one good foot. I'm making that tour!"

He hung up the phone and motioned for me to come around to the far side of the bed. I leaned down, hugged him, and kissed him on the cheek. He grabbed my wrist with his right hand in a grip so powerful I thought the blood would stop running into my fingers. I smiled at him.

"What is this 'sick' crap?" I demanded. "You're breaking my wrist, and meanwhile you're goofing off in this luxury suite. Boy, you'll do anything for attention."

He gave me what might have passed for a grin. "Come over on the other side now," he said. His voice was weak. I moved to the left side of the bed.

"Now," he commanded. "Take my left hand in yours." I gripped his left hand. It was dead. He made a mighty effort, and the fingers moved a millifraction. "Now, watch my left foot," he said. I looked at the uncovered toes. "See that?" he lied. "See 'em move?"

"I sure as hell did," I lied back. "So, when are you busting out of here so we can go play some tennis?"

He looked me in the eye. "I'm gonna beat this fucking thing. You know goddam well I'm gonna beat it."

"Well, let's see. You beat angina. You came through a quadruple bypass like you were sixteen years old. You even survived Tommy Dorsey." He laughed quietly. "And—you've smoked enough pot in your life to start a plantation. Yeah, you'll beat this like you've beaten everything else that ever got in your way."

He changed the subject abruptly. "Are you ready for what Marie came up with?"

"I'm all ears."

"The other day, I tried to hold a drumstick in my left hand. No way. It just fell right out. So then Marie gets this bright idea. She brings in a bunch of rubber bands and fastens a stick to my hand with them. I'm damned if it didn't work! Of course, moving my wrist is the main problem, but the stick stayed in my hand with those rubber bands holding it.

"So then she says, 'All right. The hell with your left hand. When you played the Paramount that time years ago, your left arm was in a sling, right? So if you have to—and I'm not saying you will, mind you—but if you absolutely had to, you could play with your right hand and foot, right?' I'll tell you, Melvin, she's one hell of a woman, my wife. And don't think I haven't been giving the 'one arm, one foot' bit a lot of thought. You heard me on the phone just now. If it comes down to it, that's precisely what I'm going to do. Believe me, I'll be playing drums again in a few weeks. A couple of months at the worst."

At that moment I wanted to believe it, even though Marie had told me he was doomed. Now other people began to drift into the room. His doctor arrived. I heard Buddy tell him he wanted the operation on his head. He was certain it was the answer to his problem. As Buddy turned his attention to another visitor, Dr. Becker looked at me and made a barely perceptible shake of his head. That move said volumes.

I went back out on the road. On March 16, my wife, Ali, called to read me a paragraph out of that day's Los Angeles *Herald Examiner*. In it Paul Werth announced Buddy's decision to undergo brain surgery that afternoon at 1:00 P.M. "Early reports that the tumor was inoperable were incorrect," said Werth. That was a crock, and everyone who knew the truth, including Paul, knew that. Werth's statement was understandable under the circumstances. It justified

Buddy's intentions and gave a speck of hope to Rich's myriad fans, who were waiting for a miracle and praying for their idol's recovery.

As Buddy was being wheeled into the operating room, a nurse prepared to sedate him prior to anesthesia. Solicitously she leaned over the gurney on which he was lying and asked, "Mr. Rich, are you allergic to anything?"

Buddy looked up at her and replied, "Yeah. Country and western music."

Chapter 37

"Jazz drummer Buddy Rich underwent four hours of surgery at UCLA Medical Center to remove a cancerous brain tumor and was listed in good condition afterward, a hospital spokesman said. Doctors said that Rich will undergo radiation treatments and should remain in the hospital for about two weeks."
Los Angeles Times, March 17, 1987

"I'm really going to miss you."
Buddy Rich to his daughter Cathy, April 1, 1987

DEAR GOD, HE looked terrible.

I had been out of town when the operation had taken place and had returned only yesterday, March 31. I had been in touch with Marie several times during the past two weeks. In all those phone calls she sounded defeated yet defiant. As ambiguous as that may seem, the impression she gave was that of a woman who knew her husband's condition was hopeless and who still refused to give up hope. Buddy had been released from UCLA Medical and was receiving radiation on an outpatient basis.

Now, April 1, he lay asleep curled up on a sofa in the spacious den of Sam Nassi's Bel Air mansion. I had to look twice to be sure it was him. He lay on his left side. He had always been short of stature; now he seemed shrunken. His color was poor, his head totally shaved. A long row of surgical staples described a horseshoe-like arc beginning behind his right ear and ending near his right cheek, evidence of the flap Dr. Becker had opened in order to operate on the three tumors that were draining the life out of him. The top of his head was yellowish with salve that had been applied to deter infection, of little consequence at this point.

Marie appeared and gave me a hug. Still beautiful in her early sixties, she showed the strain of the past few months in her eyes, the set of her mouth, the slight sag of her shoulders.

"Mel," she began, "I'm scared out of my wits. He woke up once this morning, looked at Cathy, and said, 'I'm really going to miss you.' All he wants to do is sleep. It's the treatments and the medication. He has no appetite. He hasn't eaten anything in almost five days. Maybe if you can get him interested in working on the book again . . ."

I kissed her cheek. "First let's get his attention."

I looked at him again and swallowed hard. I put my hand gently on his arm and said: "Hey, B. You gonna sleep all day? Come on. Wakie, wakie. We've got work to do."

He stirred, sighed, and slept on.

"Rise and shine, Traps. It's Melvie, and it's time for true confessions."

He opened his eyes and looked into my face. "Hey, Melvin." His voice was hoarse and weak. I turned on my tape recorder. "Ready when you are, C. B.," I informed him.

Slowly he began to talk. I had heard much of what he was telling me back in 1975, when we had gone into New York's Central Park on a balmy summer day. He had found a spot he liked, propped himself up against a tree, and reminisced about his early life. Now, even though he was going over old ground, I let him talk uninterrupted except to ask a few short, leading questions.

Amazingly, he came to life. His eyes sparkled as he recalled his early days. His voice actually became stronger. He smiled, joked, and at one point cried heartrendingly, as he remembered that particularly painful episode when he worked as a foil for a comic during the Depression. His nightly humiliation in front of audiences was a wound that had not been opened for decades. That afternoon he was reliving the experience, and tears spilled out of his eyes. The crying seemed cathartic, and shortly he dried his eyes, and we modulated to other subjects.

Marie, Cathy, and Joanne Carson moved in and out of the room, occasionally pausing to listen to Buddy's rumininations. During our talk I kiddingly asked him if he wanted this book to be a "puff piece." I said, "Do you want me to tell the world what a sweet, lovable person you are? That you're one of nature's noblemen?"

He laughed hoarsely and fixed me with one of his "Are you kidding?" stares.

"Do I look like Pat Boone?" he wanted to know.

"Only around the edges."

"Right on. Hey, Tormé, I'm like Popeye. I yam what I yam. That's the way I want you to write it."

"Warts and all, B?"

"Absolutely." His stare became even more intense. "Just one thing. Be accurate. That's the main thing. I've been misquoted so goddam many times I've lost track. I hate that. Whatever you write, be sure it's the truth. Straight life, dig?" I did indeed recall how incensed he had been when a two-part interview I had conducted with him for *Down Beat* back in 1977 had been edited to exclude some exceedingly rough language on Buddy's part. I was surprised at the time that he didn't realize how inappropriate some of the expletives he had used would have been in a pair of articles principally aimed at explaining how he played drums. When I had defended *Down Beat's* decision to soft-pedal the vulgarisms, Rich had exploded and damned the articles for not being absolutely faithful to the original interview tapes.

Now he gave me a look that I had seen on his face hundreds of times in the past: his eyebrows arched up, the corners of his mouth turned down in what appeared to be a challenging grin/smirk. He had exhibited that same "put-down" glance one evening years before when he had gone to see drummer Barrett Deems in a little club in Chicago. A sign outside the club proclaimed that Barrett was the "World's Greatest Drummer." Before Barrett even took the stand that night, Buddy walked up to him, gave him "the look," and said, in carefully measured tones: "The—world's—greatest—drummer?"

Deems delivered a nervous performance that evening. The next day the sign was changed to read BARRETT DEEMS: WORLD'S FASTEST DRUMMER. (And, of course, that wasn't true either. Swift though he was, no one was ever as fast as Buddy Rich.)

As Buddy treated me to this now-familiar grimace, he warned: "Like I said—write it right, you hear?"

"My hearing's perfect, no thanks to all those times we worked together when you played so loud I couldn't hear for three days afterward."

"Hey, you're lucky I let you sing with my band. Biggest break of your life."

"Yeah, yeah. Sure."

Abruptly he sat up straight and said he was hungry. Marie, who had been hovering in the background, smiled so brightly you would have thought he had announced he was buying her a sable coat. She and Joanne Carson made for the kitchen where they proceeded to warm up some spaghetti. Buddy and I continued to talk for a few minutes. All at once he became strident. "Where is that spaghetti? I want it NOW!"

Normally we'd have told him to shut up and hold his water. This burst of energy, however, this minitirade, was encouraging. They rushed the pasta to him. He ate it wolfishly. We talked for two more hours. He said, "See you tomorrow," turned on his side, and fell asleep. Marie apologized for his not saying goodbye. I waved her apology aside. I was happy he had taken nourishment. Plenty of time, I told her. Plenty of time. I promised to come back the next day. And the next and the next. We would work on the book. Some of the tenseness had gone out of her face. She saw me to the door.

"He actually looked, you know—animated. Interested. You two guys working on this book is the best thing that could happen to him."

I kissed her, got in my car, and drove away. The sky was clouding over. As I headed home, I realized it was April first. April Fool's Day. Was I being a fool to think there was plenty of time for Buddy? Hell no, I decided. The man's indestructible. We'll get this book done. Plenty of time.

The next day I did a few errands around town. Then, at a quarter to three, I headed west on the Sunset Strip toward Sam Nassi's house. As I neared La Cienega Boulevard, the phone in my car rang.

"Dad?" It was my daughter Daisy.

"Hi, honey. What's happening?"

"Dad—have you been listening to the radio?"

"No, Daze, I haven't. I'm headed out to Sam Nassi's house to work on Buddy's book, and I wanted to collect my thoughts. Traffic's getting heavy and . . ."

"Listen, Daddy, I wanted to tell you this myself. I have some bad news for you."

She told me. Buddy had gone in earlier that day for a radiation treatment. He had barely gotten back to the Nassi house when he suffered a seizure. He had been rushed back to UCLA, his blood pressure sinking dramatically. At 2:27, my longtime friend had died of cardiac arrest.

I hung up, pulled into an unoccupied parking spot on Sunset, and sat there for a moment, stunned. Then I started to cry. People passing on the sidewalk peered into my car at me. It didn't matter. Something important had passed out of my life, and I couldn't stem the flow of tears.

I looked at the gold ID bracelet he had given me years ago. Along with the flood of tears came a flood of memories. The silliness on the Paramount stage when we had worked there together in what seemed like another life; the twin MGs and his pride in driving his along the main stem of Broadway; sitting behind him on the Casino Gardens bandstand as he pushed and pulled the Tommy Dorsey orchestra with his old Slingerlands; his unconcealable, over-whelming joy in announcing that Marie had given birth to a baby girl; his closeness to his sisters in particular and his family in general; his undiminished love of jazz, no matter how many changes it went through; his never once "selling out," always remaining true to what he believed in, sometimes voicing those beliefs with a roughness that turned fans and critics off even as they admitted that he was a man committed to the truth no matter how unpalatably he might be dishing it out; his penchant for sometimes childish pranks wherein, like Mister Toad in *The Wind in the Willows,* he never "counted the cost"; the strange, walking, breathing anomaly he was—warm and caring and yet sometimes hugely insensitive—witty yet often abusively abrasive—thin-skinned when criticized but quick to voice his own criticism of anyone or anything he disliked or did not agree with—living to play drums yet impatient with questions about how he played—coveting friends and associates and often alienating them—and then I thought, for no good reason, about the very first time I met him, at the Palladium during the war, on that evening when he had still been in his Marine uniform, sitting in with the Charlie Spivak band, playing "Hawaiian War Chant."

The April sun was unseasonably warm as I sat in my parked car thinking about my very first encounter with Buddy, but at that moment a chill overtook me, and I felt the flesh on my arms bead and bubble.

"Hawaiian War Chant!" He had played it with Spivak that first night we met. And the very last thing he had ever done professionally had been his performance of "Hawaiian War Chant" during the PBS Tommy Dorsey special we had done only a few months before at, of all places, the selfsame Hollywood Palladium where we had originally met, decades ago. It was a coincidence that shook and saddened me. And with that thought came the powerful sense of loss. I had grown up in an era when the big bands and those musicians and singers who peopled them were the reigning heroes and heroines of the day.

A few of them were worthy idols in the best sense of the word. Even fewer transcended that category and occupied unique niches in musical history because they were "originals"; innovative, pathfinding artists who became role models for lesser talents to emulate, Louis Armstrong, Duke Ellington, Benny Goodman, Bix Beiderbecke, and Art Tatum were among the few who led the way and were worthy of the term "genius." Buddy Rich stands right alongside those giants of jazz. A musical phenomenon. One of a kind. We will never see his like again.

⊡ Epilogue

ON APRIL 5, 1987, the chapel at Pierce Memorial in Westwood was overflowing with Buddy's friends and family. Frank Sinatra, Morey Amsterdam, Robert Blake, Sammy Davis, Jr., Artie Shaw, Georgie Auld, Edie Adams, Johnny Carson, Angie Dickinson, Hugh Hefner, and Peter Falk were among the many who came to pay their last respects.

The closed casket rested beside one of Buddy's drum sets. Terry Gibbs, Al Viola, and Tom Warrington quietly played some of Buddy's favorite songs as the mourners talked to each other in hushed tones and awaited spoken remembrances by some of Rich's friends.

Sisters Jo and Marge sat somberly, nodding and thanking the many who approached them with words of comfort and condolence. Marie startled many of the guests by arriving in a red dress. She became furious with those who criticized her for it.

"It isn't my choice," she remonstrated tearfully. "It's Buddy's. He asked me—no, he ordered me—to wear this dress. I wanted to wear something black and simple. He insisted I wear this one if and when he passed away. I promised him I would and I did. End of discussion."

Buddy's niece, Barbara Corday, at that time president of Columbia Pictures Television, spoke humorously and movingly about her famous uncle. So did Frank Sinatra. Artie Shaw recalled Rich's shining year with the 1939 Shaw band, and Johnny Carson touched everyone's heart when he said: "Buddy was not afraid of dying. He was just afraid of living and not being able to play the drums." Jerry Lewis was as close to Buddy as anyone. He remembered how the drummer once "topped" him by tossing a zinger at him that went: "Dean [Martin] doesn't need you anymore. Better find another line of work."

Drummers Ed Shaughnessy and Jake Hanna agreed afterward that the memorial service was "more festive than sad." Buddy would have liked that epitaph.

Marie and Cathy handled the event bravely. Their attitudes were deceptively light. On purpose. They knew the man they had loved and fought with and lived with for so many years would have balked at anything maudlin or mawkish. They knew he would have approved of the light vein in which Carson and Sinatra and Barbara Corday had spoken of him.

Absent from the chapel was Buddy's brother Mickey. His wife, Elaine, who had distinguished herself as a supervising producer for Aaron Spelling Productions, was in attendance with her children, Josh and Lisa, but Mickey was still at war with his cancer and unable to attend.

Jack Jones had boarded an airplane on April 2, 1987, destination Europe. While the boarding process was underway, the plane's video system carried the national news. Jack and his wife, Kim, were reading, idly listening to the telecast. Jack heard the newscaster say something that sounded like "Buddy Rich" at the precise moment the plane's door noisily whirred closed.

Jones sat bolt upright and alerted Kim, but by the time the door was secure, the newsman had moved on to another item. The Joneses remained unsettled all during the long taxi run up to the active runway. The plane finally took off, and the second the seat belt sign went off, Jack got out of his seat and asked a passenger across the aisle whether he had heard something on the news pertaining to Buddy Rich. Casually the passenger said, "Yes. He died this afternoon."

Kim and Jack cried most of the way across the Atlantic. So it had all been in vain! The middle of the night trip to Mount Sinai hospital in New York. The secret exit from that establishment with Buddy wearing nothing but pants and a T-shirt. The drummer's enormous self-control on the flight to California when at one point he felt a seizure coming on and by sheer force of will controlled it, knowing that an uncontrolled spasm in flight could have resulted in Jack, Kim, and Buddy being delivered to the first available airport en route.

A performing obligation kept Jack and Kim from being on hand for Buddy's memorial service on April 5. Days later, upon the Joneses' return from overseas, a second, Jewish service was held at Pierce Brothers Westwood. A rabbi said kaddish. Jack, Kim, Marie, Cathy, Mel Brooks, and a few close friends were present. I stood with them, a yarmelke on my head, and listened while the holy man intoned the Hebrew prayer for the dead.

I looked at Jack. The rabbi's words were incomprehensible to him, but he sensed their grave meaning and was visibly moved. Kim, who had been crazy about Buddy, wept quietly. I couldn't help but be reminded of the poem that

Jones had written on his trans-Atlantic flight after hearing of Buddy's death. He had wired it to Marie, to be read at the first memorial service. Here, in part, is Jack's tribute:

IMPRESSIONS OF BUDDY

Here comes Buddy, get out of the way
Somebody pissed him off today
Dishonesty must have done the trick
That sort of thing always makes him sick

A more candid man I never met
Flat out style with no regret
A man with talent to the brim
Great drummers dream of being him

If you're alert you might perceive
A trace of heart just on his sleeve
Forget you saw him let it slip
Don't show and tell, cause that's not hip

A memorial service for Buddy Rich is slated for St. Peter's church May 17. Speakers will include Friars dean Jack L. Green, Hal Conrad, Honi Coles, Phil Leshin, Max Roach, Roy Eldridge, Joe Morello, Chico Hamilton, Sonny Igoe and others. *Variety*, May 13, 1987

Since Buddy had been born and bred in New York, it was fitting and proper that a service take place there to give his East Coast admirers, friends, and fellow musicians the opportunity to say goodbye.

Cathy set to work to stage a theatrical tribute to her late father. Originally it was Jerry Lewis's notion, and quickly Sammy Davis, Jr., Sinatra, Johnny Carson, Bill Cosby, Jack Jones, and I signed on. Unfortunately, our busy schedules never coalesced, and that particular event did not take place.

Cathy's determination to see her father's memory honored by his peers never waned. She was finally able to convince jazz entrepeneur George Wein to include a Buddy Rich tribute in the 1988 JVC Jazz Festival in Carnegie Hall. The Rich band, with Steve Marcus in command, was reassembled. Film clips of Buddy in various movies with a variety of bands and groups were projected throughout the evening, and a slew of fine performers gave of themselves in aid of a new foundation Cathy had organized: the Buddy Rich Memorial Brain Tumor Research Foundation, based at UCLA Medical Center.

The vintage Slingerland drums Buddy played in his final years belonged in a special place, and in March 1989 the Smithsonian Institution in Washington,

D.C., acquired them. Now Rich's drums belong to the ages, along with all the other meaningful memorabilia selected by the Smithsonian as representative of our long history of accomplishments in the arts and sciences.

The beat goes on. Cathy Rich has successfully resurrected her father's orchestra. She has inaugurated a new scholarship fund in Buddy's name for promising young drummers. She has successfully produced concerts with the Buddy Rich band at the famous theater in the round in Westbury, New York, and at the newly restored Art Deco classic Wiltern in Los Angeles. She plans many more such evenings. She has remarried and currently lives on Long Island with her husband, Steve Arnold, and her growing son, Nicky.

Marie Rich has settled in Palm Desert, California. The woman who could never get used to New York's frigid winters warms herself in the desert sun and thinks about the good/bad old days. There are friends on hand to comfort her. She is reasonably content. She misses her husband.

The Rich sisters thrive. Sprightly and active, Marge Rich Ritchie works in Los Angeles. Jo Rich Corday enjoyed a steady role on the long-running series "Cagney and Lacey" as the Bag Lady. When that show finally ran its course, she was paged for other TV parts and continues to work as a character actress and occasional extra player.

Elaine Rich has left the Spelling organization and has several TV projects currently in development at ABC and CBS in which she will function as executive producer.

Mickey Rich fought the good fight against his illness uncomplainingly, improving at times but eventually deteriorating. He died on July 18, 1989. A large turnout of friends, many of whom were famous, attended his memorial service.

II *Sidebars*

□ *Buddy and Drummers*

EVEN THOUGH HE knew he was the best, Buddy had kind things to say about a wide variety of drummers. Needless to say, drummers gravitated to him like bees to the hive, and he basked in the glow of admiration and proffered friendship. Jo Jones, Count Basie's elegant drummer during the thirties, the war years, and beyond, was Rich's idea of a great drummer. He saw in Jones a style of playing radically different from his own, short on technique but strong where keeping perfect time was concerned, knitting together the swinging Basie band along with guitarist Freddie Green, bassist Walter Page, and the Count himself. Jones pioneered fourteen-inch hi-hat cymbals, which he played in a very open, ringing fashion, as opposed to most drummers of his era, who played their smaller hi-hats closed or semichoked. Jo and Buddy were close personal friends, and Rich's admiration of the Basie drummer was genuine and lasting.

Buddy's early "swing" drummer influences included the legendary Chick Webb. Chick's hi-hat work and his general approach to powering a big band set standards that were copied by a multitude of drummers right through the Swing Era. Born a hunchback, often in great pain, he died young, but his records have become a correspondence course for hundreds of drummers.

As a child, Buddy had learned his predominantly military style of drumming by listening to vaudeville pit drummers; similarly, his conversion to jazz was made possible by listening to records and going to hear early practitioners in person. Gene Krupa, with the history-making Benny Goodman band, was an undeniable force in the percussion world, and Buddy emulated his playing at the inception of his own jazz-drummer career.

As I mentioned earlier, on the live-performance LP of Artie Shaw's orchestra recorded at the Café Rouge of the Hotel Pennsylvania in 1939, Rich plays a break between the bass drum and a cymbal that is clearly lifted from

Gene's repertoire. Whether it is done in homage, mimicry, or ridicule, the "break" was one of Krupa's signatures, and it stands on that recording for posterity to ponder over.

Rich's early clonings of Krupa's style—rim shots, hand-choked cymbal punctuations, cowbell licks—were always played with such purity, such positiveness, that the younger drummer seemed to be saying to the world: See? I can build a better mousetrap. He could and did—no disrespect to Gene, whom Buddy looked upon with appreciation and not a little awe for having single-handedly put drums into the forefront of the collective public mind.

He thought Ray McKinley a supremely musical drummer, if a bit light-handed when it came to "kicking" a band. He enjoyed Zutty Singleton's simplistic playing and commented favorably on Jimmy Crawford's work with the Jimmie Lunceford band. Cozy Cole and Sonny Greer were too rigid, too "unswinging" for his tastes, yet he always spoke of them with respect. Buddy Schutz, a Krupa facsimile who played for years with the Jimmy Dorsey orchestra, was "adequate" in Rich's eyes, as were Maurice Purtill with Glenn Miller and Cliff Leeman with Charlie Barnet. I once voiced my enthusiasm for Leeman's playing with the Barnet band. Buddy shrugged noncommittally. He had taken Leeman's place with the Artie Shaw band in 1939 and had made an enormous difference in the process.

Buddy's appraisal of the talents of Dave Tough and Don Lamond, who consecutively propelled the famous Woody Herman Herd, could not have been more positive. Tough and Lamond were short on solo ability, long on holding the Herman band together with strength and skill. Buddy thought they were quite special. A standout in Buddy's opinion was the peerless Sid Catlett, who had presided for a time over the Louis Armstrong rhythm section. "Sid was a guy who sounded great with a small group or a big band. He was something else," praised Rich.

Alvin Stoller, the young man who took Rich's place with the Tommy Dorsey band, played more like Buddy than anyone else. He had excellent technique, taste, and a strong, metronomic sense of time.

Buddy had a bantering relationship with Shelly Manne, who played so effectively with the hard-to-hold-together Stan Kenton orchestra, as well as having provided the rhythmic kick for a later edition of the Woody Herman Herd. One night at a small Los Angeles club called the Haig, Shelly asked a visiting Buddy Rich to sit in with the quartet that Manne was fronting. Shelly relinquished the sticks, and Rich proceeded to treat the audience to a turn that left the entire room in shock. He handed the sticks back to Shelly, who looked him in the eye and said: "Buddy, you prick." Rich grinned and did not take offense. He had delivered another lesson in one-upmanship.

He had great affection and respect for Ray Bauduc, whom he considered to be the very best of the Dixieland drummers. "He can really play," he once remarked to me. "His closed roll is just beautiful."

Louie Bellson, probably the nicest as well as one of the best drummers ever, loved Rich, and Buddy returned that affection twofold. Bellson studied the Master's work as if he were the everlasting student and Rich the professor which, of course, was exactly the case. They never had any sort of falling out, although one night during a tour they were making with Jazz at the Philharmonic, it could have happened had not Louie been the sweet, temperate human being he is.

Buddy and Louie were called upon each evening to engage in a "drum battle." Rich, because of his fondness for Bellson, had been playing with some restraint, careful not to show up his young friend. One night, as Buddy was walking toward the stage door of that evening's venue, a Bellson fan snarled a warning. "Hey, Buddy! Louie's gonna cut you a new asshole tonight." That night, as the drum challenge began, Rich, the old expert at timing and drama, paced himself, cleverly allowing Louie to dominate with his famous twin-bass-drum patterns and his undeniable technical prowess. Then it was Buddy's turn.

He began quietly with a barely discernible press roll accelerating into a more open roll, then, removing the "governor," he surged full steam ahead. As he had on so many evenings of his life, he went on to produce a historic solo. When he finished to tumultuous applause, whistles, and a standing ovation, he smiled at Louie and, with his sticks held in his right hand, indicated: your turn. Louie Bellson wisely laid his sticks down upon his large tom-tom. The drum battle was over for that evening.

Buddy maintained long-standing relationships with several drummers, among them Sonny Igoe, Sonny Payne, Mel Lewis, Freddy Gruber and Ed Shaughnessy of "The Tonight Show." My drummer, Donny Osborne, Jr., was one of the few Buddy would allow to sit in with his band. Donny was a kind of protégé of Buddy's, and after Don, Sr., resigned from Slingerland, Buddy wangled a set of WFL drums for Donny—no mean feat, since Donny was the son of the ex-president of Ludwig's number one rival company.

Excepting Max Roach, Rich did not like many so-called bebop drummers ("long on pounding, short on talent") or most rock drummers ("animals—no talent animals"). On the other hand he never in my company disparaged any of them in a personal way. On those occasions when a bop drummer or a rock drummer would come backstage after one of his performances, he was always charming and friendly.

The only drummer he had a personal aversion to was Butch Miles. I heard him order his road manager, Steve Peck, to "keep Miles off the bus" one evening when Miles attended a Rich concert, clearly indicating he wanted no part of Miles socially. Miles himself admitted in the Buddy Rich memorial edition of *Drum Tracks* magazine that in 1987 he and Buddy were "on the outs again." However, Rich never allowed his personal feelings to interfere with his professional judgment. In 1975 he recommended Miles to Count Basie. Miles played with the Count for a number of years thereafter.

Buddy and Drums

LANCELOT'S QUEST FOR the Holy Grail was no more passionate or obsessive than was Buddy Rich's lifelong search for the perfect snare drum. He fussed and fumed over a wide variety of snare drums throughout his lifetime, and I cannot recall a single one that ever really satisfied him. The snare drum, of course, is the centerpiece of the drum set. Everything a drummer does flows from the snare, and, depending on the player's range of technique, that all-important piece of equipment can make or break his performance.

No matter what he played, irrespective of size or make or model, they always sounded perfect to me. Still, he was never completely pleased with one in all the years I knew him. Well, maybe one. He used to speak with affection about the original snare drum he played as Traps, the Drum Wonder. "Now that was a snare drum," he would chirp. "Old Man Ludwig knew how to build a drum in those days." Was it merely nostalgia that prompted his outburst. Perhaps not.

Years ago, he got hold of an old Ludwig snare made back in the '20s. He fooled with it for a while in his Las Vegas home, tightening the heads and the snares, tapping the batter head, then the snare head, with his fingers like a doctor probing a patient's abdomen. I thought he had finally found the panacea. The drum really sounded crisp and rich. Because of his enormous technique, he always kept the batter head fairly tight and the snares smartly pressed against the bottom membrane. He grinned a lot whenever he addressed that old Ludwig with a pair of sticks. Yet, mysteriously, he never used it onstage and refused to explain why.

As Traps, he had been the shining jewel in the Ludwig and Ludwig diadem. When Gene Krupa became the Deb's Delight in the middle and late 1930s, that drummer's association with Slingerland drums fired most young drummers' imaginations. The long, pear-shaped lugs, the gleaming chrome rims and cymbal stands, and the soft, white Marine Pearl–covered tom-toms, bass drum, and snare drum induced many aspiring youngsters as well as a huge number of professional players to abandon whatever brand of drums they were currently banging on and opt for the Slingerland product.

When Buddy played with Joe Marsala's group at the Hickory House in New York in 1937, he used a rudimentary set of drums, the manufacturer of which was lost to his memory. Just before he left Marsala to join Bunny Berigan's big band in '38, H. H. Slingerland, who had known of the phenomenal young drummer since his early vaudeville days, offered Rich a set of drums by way of getting him to become a Slingerland endorser. Buddy jumped at the chance. He loved the look and feel of the Slingerland product, and, besides, finances were low and a free drum set was just what he needed. His only concern was Gene Krupa.

With Slingerland, Buddy would never fare better than number two in the pecking order as long as Gene was the company's prime drumming star. And perhaps not even number two. Other Slingerland users of the period included Ray McKinley with the Jimmy Dorsey orchestra, Cliff Leeman with Artie Shaw, Dave Tough with Benny Goodman, and Maurice Purtill with Tommy Dorsey.

Briefly he considered sounding out the other drum companies: Gretsch, Wm. F. Ludwig, Leedy and his old associates, Ludwig and Ludwig. The thing was, he really liked the Slingerlands, and in the end he accepted Old Man Slingerland's offer. When the Berigan band played Chicago, Buddy sat for a photo session with the famed show-business photographer Maurice Seymour. Slingerland provided a set of drums for this sitting that consisted of two bass drum–mounted tom-toms, a pair of bass drum–mounted cymbals on swivel arms, and a trap tray! Buddy's initials in large Old English-Style are framed with a "natural" sign as a bass drum logo. Rich laughed a lot over this clutter of drums, which, because of the many ads in which they appeared, gave the impression it was his special setup.

"Look at those cymbals on the bass drum," he sneered, showing me the 8″ x 10″ glossy. "How the hell could I ever get to them? I'd have to be a contortionist."

The drum set Slingerland did give him was a duplicate of the Krupa outfit. Buddy rarely varied from that setup during his long career. A bass drum (14″ x 28″ originally, later supplanted by a 14″ x 26″), a 5 1/2″ x 14″ snare drum, a bass drum-mounted 9" x 13" tom-tom, two 16" x 16" floor tom-toms, two floor stand cymbals, two bass drum–mounted cymbals, a cow bell clamped directly in front of him on the bass drum hoop, and a hi-hat stand to the left of the snare drum, sporting two deep cup 11" Zildjian cymbals, which gradually evolved into more impressive sizes.

He brought those drums to the Artie Shaw band in 1939, and Slingerland ads of the day as well as his appearances with the band in Paramount and Warner Brothers shorts reveal a rather strange bass drum insignia. Buddy's initials appear in a semi-arc in the upper left-hand corner of the bass drum head. The "B" and the "R" seem tied together with a thin line. There is no encasing shield. When the Shaw band appeared in *Dancing Co-ed* (MGM, 1939), Rich's bass drum head exhibited a script-style "BR" with a larger "AS" (for Artie Shaw) more or less centered on the head. Not until Buddy joined the Tommy Dorsey band did he finally standardize his logo, a design he would use for the rest of his professional life: a heraldic shield with his initials in block letters, angling upward and bracketed by a pair of thick, black lines, adjacent to which were the letters "TD" in considerably larger font. This was the design used by Gene Krupa during his years with Benny Goodman beginning in 1935.

Calfskin heads were the only kind of drumskins available in those days. Weather and temperature played hell with them. Heat would tighten them to the bursting point one moment, then cold would reduce them to flaccid cowhides the next. Rich constantly tuned and tightened his drums and managed to maintain a consistent sound out of the bass drum (deep and resonant), the snare drum (tight and raspy), and the floor tom-toms (pitched low for a junglelike effect).

Buddy stored his Slingerlands when he checked into the Marines in 1942 and took them out of the mothballs when he was discharged in 1944 and went back to work for Tommy Dorsey. In 1946, when he left Dorsey to form his own band, he had a new deal with the WFL drum company.

He had never liked William F. Ludwig, Jr., although he had been fond of his father, founder of Ludwig drums. Junior, however, had made Rich an offer he could not refuse. For the first time in his life, Buddy was a paid endorser. The figure (undisclosed) was enough to make him turn his back on the Slingerland company. It wasn't just the money. With Ludwig, he would be top dog. Number One. The premier drum star on the WFL roster, a position he could not hope to attain with the Krupa-dedicated Slingerland people. Being the head honcho meant a lot to Rich. And why not? He was the greatest drummer in the world. His pride dictated that he not take a backseat to anyone when it came to promotion, publicity, or status with a drum company.

Now he set out to test his strength with his new suppliers. He demanded—

and got—drums, holders, wire brushes, sticks, and cymbals until he was awash in them. He repeatedly badgered Bill Ludwig, Jr., about the Ludwig snare drum, an instrument many drummers found very much to their liking but Buddy disdained. The Wm. F. Ludwig organization tried to please him. They designed several new snare drums specifically for him. None of them would do. I once saw him kick a brand-new Ludwig snare across a room into a wall. "Friggin' drum stinks," he barked. I thought he was nuts. It sounded great to me when he played it.

He used to snort at drummers who claimed they "tuned" their drums. "You don't tune drums, dummy; you tighten them." Many disagreed with this edict from the Great One. At the beginning of the second side of Goodman's classic "Sing, Sing, Sing," Krupa "tuned" his small tom-tom to an "A" to blend with the famous Vido Musso tenor sax solo. Percussionist Chauncey Morehouse's "Ngoona Ngoona" drums were also tuned to play melodies of a sort.

Rich experimented with a number of snare drums, including a three-inch "bebop" model being used by the new wave of jazz drummers in the late '50s and the 60s. He got more noise than anyone else out of one of those freakish little toys, but the basic power he needed from a snare drum simply wasn't there. He abandoned the "bebop" drum quickly.

He clashed with Bill Ludwig, Jr., and began trying all sorts and makes of drums. A company called Fibes had entered the drum scene, and many young rock and roll drummers were using them. Rich tried them. He wasn't thrilled. Vox drums were yet another venture into the unknown for Buddy. They simply did not hold up under his merciless strength.

His legendary power *was* equaled by a new company called Rogers Drums. Their product was built like cast iron, reminiscent of the Radio King Slingerlands Buddy had used long ago. He made a deal with Rogers and for a time was reasonably happy with their output. Before long, he began to nit-pick. After a few years with that company, his relationship with them came to an end. The Rogers drums (and there were dozens of them in all sizes and shapes) were plunked into a warehouse in Bayonne, New Jersey, to sit and gather dust with the Fibes, Vox, Ludwigs, and old Slingerlands already consigned to what I used to call the Graveyard of Lost Drums. God only knows the value of all those abandoned pieces.

In a quirky mood, Rich hauled out the Fibes once more and used them during the making of a 1968 album called "The New One," usually referred to as the Buddy Rich psychedelic album. Those drums drove him crazy. In exasperation, he called an old friend, Don Osborne, who was running Slingerland Drums for absentee owner "Bud" Slingerland, Jr. (Old Man Slingerland had died years before.)

"Help!" cried Buddy.

"Gotcha!" answered a compassionate Don Osborne. A good drummer himself, Osborne had known for some time what trauma Buddy was going through, trying to find drums he could be happy with. He entered into a deal with Rich that included providing all the drums Buddy could ever want or need plus Rich's now-standard endorser's fee. Buddy was delighted. He liked Osborne enormously and was happy to be reunited with the company. Shortly after he signed with Slingerland, he visited Osborne in his home. On hand were Osborne's wife, Eddy, and Don, Jr., a budding young drummer.

Osborne led Rich down to the den. Twelve snare drums sat in a row on the floor. Buddy's eyes lit up like it was Christmas and he was six years old. For the next few hours, with Junior watching respectfully, Buddy tested every one of the snare drums. He kept going back to one in particular. Finally he picked it up, looked at the senior Osborne, and said: "This is the greatest snare drum I have ever played." Osborne was beside himself with joy.

Rich stayed with Slingerland for many years, but as time went on, the perfectionist in him surfaced, and he became more and more finicky. He had a terrible blowup with Don Osborne when the latter went to see Buddy and his band at the Plugged Nickel in Chicago and found, to his dismay, that Rich was using a Fibes snare drum.

"Goddam it?" Osborne muttered. "The same old 'snare drum' crap." After the set Osborne, a man not at all shy about speaking his mind, upbraided Buddy about using a "scab" snare drum. "Where the hell is the 'greatest snare drum you ever played,' huh? Do you know how this makes me and the company look? Like shit, that's how! Jesus! I send you drums till they're coming out of your ass and you do this to me? To Slingerland?"

A pitched verbal battle ensued, and it was inevitable that sooner or later Rich would be "moving on." Surprisingly, Bill Ludwig, Jr., came back into the picture. He had heard of the falling out between Buddy and Osborne. He offered Buddy even more money than he was getting from Slingerland if he would once again endorse WFL drums. Rich, always in debt, accepted.

Ludwig shipped a slew of drums to Buddy. If the drummer had to do "The Tonight Show" and did not have a set on hand, Bill, Jr., obediently placed a brand-new kit at his disposal, after which Rich either stored them or, more often, gave them away. Jerry Lewis, Johnny Carson, and Sammy Davis, Jr., were three of the many recipients. Buddy's original antipathy toward Bill Ludwig, Jr., eventually surfaced again. Several years—and hundreds of pieces of equipment—later, he flew the Ludwig coop.

In the middle 1980s, unsponsored and unaffiliated, Buddy laid his hands on a vintage set of Slingerland Radio Kings. He had come full circle: Slingerland to

Slingerland. Drummers who came to see and hear him play during the final years of his life grinned with approval and envy when they saw those drums.

And the snare drum?

During one of our last performances together, he smiled at me and, petting the old Radio King snare affectionately, said: "Best goddam snare drum I ever played."

◙ *Buddy and Drumming*

EVEN THOUGH HE denounced *Down Beat* magazine for deleting most of the expletives in our two-part interview (February 9 and 23, 1977), he was unusually voluble about how he played drums in those twin sessions.

When I asked Buddy about the radical angle of his snare drum during his Artie Shaw days, he replied:

"I was using a 26" bass drum at the time, and consequently I had to sit two inches higher, and I had to bring the snare drum up that high. I'd be playing above the drum; instead of my hands falling on top of the drum, they'd be above, and I'd be wasting all of this energy. I couldn't very well keep the drum at a flat angle and be down low, so the only way that I could hit a rim shot would be to have the drum below me. . . .

"After about a year with Artie's band, I changed the setup and started sitting a little lower, bringing the snare drum down a little bit so that it was in about the same area as the 9-by-13 tom-tom. By not having to raise your hand to play the drum, you can get around the drum because everything is on the same level as your hands."

TORMÉ: "More the economy of motion?"

RICH: "That's the idea of playing. Maintaining some kind of stamina is to be able to get around the drums with the least motion. You have everything just exactly where your hands would automatically be. The position [of the drums, cymbals, etc.] is everything."

TORMÉ: "You once told me that if you can master a roll, both closed and open, that was the center, the core of playing."

RICH: Most drummers who can't roll really don't have any techniques with the hands. You must have the ability to control your wrists to a point where you can make your roll sound like you're tearing a piece of sandpaper. Most teachers teach kids today that there is a definite way of playing; start with the right hand or start a pattern with the left hand. Wrong. You play the way your hands automatically fall. Not left or right or right or left—as long as you have the control and ability to play what you have in mind."

On the subject of solos:

RICH: "All solos should be paced. You start with an idea. I like to think of my solos as telling a story. You tell the beginning of a story and you build up to a punch line. But if you tell a story and tell the punch line first, where are you going? That's the way I play, according to my moods. I know exactly what I want to do and where I want to go. I pace myself to where I know that at the very end of my solo, I'm going to play a roll or I'm going to knock some cymbals around, but I know I must conserve energy to get me through the ending. I don't use my body. It's all wrists. The only reason you raise your arms is to hit a cymbal or reach behind you to hit a tom-tom. The actual playing all takes place down here, so that you're not breathing heavily. You're just using your wrists."

We explored the specific kind of semi-closed, choked hi-hat cymbal sound he produced with the old Artie Shaw band.

RICH: "In those days, I used a much smaller 11″ hi-hat. And both cymbals were the same weight, medium thin. I didn't need the overwhelming sound of large cymbals [for the Shaw instrumentation]. So the whole concept was different. I always played so that I managed to hit two [hi-hat] cymbals at one time. Instead of just playing the top [hi-hat] cymbal which gives you that 'te te bah te te bah.' This way you get 'thw thw thw thw thw.' The only way you can do that is to hit both cymbals at the same time."

I asked him about the "lever action" of his right hand when he played the hi-hats. He admitted that he did not play with his "fingers," that his hi-hat playing stemmed purely from his wrist.

RICH: "You don't get a sound with the fingers. They don't control the stick; your hand controls the stick, and if you can't use the wrist action, then you don't have stamina and power to play hi-hats at any given tempo for any length of time."

He allowed that tap dancing was one of the reasons he had such great coordination between his hands and feet behind a set of drums. When I asked him how young kids coming up could learn to play jazz drums, he recommended listening, listening, listening to early Basie and Woody Herman records until they "get into your ear, into your body. It's just something that you feel. If you're going to play jazz, you have to listen to the jazz list."

TORMÉ: "What about people who intellectualize the art of drumming and equipment? For instance, recently in *Down Beat,* there was a whole thing by Billy Cobham and Louie Bellson on cymbals. Did you read it?"

RICH: "Ah, yes, I always read the comics on weekends. . . . I think that to use different type cymbals for recording, for a theater, and for a club is ludicrous. I mean, if you can't control the sound of your cymbals wherever you play. . . . When you play them, if they feel good, that's it. You don't deaden cymbals, you don't get bigger cymbals because you're playing a bigger hall. You don't get smaller cymbals because . . ."

His face was getting red. He looked positively apoplectic. I changed the subject.

TORMÉ: "How about the quest for the perfect snare drum? I have never known you yet to like a snare drum."

RICH: "I only played on one snare drum in my whole career that I really loved, and that was an old Slingerland Radio King."

TORMÉ: "The old Gene Krupa model?"

RICH: "It could have been a Gene Tierney model for all I know. The construction of that drum was perfect for the kind of drum sound that I'm looking for."

Since he demanded crispness out of a snare drum. I was not surprised when he commented: "I don't like loose snares. I'm constantly turning the wheel to pull the snares up."

What about his bass drum?

RICH: "All drummers muffle [bass drum] heads; otherwise you get such a boom that the drum is unplayable. I use two-inch strips of felt, one on each side of the head. It takes the overtone away, but you still get the volume and you still get the bass sound. When I joined Artie Shaw's band, instead of accenting things with the brass on the snare drum, I would accent on the bass drum. It would drive [Artie] crazy because he was used to hearing 'four' and not having the drummer make the accents with the brass.

"Then, when I didn't do it, Artie missed it, because the bottom wasn't there, and it was all highs. I started to develop the foot by playing not only the accents, but then I started to incorporate it into solos, by simply leaving two or three beats out with either hand and using my foot."

Considering that he absolutely hated talking about the pyrotechnics of playing drums, these interviews were a rare dialogue indeed—probably dry and boring to the average reader, but instructive and perhaps even inspirational for drummers reading this book.

Buddy on Film

BUDDY RICH'S FIRST encounter with the motion picture camera occurred at Warner Brothers' Vitaphone studios in New York. The year was 1929. He was twelve. The seven-minute one-reeler in which he starred was called "Buddy Traps in Sound Effects." In it he sang, danced, and finally wound up playing the familiar "Stars and Stripes" finale that had won the hearts and applause of so many thousands of people during his younger years.

The next time he was seen on film was ten years later, with the Artie Shaw band in a sappy Paramount short called "Class in Swing." The band is seen in a glossy Hollywood setting. Unfortunately, the opening tune, "Table d'Hote," is performed in a series of annoying cuts in which first the rhythm section, then the saxophones, and finally the brass appear. To compound this idiocy, an offscreen narrator who sounds like he should be announcing newsreels talks almost incessantly throughout the entire program, explaining to us dumbbells how the rhythm section functions, why the saxes and brass come in where they do, and what this thing called Swing is really all about. Helen Forrest takes a turn, singing "I Have Eyes," and then the band cuts loose with "Shoot the Likker to Me, John Boy." Even the irritating narrative cannot ruin the sparkling performance by the Shaw band, and Buddy, looking young, trim, and enthusiastic, comes in for his share of closeups, tom-tomming in support of Shaw's solo clarinet at the end of the tune.

Artie had made a short subject for Warner Brothers in 1938 called "Artie Shaw and His Orchestra," with Buddy's predecessor, Cliff Leeman, on drums. Now that same studio paged him for a second effort, "Symphony in Swing."* This time the band is let pretty much alone on the opening number, "Alone

* Sources vary as to which "Short" ("Class in Swing" or "Symphony in Swing") was the first to be produced.

Together," as well as on Johnny Mercer's "Jeepers Creepers," with a breathless, kicking Tony Pastor vocal gracing the arrangement. Rich is seen mainly in background shots during this tune, but his drumming is *felt* in no uncertain terms. Helen Forrest sings "Deep Purple" beautifully but is only seen in the first few frames of the song. Director Joseph Henabery (who, incidentally, played the role of Lincoln in D. W. Griffith's *Birth of a Nation*) chose to cut away from Forrest to a garden where two lovers dressed in period costumes say their tearful goodbyes. Finally, we see Helen again for the last few bars. Ridiculous.

The closer is more like it, although for pictorial purposes the band is set up in opposite rows, saxes on one side, brass and rhythm facing them. I doubt if any band in the history of music ever set up this way. Anyway, it's a pleasure to hear the Shaw band go through the paces of "Lady Be Good," complete with a fluid Georgie Auld tenor solo and an "out" chorus reminiscent of Basie's "Every Tub." Rich's overhand snare drum–hi-hat technique is very much on display. In those days he, like most drummers, played in that fashion, with the snare drum tilted at a more radical angle. Looks awkward, but at the time, it worked.

Prior to this little Warner Brothers tidbit, the band had been toiling over in Culver City on the MGM lot in *Dancing Co-ed,* starring Lana Turner and Richard Carlson. The plot (?) revolved around a professional dancer (Turner) enrolling in a midwestern college in order to be eligible for a nationwide contest designed to choose a new dancing partner for movie star Lee Bowman. The Shaw band tours around the country, accompanying the young college hopefuls.

While the band is seen briefly in a few of these college contest scenes, the only featured Shaw number is "Traffic Jam," which spotlights Buddy at the beginning, playing a drum break that leads into the instrumental. Unfortunately, there are many cutaways while the band is playing. Considering Shaw's enormous popularity that year (his band was chosen best Swing band by virtually every music magazine in the country), you would have thought they'd let the band have its head without intrusive and largely unneccessary cuts to some of the principal (and not-so-principal) players. No such luck, and we have to be content with snatches of Artie and the boys as they powerhouse their way through "Jam."

Buddy was not to be seen again on film until after he joined Tommy Dorsey. TD's gang checked into Paramount studios to appear in *Las Vegas Nights* in October 1940. Constance Moore, Bert Wheeler, and Phil Regan were among the cast members. Aside from the immensely popular "I'll Never Smile Again," sung by Sinatra and the Pied Pipers, the band was featured in two slots. "Song of India" was a Dorsey evergreen that Buddy roundly detested playing. It was an icon, however, in Tommy's library and a logical, if unexciting, choice for the first film in which his band appeared.

"The Trombone Man Is the Best Man in the Band" is a novelty number that eventually finds Buddy playing a rather long drum solo. The tune was a lightweight entry, but better "Trombone Man" than nothing.

Ship Ahoy, made at MGM in the spring of 1942, was excellent. Tommy's theme, "I'm Getting Sentimental over You," immediately follows the opening titles, after which the film gets off to a roaring start with "Hawaiian War Chant," beautifully photographed and featuring a Don Lodice tenor solo and some smashing duet work by Buddy and Ziggy Elman.

To begin this segment, Buddy's drums were placed on a camera platform, and as he plays the opening tom-tom gambit, he and his drums, with the camera directly in front of him, are transported as if by magic carpet from the forefront onto the bandstand. It was a favorite cinematic ploy at MGM, extremely effective, and was used during Harry James's "Trumpet Blues" number in *Bathing Beauty* (1944).

Buddy is heavily featured in "I'll Take Tallulah," pairing with Eleanor Powell in a combination drum-tap routine. The byplay between these two artists tossing drumsticks and a tom-tom at each other in perfect rhythm is a highlight of the film.

During a Frank Sinatra rendition of a nice Burton Lane tune, "The Last Call for Love" (based on the bugle call "Taps"), there is a trombone interlude after the vocal chorus. Dorsey, his trombonists, and part of the rhythm section, with Buddy very visible, are dressed in quasi-Russian costumes in keeping with the festive "Captain's Night" being celebrated aboard the ship on which the band is performing.

I once brought a videocassette of *Ship Ahoy* to Rich, and we watched it together. During the trombone interlude in "Last Call," I noticed that in the film Buddy was grinning like the Cheshire cat to begin with, and then actually breaking up. "What was so funny?" I asked him.

"Well, we were 'sidelining,' you know?" "Sidelining" means that the musical number in question is prerecorded before filming of that number begins. When the cameras roll, the recorded music is played back, and the musicians merely "mime" what they have previously recorded. What the moviegoer hears is the prerecorded version of the song or instrumental.

Buddy continued. "So, we get to that trombone interlude, right? And Tommy and the 'bones are making the worst kinds of sounds imaginable on their horns. Really horrible. It looked like they were playing the chart beautifully, but, since what was coming out of their horns wasn't actually being recorded, they blew some of the worst-sounding stuff you ever heard. If you think I was breaking up, you should have seen the sax section. They weren't in the shot, and they laughed right through that part of the chart."

Maverick Buddy moonlighted in a little Universal movie in early 1943. Without getting his boss's permission, he appeared as a bandleader in *How's About It?,* an innocuous bit of frippery that starred the Andrews Sisters and Shemp Howard. The main premise of this movie is the Andrews Sisters' overwhelming desire to quit their jobs as elevator operators in a music publishers' building and sing with Buddy Rich's orchestra. Again and again, Patty Andrews sighs dreamily as she contemplates the joy that singing with Buddy's band would bring her and her siblings.

Finally, Shemp Howard, acting as the girls' agent, arranges to have them appear with Rich's orchestra. Buddy is seen near the end of the film, dressed in a white dinner jacket, as the leader of a studio orchestra put together for the movie. He does a featured number called "Take It and Git," with loudly shouted encouragements from the band as a few unidentified musicians play their twelve-bar blues solos.

Rich plays an extended solo that is almost a carbon copy of his "Trombone Man" work. When Tommy Dorsey found out that Buddy had done *How's About It?* without getting his permission, he raised merry hell with the drummer, creating another tear in the delicate fabric of their relationship. Rich couldn't have cared less.

By the time the band checked into MGM for work on *Du Barry Was a Lady,* Buddy had made his commitment to the U.S. Marines and was awaiting his orders to report for duty. Consequently, his near-disinterested demeanor during the playing of "Well, Git It" is somewhat understandable. Even an obvious concession from Tommy, the placement in front of the instrumental of a brief Rich solo, did not mollify Buddy, who wanted out of the Dorsey organization and into the service.

To make matters worse, the band was made to dress in powdered wigs and eighteenth-century costumes during a long dream sequence that takes up the largest portion of the film. The hot lights needed for the Technicolor cameras and the uncomfortable costumes the band had to wear had everyone grumbling, Buddy loudest of all.

Before Rich actually reported to the Marines, he played on a pair of soundtracks that featured the Dorsey band. His distinctive drumming is easily recognizable in the "Broadway Rhythm" number toward the end of MGM's *Presenting Lily Mars,* which featured the Dorsey orchestra and Judy Garland. Likewise, he is heard on the sound track of MGM's *Girl Crazy,* which starred Mickey Rooney and Judy Garland. Close scrutiny of the drummer photographed with Dorsey's band identifies him as Maurice Purtill, former Glenn Miller rhythmkeeper, who replaced Rich when the latter went into the service.

Buddy was discharged from the U.S. Marines in mid-1944 and rejoined

Dorsey shortly thereafter. Late in the year, the band was once again on the MGM lot, appearing in an Esther Williams picture called *Thrill of a Romance*. As if to say "Welcome back," Tommy saw to it that his prodigal drummer was featured in a sequence that takes place in a hotel lounge. The occasion is a jam session with a few Dorsey men participating, among them Buddy De Franco on clarinet and Milt Golden on piano. At one point, everything stops and Rich takes off, again sounding and playing pretty much as he did in *How's About It?* and *Las Vegas Nights*.

"The Buddy Rich Orchestra" receives billing in a Republic Pictures feature called *Earl Carroll's Sketchbook*, made in March 1946. Rich is only seen buried within the confines of a large studio orchestra (with strings yet—Buddy's unfavorite instruments). Whether he actually played on the soundtrack, or perhaps was left on the cutting room floor, is moot. Certainly nothing of his identifiable drumming is heard during the course of this celluloid turkey.

In 1948 the new—the real—Buddy Rich orchestra was seen and heard to fine advantage in a Universal two-reeler. Allen Eager and Terry Gibbs are featured on the opening track, and Terry surfaces again on "John Had the Number." The Mello-Larks, one of the best vocal groups of the time, sing "Let's Get Away from It All." The golden nuggets of this little short, though, are Buddy's contributions—singing "But No Nickel," tap dancing with choreographer Louis Da Pron while the Rich band accompanies with Basie's "Swinging the Blues," and finally pulling out all the stops in an explosive performance of his old Dorsey feature vehicle "Not So Quiet, Please."

It's fun to watch this number, because the opening band portion is prerecorded, and Rich doesn't quite make it in the "synchronization." The long solo, however, is photographed and recorded live, with the camera placed forward of and slightly above Buddy's drums. His tom-tom work, interacting with his bass drum during this solo, results in one of the most exciting pieces of film ever shot of any musician.

Once again in 1948 the Rich band was signed for a short subject, the one-reel "Thrills of Music" at Columbia Pictures. This time Buddy dances with the great Steve Condos, sings a duet with Betty Bonney ("A Man Can Be a Wonderful Thing"), and solos on "Kicks With Sticks," a nice outing but not as impressive as the Universal short.

By the time Buddy joined Harry James's band in the early 1950s, the big studios had become apathetic about using name bands in feature films. Universal (now Universal-International) hung in there, though, churning out band shorts produced and directed by big-band fan Will Cowan. In a short titled "Harry James and His Music Makers" (1953), Buddy is seen but not featured to any great advantage.

Here's a weird one. In the summer of 1955 Rich appeared in another Will Cowan band short, this time as a solo artist with Freddy Martin's orchestra. (He smirked when I kidded him about this one. "I'll do anything for money— almost," he said nonchalantly.) Buddy is featured at the very end of this two-reeler. The Martin band plays no more than a few bars of some undistinguished "lead-in" instrumental, then it's all Buddy, once again playing an extended solo.

Rich also was filmed with the James band in a pair of 1965 20th Century Fox half-hour syndicated TV specials called "The Big Bands." In one of them he comes to the fore with a drum-feature arrangement of Juan Tizol's "Caravan." On the second program he is merely the driving force within the James rhythm section.

Throughout the ensuing years, Buddy was seen again and again on TV— "The Tonight Show," "The Merv Griffin Show," etc., as well as several "specials": "One Night Stand" with Lionel Hampton, Gene Krupa, Gerry Mulligan, and others; "Concert of the Americas" with Frank Sinatra in Central America; on his own videocassette, "Mr. Drums"; and finally on PBS's "Sentimental Swing: The Music of Tommy Dorsey."

An interesting piece of information has surfaced thanks to the efforts of Buddy Rich fan club members Steve Lederman and Hugh Turner. They have apparently found out that Rich recorded a frenetic solo used in a 1944 Universal thriller written by Cornell Woolrich entitled *Phantom Lady*. Elisha Cook, Jr., "mimed" the Buddy Rich effort in the film, and well-known film historian/ critic Leonard Maltin wrote that the "drumming scene with Cook is simply astonishing." Years ago I had heard that Rich was involved in this movie, but when I asked him about his participation in it, he couldn't remember whether or not he had done it. His solo work is so distinctive, however, that I am sure Lederman and Turner are correct in attributing the drumming in *Phantom Lady* to Rich.

Dr. Klaus Stratemann's filmo-discography of Buddy and Gene Krupa, published in 1980, is an enjoyable overview of their work.

HE LOVED CARS. All kinds. The first really glamorous machine he ever owned was a 1940 Lincoln Continental, metallic blue with the exposed steel-encased spare attached to a luggage-shaped trunk. There is that great picture of Buddy in the Lincoln in front of the Astor Hotel in New York, surrounded by dozens of fans. Frank Sinatra sits in the backseat. Buddy still had that pride and joy of his when he went into the Marines. Almost immediately following his discharge, he laid his hands on another Continental, this one in an arresting shade of yellow. Driving out to the Casino Gardens in that beautiful car was one of the few redeeming pleasures that offset Rich's rejoining the string-infested Tommy Dorsey orchestra of 1944. One thing about Buddy: he never became jaded where cars were concerned. With the top down and the sun setting far out in the Pacific, he would turn to me, pat the steering wheel of the Lincoln, and beam.

When he bought his MG-TC Midget in 1947, it was meticulously kept, just like his previous cars had been. The little right-hand drive beauty was not really comfortable or quick, but Buddy had a soft spot for his. After he disposed of it, he regretted his decision and constantly asked me to stay on the lookout for another one of 1947 vintage. He never did own a second MG, but he had great nostalgic feelings for his original one.

Among other automobiles, he drove Jaguars, a Mercedes-Benz 450, and a Silver Shadow Rolls, which he roundly detested and consigned to Marie. On the occasion of the PBS special we were both involved with during January 1987, he led me by the arm into the parking lot of the Hollywood Palladium and walked me up to a gleaming black Porsche 928S. "How about that?" he grinned at me.

"Killer car," I answered enviously. "A gem. I suppose you're driving it way too fast?"

"Took it to Vegas a few weeks ago. Went 135."

"A hundred and thirty-five? What about cops?"

"Got four tickets on the way," he boasted proudly.

"Ouch! That must have cost you a fortune."

"No way, José!" he laughed. "I've got a friend downtown. On top of which, if they're gonna keep making stupid fifty-five mile-an-hour speed laws, I'm gonna keep breaking them!"

That Porsche was the last car he ever owned, and when he died, I remember thinking what a shame it was that he didn't live to see the hated limit amended in favor of a more sensible sixty-five on most interstate roads. Not that it would have mattered. He would have still driven, with the same precise skill he exhibited behind a set of drums, at 135 and gotten dozens of tickets, which he would have blithely turned over to his "friend downtown."

Overturning the national speed limit was one of his consuming passions. His face would purple with rage just thinking about the restrictive law. He would launch into a tirade about freedom of choice and the gross injustice of hogtying anyone who wanted to push the pedal all the way down to the metal. On several of his "Tonight Show" guest shots, he went on and on about his rights as a driver and an American citizen. Johnny Carson suffered Buddy's rantings with equal parts of amusement and bemusement.

Of ongoing concern and interest to Rich was his crusade to legalize pot. He saw no reason why it should not be as legal as scotch or vodka. He claimed, as have so many thousands of others, that marijauna is less harmful than alcohol and that the stigma of pot-smoking, the illegality of it, was purely political.

Unfortunately, Buddy's tiresome dissertations on the joys and benefits of using "boo," as he sometimes called it, could induce deep sleep in an insomniac. Whether the tumors that caused his death were the result of years of marijauna abuse is something that can only be speculated upon. Some doctors I have spoken with think Buddy's pot-smoking contributed to his fatal sickness: others shrug their shoulders.

Yet another rabid passion of Rich's was karate. Certainly, he was one strong individual who knew the rudiments of the sport. I have seen him grab someone's arm playfully, apply a wrist lock, and bring his unsuspecting victim to his knees. On a Saturday several years ago, he appeared on a segment of ABC's "Wide World of Sports" with several karate experts. He acted as guest moderator, and he spoke with authority and understanding. Later he demonstrated various "katas," those now-familiar stances and movements endemic to karate. Weeks later, he showed me the black belt he said he had earned. A friend of his, who wishes to remain anonymous, says that Buddy's black belt was an honorary one, not an earned one. You could have fooled me. B certainly acted as though he knew all the moves.

Getting him started on UFOs was yet another way to let yourself in for a rambling monologue. His belief in flying saucers and other unexplained things that go bump in the night sky was unshakable. He devoured magazines on the subject and delighted in going head to head with "unbelievers." By the time he finished with these infidels, they were usually ready to look toward the heavens for close encounters of any kind; that's how knowledgeable and well-versed Buddy was on the subject.

And then, of course, there was jazz. After all the years he spent playing with a stellar list of the best musicians in the world, after the countless records, the endless one-nighters, the innumerable clubs and ballrooms and concert halls in which he appeared, the luster of jazz never dimmed in his mind or his heart or, indeed, his ears. He loved the trappings, the people, the fans, the respect of his peers, the excitement of collaborating with the likes of Bud Powell, "Sweets" Edison, Count Basie, Dizzy Gillespie, Ella, Frank, and so many others far too numerous to mention. He disliked sham in a musician. He idolized "originals" and paid them the same obeisance he enjoyed from fans and colleagues alike.

◨   *Buddy's Pranks*

HE WAS AN unreconstructed prankster, dating back to his childhood and the not-inconsiderable influence of that other compulsive prank-player, Robert Rich. Buddy's pranks were sometimes funny, inventive, and harmless. They could also be destructive, demeaning, and downright dangerous in their childish thoughtlessness. I am certain I could have gathered a glossary of Rich's "gags" from a wide variety of people who knew and worked with him. I have chosen some, however, from personal experience that serve to illustrate the workings of his mind in the pursuit of his duties as the "Anything for a Laugh" champion.

One night, during the existence of his first "Buddy's Place" club on Second Avenue in Manhattan, I called to tell him I was coming over to see his final set of the evening. It was a Saturday night, and the place was jammed. After doing a particularly impressive turn, he went to the microphone to thank the audience and then announced: "Ladies and gentlemen, one of my favorite people is with us tonight. I love him, and I know you do too, so it's a pleasure to introduce Mr. Mel Tormé."

I stood up. Not one single person applauded. Absolute dead silence. The "quiet" in the room was stunning. I looked around, my jaw unslung, until in that split second I realized that Buddy had set me up, warning the crowd beforehand not to utter one whistle, cheer, or handclap when he announced me. The room then broke up into long, loud laughter. No one laughed longer or louder than I. Harmless.

We were standing in the wings at a jazz festival. Buddy's band had been on, and now he and Cathy were keeping me company backstage as an announcer was about to introduce me.

"And now, folks," the MC on stage was saying, "it is my pleasure to bring out a singer who . . ."

Buddy and Cathy stood close to me, smiling expectantly.

Just as the announcer pointed toward me and said: "And here he is—Mr. Mel Tormé!" Buddy took a bottle of blue ink out of his pocket and casually spilled it all over the front of my tux shirt.

I looked down, horrified. The audience was applauding. The MC was waving me on. Rich grinned his devil's grin and pushed me onstage. I walked toward the mike, shocked and mortified. How could I possibly explain . . .

I got to center stage, cleared my throat, and said: "Before I begin, ladies and gentlemen, I want to tell you about . . . " I looked down at my shirt. It was perfectly clean! Not a trace of ink! I looked into the wings. Buddy and Cathy were convulsed with laughter. Disappearing ink! I shook my fist in their direction and cracked up along with them.

Harmless.

In September of 1975 I showed up at Buddy's Place II. We had rehearsed all afternoon for the opening taking place that evening. As I walked in, Buddy was in a high state of distress. I had never seen him so furious. He dragged me back into the dressing room and indicated the closet. Empty! All the clothes, his and mine, were gone.

"Bastards got in here this afternoon, right after rehearsal. Took every frigging suit of mine and yours." He turned to Stanley Kay. "How soon did those cops from the Seventeenth say they'd be here?"

Stanley shook his head. "I don't know, B. They said as soon as they could."

"Shit," Rich exploded. "Typical! This is what we pay our taxes for, huh? So they can sit on their butts and show up any goddam time they please. Wait'll they ask me to do another police benefit. I'll . . ."

But this time I wasn't buying. "Take it easy, B," I soothed him. "They're only clothes. I mean, what the hell."

He looked sideways at me. "Only clothes? ONLY clothes! What about all those new outfits you just had made for this opening? How do you think I feel, knowing that . . ."

Hey, I'm insured. These things happen." I indicated the corduroy pants and windbreaker I was wearing. "Don't sweat it. I'll work in these."

He couldn't suppress a grin. He looked at Stanley and Marty Ross, shrugged, and said: "Well, I guess you can't win 'em all." All the "stolen" clothes mysteriously reappeared in five minutes.

Harmless.

Not so harmless, not so funny, were two other "gags" he pulled during that engagement. I had been dieting all through the month of September. By closing night, I had shed around twelve pounds and was proud of my accomplishment. The final show was attended by a sellout crowd.

I had performed only twelve minutes of my projected sixty- to sixty-five-minute act when Buddy appeared onstage, one hand waving the band to a halt, the other hand behind his back.

"Hey, folks," he explained. "Before we go any further, I want you to know how proud I am of my best friend here. He's been dieting like crazy, and he's lost over a dozen pounds in the two weeks he's been here." The audience applauded. "Melvin," he continued, "I know how much you love sweets, and I know what a sacrifice it's been, giving them up while you've been playing here. So—I think, on closing night, you deserve some dessert." With that, his right hand shot out from behind his back, and he slammed me in the face with a lemon meringue pie.

Now, we're not talking about a "shaving cream" pie, like the ones the "Laugh-In" gang used to pepper each other with. We're talking sticky, gelatinous, gooey lemon meringue. Sadly, in addition to ruining my suit and the rest of the performance, the contents of the pie sailed way beyond me, spattering patrons right and left with staining, soiling goop. Women at ringside screamed as the meringue and the thick lemon custard stuck to their faces, blotched their dresses, slid their slippery way down their *décolletages*. Men jumped out of their chairs, shaking their hands free of the clinging mess that had suddenly attacked them. Buddy laughed uncontrollably. He was the only one.

I threw up my hands in disgust, apologized to the audience, and made for the dressing room and soap and water. For once, Stanley Kay jumped all over Rich. "For Christ's sake, B. Women are screaming out there, men are cursing. We gotta give back most of their money because Mel couldn't do a full show. What the hell is the matter with you? Couldn't you at least have waited till Mel's last number?"

Buddy fixed him with a fisheyed stare. "No, man. I couldn't." Marty Ross, the real owner of Buddy's Place and a pussycat of a guy who would later figure heavily in my career as the proprietor of a classy East Side club called Marty's, abandoned his usual placid demeanor and put in his two cents. "Damn it, Buddy. We're going to get sued, that's all there is to it. Those people out there are furious. The ruined suits and dresses alone are going to cost us a fortune. Jesus!"

Buddy looked at them petulantly, nodded his head slowly, and pouted. "Okay, so we just won't have any fun around here anymore." We were all astounded by his attitude. It was the kind of remark one might have expected out of a twelve-year-old's mouth. Sometimes Buddy was extremely childish.

Much more serious was a failed prank that, had it taken place, might have had some really dangerous repercussions. Early in the run at Buddy's Place, Marty, Stanley, and Marie pulled me aside one evening as I entered the club. The strained looks on their faces told the story; something had happened or was about to. Something dire. We sat down at a table. Marie said, "Honest to God, Mel, I sometimes think Buddy is crazy. Really crazy."

"Now what?" I laughed. "Did he hide all the clothes again?"

Marie looked at Marty Ross, who said: "No, nothing like that. Are you ready for this? He arranged with two of his Seventeenth Precinct buddies to come down here tonight before the first show, pretend to be mob guys, drag you out of here, throw you in the trunk of their unmarked car, and drive you around town for an hour or so before bringing you back here for the first show."

Stanley wiped his perspiring forehead. "Thank God, he let us in on it before those guys got here."

"Do you know, we actually had a fight with him over this? We had to threaten him, warn him, twist his arm to make him stop these guys from coming over and doing it," advised Marie. "Doesn't he have any idea how dangerous that could have been? You could have suffocated in that trunk."

"Or had a heart attack," added Marty. "I don't understand Buddy. It's like he doesn't think before . . ."

"I know, I know. He comes from a family—at least a father—who thought that pranks were a way of life," I said.

"Okay, pranks. Fun," Stanley interrupted. "This wasn't a prank. This was a potentially serious idea that—Mel, what would you have done if we hadn't talked him out of it?"

"Well," I answered him, "I would have either screamed all the way to the cops' car and continued screaming while I was in the trunk. Or I might have choked to death in that trunk. Or had a heart attack. Or—"

"Or?" Marie interrupted.

"Or," I said taking a deep breath and looking Buddy's wife square in the eye, "I might have come back from this ride, walked into the club, grabbed a butcher knife, and plunged it directly into your stupid, childish husband's heart."

Marie was taken aback. I touched her hand gently and said, "I'm not kidding, Marie." At that precise moment, I meant what I said.

☐ *Cathy Rich: I Remember Dad*

"WHEN I WAS young, he really wasn't around much. It wasn't like he had a nine-to-five job. The thing I really remember about him is that anytime there was an important event, a bake sale, a school play that I was in, or a recital of any kind, anytime I was ever doing anything, he was there. Whether he had to cancel a show or be late for a show. That was pretty amazing to me, considering the kind of schedule he had.

"He was so many different people at different times. The performing type person was a different guy from the guy that tucked you in at night, and the guy that was talking to young fans was different than the one yelling at the guys in the band.

"There was a side of him that a lot of people did not get to see. He really was a soft-hearted person. He was a kind, passionate, and gentle soul . . . he was very humble. I remember one time at a symphony concert. After Dad finished, the conductor came off, and he was crying. 'I have seen Heifetz play. He is the greatest that will ever be at what he does. You are Heifetz on the drums. I have never seen anything like this.' My father began crying. Everyone was crying. He was quite modest about his abilities and always respected other people's talents, whether it be athletes, artists, singers, or anything. He was the first person to say to someone 'That's great.'

"We moved around a lot. I was born in Los Angeles. I stayed there till I was about three. Then we moved to New York, and then to Florida, then to Las Vegas. We lived there for about nine years. Then to Palm Springs, then back to New York.

"I always sang in school. I was in the chorus, the honor chorus. When my dad formed the 1966 band, that was the year that Sonny and Cher's version of "The Beat Goes On" came out. One day we were driving around, and it came on the radio. I told Dad to listen to it, and he said, 'Why don't you sing it with the band?' Just like that! Everything was so matter-of-fact with him. I said okay, and that was it.

"I got my courage up, walked into the club [The Chez] that night, and the first person I see, sitting ringside, is Judy Garland. I lost control. I ran backstage and said to Dad, 'No way I can get up there and sing in front of Judy Garland.'

"'What are you talking about?' he said. He walked over and talked to Judy, who called me over and talked to me for about a half hour. She was wonderful. She said: 'Don't ever let anybody intimidate you. You just get up there and do it!'

"And I did.

"As far as how dad and I got along? Oh, we had our knock-down-drag-out fights once in a while. I remember one time, there was this guy I was dating who just rubbed him the wrong way. This guy was not intimidated by my father. This guy went toe to toe with my father, and until the day he died, if you mentioned this guy's name, Dad would get so furious you couldn't even speak to him.

"But that didn't hurt my relationship with my dad. We had such a special kind of thing. I mean, we were pals. He would talk to me, from early, early on, about things in the world, the way you should feel about other people. If nothing else, he had compassion, which is not what you would expect from him.

"There were many times when he was rough on people, and I would open my mouth, and I would say, 'You're completely out of line.' At first he would be upset with me, and he'd say: 'How can you take someone else's side?' And I'd say: 'Well, you taught me to see things from both sides. If I see you do or say something that I think isn't fair, I'm going to say it to you.' He would think about it for a while, and if he really thought that I was right, he would go back and make amends for it.

"I was able to calm him down by just sitting and discussing a problem he might have. So many times, band managers would come to me and say: 'Please, Cathy, you gotta go in and talk to him.' I was a mediator, early on.

"I mediated many of the fights he had with Mom. That put me in a very strange position as a child. Having to be an adult/child is very hard. But I always knew that if I went in and got in the middle of it, it would stop.

"I remember one time, they had gone grocery shopping together. Now, you gotta imagine my father as a 'civilian,' going grocery shopping, bringing the groceries home, which was so foreign to him. Well, somewhere between the store and the apartment, they 'got into it.' My mother began unpacking the groceries, I was in my room, and I heard it start. I came out of my room, and the next thing I knew, all the groceries were flying; I was dodging chicken and apples. My mother was throwing the food, he was yelling. 'What are you doing?' I said, and I started to laugh, because it was so ridiculous. Then they started to laugh, and then it stopped.

"Another time they were having a fight, and Mom picked up a very heavy glass ashtray. He looked at her and said, 'Don't even think about it.' That infuriated her, so she threw it at him. He raised his arm to deflect it from hitting him in the head. It hit him in the elbow, and he heard a crack. Very calmly, he said to her: 'I'm going to drive myself to the hospital now. Don't be here when I get back.' Of course, Mom was there when he got back. It all blew over.

"About his temperament: I would talk to my aunts about him and his childhood, about the things that happened to him as a child. I think it had so much to do with the way he was treated. His father was a real tough guy and treated him probably not the greatest way to treat a child.

"On the happy side, you know he was a prankster. He loved practical jokes, and he did have the ability to laugh at himself. I remember one time, we were staying at the Continental Hyatt in Boston. He had gotten back to the room very late from his evening's gig. He had barely gotten to sleep when construction workers began hammering and banging away in the hotel. Now, he had been going through a plague of construction noise in several hotels prior to this, and he just flipped out. He was wearing a hairpiece at the time. He grabbed the 'piece' off his nightstand and slapped it on his head. Sideways! He had one leg in a pair of pants and one arm in a shirt. He ran out into the hallway and started tearing up and down the hall, yelling: 'I'm going on Johnny Carson, and I'm going to RUIN this hotel!' He ran down to the lobby and began pounding on the front desk, like a total maniac, just freaking out! This is about six o'clock in the morning, and the poor front desk clerk is saying, 'But Mr. Rich! But Mr. Rich!' All of a sudden, he comes back to the room, takes off his hair, takes off his shirt, laughs, and calmly goes back to sleep.

"One night in Palm Springs, when I was about seventeen or eighteen, we were talking, and I said, 'Gee, I've always wanted to get hit with a pie,' and he said, very casually, 'Oh? Okay.' So the next night he comes home with an apple pie, and we had dinner and were washing the dishes, and he comes in and says: 'Cath!' I turn my head, and I see this apple pie flying in my direction. Because I turned my head, it only got me on the backside of my head. I looked at him and said: 'I don't believe you! You didn't do it right! And it's supposed to be a cream pie.' So he said; 'Oh, well, all right,' and it was totally forgotten. So I went to the shower and washed the apple pie off. There was a knock on the door, and Dad said: 'Hey, Cath. Baron [the Rich family dog] is crying. He wants to come in with you.' I said okay. I opened the door, and bang! A lemon meringue pie, right in the middle of my face. It splattered all over the bathroom. The entire room was filled with lemon meringue pie. I looked at him and said, 'Great! That was great!' [I reminded her of my lemon meringue episode at Buddy's Place. I guess that kind of humor is in the eye of the beholder.]

"Dad loved to play golf, but he didn't really have the patience for it. One morning when we were living in Vegas, he was part of a foursome playing at the Tropicana golf course. By the time he got to the eighteenth hole, he had played so badly and was so furious at himself that, after he had hit a ball into a pond, he picked up his golf bag and heaved it and all his clubs into the same pond. Then he turned and started walking back to the clubhouse. The others in the foursome looked at him disappearing over a small hill and shrugged and said, 'Oh, well, that's Buddy.' All of a sudden, they see him coming back. Now what? He walks past them, a calm look on his face, goes to the edge of the pond, rolls up his pants, wades in, fishes around for the golf bag, finds it, lifts it out of the water, and removes his car keys from the bag. Then he lets the bag drop back into the water and, without another word, walks by his friends once more and makes for the clubhouse. It's like a scene out of a Chaplin movie. The people just stood there with their mouths open. He didn't say a word. Just walked away. The end.

"When my son Nicky was born, on September 21 of 1984, Dad was in England on tour with Sinatra, so he didn't see Nicky until he was a month old. He was crazy about his grandson. He would baby-sit at every opportunity. He would come and stay with me, and he was always trying to hustle me out of the house so he could baby-sit. He would sit for hours with Nicky, who was the 'great sleeper' at that time. Nicky was also colicky right around then. Dad would sit on the floor and just rock that baby for hours and hours.

"When Dad got sick and was in the hospital taking radiation, he would constantly ask the nurse, 'Am I gonna be okay? Am I gonna live long enough to see my grandson grow up?'

"He wanted to visualize his sickness like it was a war. There was a good team and a bad team, and the good team had the guns and were shooting down the bad team, you know, meaning all his tumors. I'd come into his room and he'd say: 'I shot 'em all down today.'

"He had a very positive attitude at first. After the surgery, when he saw he wasn't going to get well, he just wanted to leave this planet. He kept saying to me: 'If I can't be what I've always been, I don't want to be here. I can never be less than what I've been.'

"I just kept telling him he was going to be okay. Maybe that was selfish, but I just couldn't give in to the thought that he was going to die. We were so close, and it was such a horrible experience to sit there and see it happen. At the very least, I thought I would have a few more years with him.

"He was a great father. He was always there for me, always supportive. He never, ever failed me."

◘ I Remember Buddy

STEVE MARCUS: The predominant thing was to produce good music. Buddy made it tough on some people for a variety of reasons, but he just wanted the band to be perfect. Not to stay with him would be to walk out on the greatest teacher anybody could fall into a relationship with. A man who knew music and show business and audiences and life and humor back and forth, inside and out. I could spend all day hanging out with him and never get bored. Buddy may have been a little cruel at times with certain people, but overall he made better players out of people. He was the greatest human being that I have ever known. I just can't stress this strong enough.

LOUIE BELLSON: I think he'll be remembered for many things. He was among that group of players including Chick Webb, Baby Dodds, Jo Jones, Sid Catlett, and Gene Krupa who were all innovators. Players like that come around only every so often.

ALVIN STOLLER, drummer: What Buddy could do with a couple of pieces of wood was uncanny.

ROY BURNS, drummer: To Buddy, the drums and music were the most important things in his life, next to his family. What sticks most in my mind is the example he set for the rest of us. His dedication, his drive, his ability to keep going in spite of a number of health problems, and the fact that he played so well right up to the end shows all of us that we could try a little harder. I sure miss him.

BOB BOWLBY, saxophone player with the Buddy Rich Band: Sometimes, when Buddy disapproved of our playing, he would call for an 8:00 A.M. rehearsal the next morning. We called these "hate" rehearsals. Also, some rehearsals were devoted entirely to standing up, bowing in unison and sitting down again, over and over and over, until we got it correct. If I heard it once, I heard it a thousand times—when we were on the job, Buddy wanted us to be "professional," and he wanted his music rendered to "perfection."

You may not believe this, but it really bothered him when someone didn't like him. He would never admit that, though.

ANDY GRAVISH, trumpet player with the Buddy Rich Band: Buddy was always in control of himself, the band, and the audience. However, there was one time in Dallas . . . a fellow was in the audience who knew Buddy from years ago and had replaced him at the drums after one of Buddy's stints with Harry James. Right in the middle of a quiet passage of Buddy's "Channel One" solo, this guy yelled out: "It looks like the drummer is getting fat." Buddy abruptly interrupted his solo, jumped off his drum throne, and emphatically shouted "SCREW YOU," which is a polite way of restating what he actually said. This guy came backstage to apologize, but Buddy was already gone.

ED SHAUGHNESSY, drummer on "The Tonight Show":   It was the late forties. B. R. was working Birdland in NYC, and on the Monday night (his night off) he shows up with a PR [public relations] guy at Birdland where I've just finished a Terry Gibbs set. A well-known musician-composer's group was just starting their set. B. R. invites me to join his table and starts to berate the band and the eminent leader's compositions. I, being a friend and fan of the guy, got my Irish up and said something like, "Why are you here on your night off, if it's such worthless music?" The PR guy says: "You can't talk to Buddy Rich like that." B. R. tells him to take a walk. I say to Buddy: "We may have to have bad feelings about this. I don't really care, 'cause I can always buy your records."

B. R. goes into a fit of laughter and starts banging the table. He loves it and says: "Kid, I think you and I are going to get along real good." And we did.

ROSS KONIKOFF, trumpet player with the Buddy Rich Band: Buddy never felt comfortable in Germany. One afternoon we were doing a broadcast from a Hamburg radio station with a live audience that wasn't very responsive to the band. Buddy had been muttering under his breath the entire show. After it was finished, a few of us went with Buddy to hear a tape of the show, which had gone out live. Clearly on the tape in Buddy's unmistakably bitter tones were the words *Nazi motherfuckers!*

One would have thought that after all the years of playing drums surrounded by sixteen guys blasting in his ears, Buddy would have been slightly hearing-impaired. And yet one night, he was stretched out over two seats on the bus, trying to get some sleep. I sat nine rows back, munching on a package of almonds. The bus was going about seventy-five miles an hour, the air-conditioning was going full blast, and less than a minute after I had begun chewing my almonds, I saw Buddy sit up quickly, look back in my direction, and growl: "Who's making all that noise?" He looked at me and said: "Shut up, Konikoff, I'm trying to sleep."

JOHN BUNCH, pianist with the Buddy Rich Band: Buddy played great every night. He was so consistent. A lot of players are up one night and down the next. Buddy was always up.

JOHNNY CARSON: The world lost a genius, and I lost a friend.

Buddy's Mouth

BUDDY'S VITRIOL COULD easily match the Wrath of Khan when it came to tearing strips off his band members for real or imagined transgressions. Dogged perfectionist that he was, he simply could not tolerate anything less than a flawless performance from each and every musician working for him since he was committed to giving his all night after night despite back pains, fatigue, or the threat of an imminent heart attack.

His fury over indolence, apathy, or careless appearance was usually vented upon his employees during or after working hours—between sets in the band room or inside the band bus, away from curious civilian ears.

On a few occasions, one of his enterprising sidemen turned on a tape recorder (surreptitiously, of course) to capture these tirades in all their expletive-laden glory. Rich never heard these tapes, but he knew of their existence. On the day before he died, he begged me to bring him a copy. He was aware of the content and insisted it be included in this book. I doubted the wisdom of his command; I still do. But here they are. (I have, however, chosen to delete the almost constant repetition of the "F" and "MF" words. The steady stream of those expletives becomes tiresome and serves no constructive purpose. This is strictly my "call.")

What you are about to read is not in the tradition of a Knute Rockne inspirational pep talk. However, it is important to remember that it was *his* band, *his* reputation on the line each time his players lifted their horns, *his* unique outlook on appearance, attitude, and dedication to excellence that prompted the outbursts that follow.

There are three distinct episodes involved here. The first one took place at a club during a one-nighter tour. The year? Anybody's guess—probably sometime in the late 1970s or early 1980s. The Rich band was populated, as usual, by many youngsters just out of Berklee or North Texas State music school. The ensemble playing on that particular night was apparently something less than wonderful. Buddy summoned the band to gather in the band room right after the first set of the evening.

Close that door. [pause] What kind of playing is being played here the past two nights? What is this? New phrasing, new bending, new sounds. No time. What do you think I'm running here? Everybody gets two weeks notice tonight! . . . You're not my kind of people. I'm working my ass off. . . . You're blowing my eardrums out. . . . All I hear is NOISE! Sit down and play some *music*. I'm accustomed to working with number-one musicians. I'm not accustomed to working with half-assed kids!

Episode two took place on the band bus as the Buddy Rich orchestra was traveling toward that evening's performance. Many of the band members sported beards, which aroused Rich's ire no end. He was especially hostile toward an Australian trombonist-arranger who had the temerity to stand up to him on several occasions. Buddy had tolerated the "beard brigade" as long as he could; the time had come to put an end to hairy facial appendages:

RICH: This is not the House of David baseball team. It's the Buddy Rich band. No more beards. Shave 'em off! I'll treat you just like they treat you in the Marine Corps. If you don't like it—get out. You got two weeks to make up your mind. This is no idle request. I'm *telling* you how my band is gonna look. You're gonna do what I want as long as you take my money. [He now addresses the Australian musician.] You seem to be giving me more trouble than anybody else. You want to do something about it? It's up to you. [louder] You wanna do something about it. . . . You go to work tonight—if I catch that beard on you, I'll throw you off the bandstand, okay?

THE AUSSIE: I'm not shaving it off.

RICH: WHAT?

THE AUSSIE: I'm not shaving it off.

RICH: That's it. You're through! Right now. Get OFF! Get your clothes and get off. Right now! [to the bus driver] Pull the bus over.

THE AUSSIE: You're supposed to give me two weeks' notice.

RICH: I give you two weeks? For what? You learn the rules of my band. You don't like it? That's it. Get off! I don't like the way you write, and I still play your lousy charts. For you, do you understand that? Not for me.

THE AUSSIE: I think you play my charts because "Manhattan" is the best chart in the book.

RICH: It is? Then take "Manhattan" and get off. Go back to Sydney and whatever you do over there—good luck.

THE AUSSIE: [responds, unintelligible on the tape]

RICH: Keep talking. You want to start some shit with me?

THE AUSSIE: I just don't appreciate being talked to like this.

RICH: I tried to talk to you like a human being. You talk back all the time. Keep your mouth shut or I'll show you what it's like! That's all.

THE AUSSIE: Okay, but you have no right to threaten me.

RICH: I'm TELLING you! You don't want to do what I want in my band—shut up!

THE AUSSIE: I will. All right.

RICH: [to the rest of the band members] Let's get that understood by everybody. I want him off. I don't want him on the bandstand.

In what may qualify as the most horrific harangue of all, episode three plays itself out on the bus as it is parked outside an evening's venue somewhere in the Great Nowhere. Buddy has called an emergency meeting of his "Killer Force," and his fury is terrible to behold. He opens, screaming at the top of his lungs:

What do you think is going on here? You had too many days off? You think I'm the only one that's gonna work out there? I'm up there working my balls off, and you are sucking all over this joint! What kind of trumpet section do you call that tonight? And the saxophones! You gotta be kidding me. How *dare* you call yourselves professionals? Playing like children up there.

Everybody could hear "clams" out there. You stand out here all night, and what do you play? Clams. You got nowhere to go next set, 'cause if I hear one "clam" from *any*body—you've had it. And this whole band is through tonight. Try me!

You got some nerve. Nights off, nothin' to do, and you play like this for me? Screw all of you! You're not doing me any goddam favors; you're breaking my *heart* up there. I gotta go up there and be embarrassed? I've played with the greatest musicians in the world. How DARE you play like that for me?

You try screwing up the next set, and when you get back to New York, you'll all need another job.

Now—get outta my fuckin' bus!

IN SEPTEMBER OF 1975 Buddy and I once again ventured into Central Park in Manhattan. We bought a couple of hot dogs from a vendor and sat under a tree. It was a beautiful early autumn day. My friend was relaxed, happy, and talkative. I mainly listened that day as he expounded on various subjects: crime in New York, gun control, sci-fi, religion.

And death.

"You're going to be fifty-nine years old, and you'll probably outlive all of us but—do you ever think about death?" I asked him.

"All the time," he replied.

"What do you think?"

"I think—what a waste of life! Why die? If you look at the causes of death—old age, parts wearing out—well, I could understand that if it were 1940. Or even 1950. But with the advances made in science, in medicine, transplants—kidney, heart, lungs—. Look, if one day we had a man who was a humanitarian in the office of president, and he decided that, instead of spending twenty billion dollars on a B-1 bomber that will kill maybe a hundred thousand people in one shot—if we took that twenty billion dollars and put it into medical science to find out why we have blood clots, why the heart gets tired of beating, if we had the money to make new 'parts' for the extension of life—"

"What would that do to overpopulation? For people to live to, say, 140 or even 200 years?"

"Well, I think it would have a great effect on all of us. If you glean as much knowledge as a man like Einstein did in seventy or eighty years, think what he might have discovered if his life could have been extended another fifty or sixty years."

"Do you believe in God?"

"I suppose."

"Does that mean you're an agnostic?"

"Wait a minute. God. A lot of people looked upon James Dean, Clark Gable, Charles Lindbergh as 'gods.' People who have accomplished great things—a lot of people like to think of them that way. Yeah, I believe in God, but I don't go with organized religion. I don't see why you have to go to St. Patrick's to pray. Why not just sit in front of a lamp and pray? If, in your head, you believe God is there, you don't have to go anyplace else."

Near the end of his life, Rich's faith in God was strong. It had to be. As a World War II saying went, there are no atheists in foxholes, and so did Buddy come out of his agnostic foxhole and pray to a benign and compassionate God to somehow overturn the rotten hand fate had dealt him. It was not to be, but that didn't mean God wasn't listening. I think Buddy knew in his heart it was simply his "time."

Index

Adams, Edie, 178
Adler, Henry, 29–30, 33–35
Aladdin (Las Vegas hotel), 121
Albam, Manny, 137
"All or Nothing at All," 52
"Alone Together," 196
Alpert, Trigger, 90
Alvin, Danny, 33, 35, 36
"A Man Can Be a Wonderful Thing," 200
Amsterdam, Morey, 104, 178
Andrews Sisters, 36, 78, 199
"Another One of Them Things," 59
Apollo (Harlem theater), 98–99, 104–5
Aquarium (New York City club), 94
Arcadia ballroom (New York City), 96
"Aren't You Glad You're You," 92
Armed Forces Radio Services, 69, 87
Armstrong, Louis, 115, 177, 186
Arnaz, Desi, Jr., 132
Arnold, Steve, 181
"Artie Shaw and His Orchestra" (movie short), 196
Arus, George, 45, 54
Astaire, Fred, 46–47
Astor Roof (New York City club), 60–64, 68, 72–73, 75
"At Sundown," 114
Auld, Georgie, 38–41, 43–44, 45, 47, 48, 50, 178, 197
Australia, tours in, 20–21, 24, 115, 137–38
Avola, Al, 47

"Baby, Baby All the Time," 92, 94
Bailey, Buster, 94
Baker, Ginger, 135
Baker, Josephine, 105
Balliett, Whitney, 117, 139
Bandbox (New York City club), 111
Bands of Buddy Rich: and The Big Four (1951), 106; and the black community, 98–100; Buddy Rich and His V-Disc Speed Demons (1945), 90; Buddy Rich and the Big Band Machine (1975), 141; Buddy Rich and the Killer Force (1976–78), 144, 146–48, 217; Buddy Rich–Buddy Bregman Orchestra (late 1950s), 117; Buddy Rich–Flip Phillips Trio (1953), 111; Buddy Rich–Harold Mooney Orchestra (late 1950s), 117; Buddy Rich Orchestra (1942), 78; Buddy Rich Orchestra (1946–47), 91–95, 200; Buddy Rich Orchestra (1948–49), 95–102, 124, 200; Buddy Rich Orchestra (1952), 106; Buddy Rich Orchestra (1966–74), 121–38, 210; Buddy Rich Orchestra (1978), 148, 149–50; Buddy Rich Orchestra (1980s), 156, 158, 161; Buddy Rich Orchestra with Steve Marcus (1990s), 180; Buddy Rich Quartet (1953), 111; Buddy Rich Quintet (late 1950s), 117; at Buddy's Clubs (1974–76), 138–43; Buddy "Traps" Rich and his Orchestra (1929), 28, 29; Cathy Rich resurrects the Rich band, 181; and finances, 97, 102, 138; Gene Krupa–Buddy Rich All-Stars (late 1950s), 117; and the

Bands of Buddy Rich (*Cont.*)
  Josephine Baker tour, 105; Lester Young–
  Buddy Rich Trio (1946), 90; in the movies,
  26, 27, 28–29, 78, 196, 200; Piccadilly Hotel
  combo (1938), 38; pick-up, 104–5, 106, 116,
  120; recordings of, 94, 98, 104, 117, 120,
  129, 131, 132, 133, 139, 147, 154, 191, 201;
  and Rich's relationship with band members, 93, 135, 137, 139, 212, 213, 215–17
Barnet, Charlie, 40–41, 98, 186
Barron, Blue, 43
Basie, William (Count): and a favorite of
  Rich's, 46; gives Rich a watch, 87; in
  Harlem, 98; and Jones, 185; and the
  Metronome All-Stars, 66; as a model for
  Rich, 194, 197; popularity of, 43; and the
  rhythm section of the band, 48; Rich plays
  with, 66, 86–87, 100, 114, 204; Rich recom-
  mends Miles to, 188; TV appearances
  of, 104
Basin Street East (New York City club), 126–
  27
Bathing Beauty (movie), 198
Bauduc, Ray, 37, 187
"The Beat Goes On," 128, 210
Beau, Heinie, 68, 72
Bebop, 48–49, 92–93, 94, 95–96, 100, 102, 104,
  117, 187
Becker, Donald, 167–68, 169, 170, 171, 172,
  173–74
"Begin the Beguine," 43, 44
Beiderbecke, Bix, 39, 177
Bellson, Louis, 120, 135, 187, 195, 212
Beneke, Tex, 66
Bennett, Tony, 130
Benny, Jack, 87
Berigan, Bunny, 38–40, 44, 53, 60, 64, 111,
  189
Berle, Milton, 74–75, 170
Berle, Ruth, 170
Bernstein, Artie, 66
"Bei Mir Bist Du Schön," 36
"The Big Bands" (TV special), 201
"Big Swing Face," 128
Birdland (New York City club), 104, 105,
  120, 213
Biviano, Lin, 136

Black musicians/community, 42–43, 46, 98–
  100, 131
Blake, Robert, 178
Blakey, Art, 120
Bluebird records, 44, 46, 49, 50n, 59
"Bluesette," 154–55
Bonney, Betty, 200
Bose, Sterling, 55
Bowlby, Bob, 135, 213
Bregman, Buddy, 117
Briglia, Tony, 29, 33
Broadway Melody of 1940 (movie), 46–47
"Broadway Open House" (NBC-TV), 104
"Broadway Rhythm," 199
Broadway shows, Rich's appearances in, 18–
  20, 31
Brooks, Mel, 179
Brown, Ben, 144
Brown, Joe E., 166
Brown, Lawrence, 94
Brown, Les, 104
Brown, Ray, 104, 105, 106
Buddy Rich Memorial Brain Tumor Re-
  search Foundation, 180
Buddy Rich scholarship fund, 181
Buddy's Place (New York City club), 135,
  138–40, 204–5, 207
Buddy's Place II (New York City club), 140–
  43, 205–6
"Bugle Call Rag," 66, 128
Bunch, John, 121, 214
Burns, Bobby, 68
Burns, Roy, 213
Bushkin, Joe, 60, 72, 75
"But No Nickel," 200
Butterfield, Billy, 50n

Café Bohemia (New York City club), 120
Café Rouge (New York City club), 48, 50, 51,
  68, 141, 185–86
Café Society Downtown (New York City
  club), 116
Cahn, Sammy, 85
"Call of the Canyon," 59
Canada, tour in, 106
Capitol recordings, 88
"Captain's Night," 198

"Caravan," 201
"The Carioca," 48
Carlson, Richard, 197
Carnegie Hall, 107, 180
Carney, Harry, 94
Cars, Rich's love for, 56, 61, 81, 84, 98, 99, 105, 111, 132, 202
Carson, Joanne, 168, 169, 170, 174, 175
Carson, Johnny: and anecdotes about Rich, 123–24, 127; and Rich as a prankster, 154; Rich's appearances with, 122–23, 124, 153, 203; and Rich's brain tumor, 168, 170–71; and Rich's funeral, 178, 179; Rich's gifts to, 123, 192; and a theatrical tribute to Rich, 180; tribute to Rich by, 214
Carter, Benny, 66, 106
Carter, Jack, 116
Casa Loma band, 29, 32–33
Casino Gardens ballroom (Ocean Park, Calif.), 85, 88
Castle, Millie, 103
Castle, Nick, 103, 116
Catlett, Sid, 186, 212
Champion, Marge and Gower, 116
"The Channel One Suite," 130, 131, 213
The Chez (Hollywood club), 122, 124, 128, 131, 210
Christian, Charlie, 66
Christy, June, 94
Clambake Seven (Tommy Dorsey band), 51
"Class in Swing" (movie short), 196
Clayton, Buck, 43, 94, 95
Clef recordings, 90
Cobham, Billy, 195
Cohn, Al, 124
Cole, Cozy, 186
Cole, Nat King, 88–89, 90, 94, 147
Coles, Honi, 180
College appearances, of Rich bands, 144, 150, 151, 156
Collins, Phil, 168
Columbia recordings, 89–90, 114
Columbus, Chris, 79
Comedy Store (Los Angeles club), 154
"Concert of the Americas" (TV special), 201
Concord Jazz Festival, 145, 146
Condon, Eddie, 103–4

Condos, Nick, 32
Condos, Steve, 32, 98, 200
Conrad, Casey, 167
Conrad, Hal, 180
Cook, Elisha, Jr., 201
"Cool Breeze," 94
Corday, Barbara (niece), 22, 178, 179
Corday, Jo Rich. *See* Rich, Josephine
Corre, Jay, 121
Cosby, Bill, 170, 180
Cowan, Will, 200, 201
Crawford, Jimmy, 186
Crosby, Bob, 37, 80
Crystal Club (Brooklyn), 29, 30, 31, 33

Dailey, Frank, 92, 98
Dameron, Tad, 92, 94
Dancing Co-ed (movie), 45–46, 49, 65, 190, 197
Dane, Pat, 86, 87, 89
Da Pron, Louis, 200
Darin, Bobby, 130–31
Davis, Sammy, Jr., 122, 178, 180, 192
Davison, Bill, 104
Death, Rich's belief about, 218
Deems, Barrett, 175
"Deep Purple," 197
"Deep River," 69
De Franco, Buddy, 88, 115, 200
Dempsey, Jack, 17
De Musio, Lenny, 131
Depression, Great, 26–31
"Desperate Desmond," 124
Devore, Sy, 84–85
Dickinson, Angie, 178
Dodds, Baby, 212
Dorsey, Tommy: arrest of, 86; and the Casino Gardens ballroom, 85; drinking of, 54–55, 68, 73, 86; and the Hall incident, 86, 87; and Lana Turner, 71, 74, 75; and the *Metronome*-poll recording, 66; personal problems of, 68; Sinatra's relationship with, 53, 57, 63–64, 67, 91–92; TV special about, 164–66, 177, 201; and World War II, 87
Dorsey, Tommy—Rich's relationship with: and Bushkin, 60; and Dorsey as harsh

Dorsey, Tommy (*Cont.*)
  with Rich, 41; and Dorsey misses Rich, 82;
  and the Dorsey TV special, 165; and Rich
  as a pain in the ass, 53, 90; and Rich's enlistment, 79, 84; and the Rich-Sinatra conflict, 57, 63–64; and Rich's leaving, 86, 88–
  90; and Rich's moonlighting, 78, 88, 89–90,
  199; and the string section, 70, 84
Dorsey (Jimmy) band, 37, 186
Dorsey (Jimmy and Tommy) band, 115
Dorsey (Tommy) band: and the Clambake
  Seven, 51; Dorsey fires the, 73; and the
  movies, 64, 65, 71–72, 75, 76, 78, 86, 87–88,
  197–98, 199–200; popularity of the, 51, 68,
  69; on the radio, 66, 69, 72, 75, 80; recordings of the, 51, 58–59, 66–67, 68, 69, 76;
  Rich plays with the, 51–78, 80, 81, 84–90,
  190, 199–200; Rich's views of the, 51, 89;
  and the Sentimentalists, 59; size of the, 53;
  TV special about the, 164–66, 201; and the
  union, 76; and World War II, 75–77, 78.
  See also name of specific person
Douglas, Mike, 130, 139
Down Beat (magazine), 45, 70, 82, 175, 193
Drugs/marijuana, 82–83, 134–35, 137–38,
  150–51, 203
Drumming: and the bass drum, 116, 195;
  and bebop, 93; with the Dorsey band, 85–
  86; and hi-hats, 33, 48–49, 64, 194, 197;
  and how Rich played the drums, 193–95;
  and the Killer Force band, 144; of Krupa
  and Rich, 106–7, 109; in the movies, 200;
  at the Newport Jazz Festival, 120–21; Rich
  wants to quit, 118–20; and rolls, 33, 125–
  26, 193–94; on the "Tonight Show," 153–
  54; and the Tormé-Rich relationship, 85–
  86, 101–2; in "West Side Story," 125–26
Drum teachers, 136
Du Barry Was a Lady (movie), 76, 79, 199
Durbin, Deanna, 87
Durgom, George "Bullets," 77

Eager, Allen, 96, 104, 106, 119, 135, 200
Earl Carroll's Sketchbook (movie), 200
"East of the Sun," 58
Ebbins, Milt, 86
Eddie Condon All-Stars, 104

"The Eddie Condon Floor show" (NBC-
  TV), 103–4
Edison, Harry (Sweets), 43, 104–5, 114, 115,
  117, 204
"The Ed Sullivan Show" (TV show), 122,
  129
Eglash, Jack, 124
Eldridge, Roy, 38, 46, 104, 106, 108–9, 115,
  180
Ellington, Duke, 42–43, 57, 93, 98, 177
Elliott, Don, 111
Elman, Ziggy, 55, 57, 64, 66, 67, 72, 78, 87,
  198
Embassy (Los Angeles club), 94
England, Rich's tours in, 131, 135, 140, 149–
  50, 158
Essex House (New York City hotel), 33
European tours, 128, 132–33, 136, 140, 146,
  158
"Every Tub," 197

Falk, Peter, 178
Famous Door, the, 33
Far East tours, 120, 129
Fatool, Nick, 50n
Fibes drums, 191, 192
Fields, Greg, 164
Fields, Shep, 79
Finckel, Eddie, 92, 93, 96
Fitzgerald, Ella, 90, 95, 115, 134, 204
Fitzhugh, Francis W., Jr., 117–18
Flamingo (Las Vegas hotel), 121–22
"Flash," 114
Flynn, Errol, 65
Forrest, Helen, 43, 45, 196, 197
Fortune, Kenny, 138
400 Club (New York City), 89
Fox and Considine (agents), 16
Freeman, Hank, 47
"Frenesi," 50n
"The Frim Fram Sauce," 94
"From Rags to Riches," 93
"From the Top" (GE Theater), 116
Frye, Marie, 67

Garland, Judy, 65, 78, 199, 210
Germany, tours in, 132, 214

GE Theater, 116
Getz, Stan, 114
Gibbs, Terry, 120, 178, 200
Gibeling, Howard, 117
Gillespie, Dizzy, 92, 94, 115, 204
Ginger Man (Los Angeles restaurant), 157–58, 159, 162–63
Girard, Adele, 33
Girl Crazy (movie), 78, 199
God, Rich's beliefs about, 218–19
Golden, Milt, 200
Goodman, Benny: as an innovator, 29, 177; Krupa's relationship with, 82, 91; and the *Metronome* All-Stars, 66; Rich's relationship with, 100; and Tormé, 91
Goodman (Benny) band: popularity of the, 43, 49; radio broadcasts of the, 42; recordings of the, 89, 90, 191; Rich plays with the, 89, 90, 91; Rich's views of the, 32. *See also name of specific person*
"The Goof and I," 124
Grable, Betty, 65, 129
Gramercy Five (Shaw band), 50n
Granz, Norman, 86, 95, 104, 106, 114, 115–16, 120, 134
Gravish, Andy, 213
Gray, Erin, 140
Gray, Glen. *See* Casa Loma band
Gray, Jerry, 45
Gray, Wardell, 114
Great America (Santa Clara, Calif., amusement park), 160
Greco, Buddy, 128–29
Green, Freddie, 43, 185
Green, Jack L., 180
Greer, Sonny, 186
Gretsch drums, 29, 189
Griffin, Merv, 148, 201
Groove Merchant International, 137, 139
Gruber, Freddy, 167, 168, 170, 171, 187
Gryphon recordings, 147
Guarneri, Johnny, 50n

Haig (Los Angeles club), 186
Haines, Connie, 53
Hall, Jon, 86, 87
"Hallelujah!" 59

Hallett, Mal, 29
Hamilton, Chico, 180
Hampton, Lionel, 87, 115, 116, 137, 201
Hanna, Jake, 178–79
"Happy Days" (TV show), 132
Harris, Bill, 111
"Harry James and His Music Makers" (movie short), 200
Hartman (Stamford, Conn. theater), 145
"Hawaiian War Chant," 64, 72, 83, 166, 177, 198
Hawkins, Coleman, 38, 66, 94
Haymer, Herbie, 88–89
Haymes, Dick, 52, 53, 75
Hefner, Hugh, 132, 178
Hefti, Neal, 92
Henabery, Joseph, 197
"Here's Lucy" (TV show), 132
Herman, Woody, 186, 194
Hickory House (New York City club), 33–36, 38, 189
Higginbotham, J. C., 66
High school auditoriums, Rich's performances in, 131, 144
Himber, Richard, 74–75
Hitchcock, Raymond, 17
Hodges, Johnny, 94
Holiday, Billie, 39
"The Hollywood Palace" (TV show), 122
Holman, Bill, 131–32
Hope, Bob, 64
Howard, Shemp, 199
Howard (Washington, D.C., theater), 98
How's About It (movie), 78, 199, 200
Hucko, Peanuts, 90
Huddleston, John, 54–55, 64
Hull, Warren, 45

"I Could Make You Care," 59
"I Found a New Baby," 119
Igoe, Sonny, 180, 187
"I Got Rhythm," 78
"I'll Be Seeing You," 58
"I'll Never Smile Again," 58–59, 197
"I'll Take Tallulah," 198
"I'm Comin', Virginia," 44, 46

"I'm Getting Sentimental Over You," 198
"Indian Love Call," 43
IRS (Internal Revenue Service), 129–30, 133, 134
"I Surrender, Dear," 48
"It's About Time," 94

Jack the Bellboy (disc jockey), 81
"The Jackie Gleason Show" (TV show), 128–29
Jackson, Chubby, 106, 111
Jacquet, Illinois, 87, 140
James, Harry: as best man at Rich's wedding, 113–14; and Lana Turner, 75; leases a house to Rich, 129; and the *Metronome* All-Stars, 66; playing of, 114–15, 198; plays with the Rich band, 111
James (Harry) band: financial problems of the, 52; formation of the, 111; and the movies, 200, 201; in the 1960s, 121–22; recordings of the, 52, 72; Rich plays with the, 111–12, 114–15, 117, 121, 129, 200, 201; singers with the, 52; string section of the, 70
"Jam Session" (AFRS program), 87
Japan, tours in, 120, 129
Jazz: as a passion of Rich, 204; Rich's initial interest in, 28–30
Jazz at the Philharmonic: in the 1960s, 121; recordings of, 110, 114, 120; Rich plays with, 94, 95, 104, 105, 106, 107, 110, 114, 115–16, 120, 187
Jazz polls, 45, 66, 70, 82, 94
"Jeepers Creepers," 196–97
Jenny, Jack, 50n
"Jim Jam Stomp," 35
"John Had the Number," 200
Jones, Elvin, 120
Jones, Hank, 105, 111
Jones, Jack, 154–55, 164, 167, 168, 170, 179–80
Jones, Jo, 43, 46, 49, 70, 86, 98, 185, 212
Jones, Kim, 166, 167, 170, 179
JVC Jazz Festival (1988), 180

Kannon, Jackie, 138
Kay, Stanley, 94, 133–34, 138, 139, 140, 141, 144, 148, 160, 205–6, 207

Kelly's Stables (New York City club), 38
Kenton, Stan, 43, 47, 92, 186
Kern, Jerome, 85
"Kicks with Sticks," 200
Kirk, Lisa, 116
Kitsis, Bob, 47–48
Konikoff, Ross, 144, 214
"The Kraft Music Hall" (NBC-TV), 130–31
Kraus, Arthur, 27, 28
Krupa, Gene: as a bandleader, 70, 84; death of, 137; with the Dorsey (Tommy) band, 82–83; and the *Down Beat* polls, 82; and drugs, 82–83; as a drummer, 106–7, 110; and the Goodman band, 37, 82, 91, 185, 190, 191; Goodman's relationship with, 82, 91; hi-hats of, 49; image of, 16; as an innovator, 107, 212; and Lana Turner, 75; logo of, 190; and Marie Allison Rich, 107–10, 112; as a model for Rich, 114–15, 185–86; recordings of, 110, 117, 120, 191; Rich's relationship with, 29, 70, 82, 84, 106–10, 117, 120, 137; and Slingerland, 37, 96–97, 189, 190; Stratemann's work about, 201; and Tormé, 106–7, 137; TV appearances of, 137, 201; Webb's influence on, 29
Kyle, Billy, 94
Kyser, Kay, 43

LaBarbera, John, 136
"Lady Be Good," 46, 197
Laguna, Eddie. *See* Cole, Nat King
Lamond, Don, 186
Lane, Burton, 198
"The Last Call for Love," 198
Las Vegas Nights (movie), 64, 65, 69, 197–98, 200
L.A. Voices, 164
Lawyer, Nicholas Rich (grandson), 161, 168, 181, 211
Lederman, Steve, 201
Leedy drums, 189
Leeman, Cliff, 40–41, 52–53, 186, 189, 196
Lennie's-on-the-Turnpike (Boston club), 131
Leonard, Jack, 51
Leonard, Jack E., 104
Leshin, Phil, 180
Lester, Jerry, 104

"Let's Dance" (radio program), 42
"Let's Get Away from It All," 200
Lewis, Jerry, 137, 156, 178, 180, 192
Lewis, Mel, 187
Linn, Ray, 68
Lippman, Joe, 38
Living Room (New York City club), 118
Lodice, Don, 53, 67, 72, 198
Lofgren, Bruce, 141
Lombardo, Guy, 43
London, Rich in, 130, 131, 145
Long Beach (Calif.) Auditorium, 107, 108–9
Longo, Mike, 141
"Loose Lid Special," 69
"Losers Weepers," 59, 69
"Love for Sale," 128
Lowrey, Chuck, 62
Ludwig, William F., Jr., 96–97, 190–91, 192
Ludwig, William F., Sr., 188, 190
Ludwig drums, 14, 16, 19, 37, 96–97, 187, 188–89, 190–91, 192
Lunceford, Jimmie, 43, 52, 98

McGarity, Lou, 90
McGovern, Maureen, 164
McKinley, Ray, 49, 100–101, 186, 189
McRae, Carmen, 141
"Make Me Know It," 59
Maltin, Leonard, 201
Mandel, Johnny, 94
"Manhattan," 216
Manieri, Mike, 120
Manne, Shelly, 124, 186
March, Hal, 108, 110
Marcus, Steve, 141, 154, 161, 165, 180, 212
"Maria," 125
"Marie," 51
Marijuana. *See* Drugs/marijuana
Marines, U.S., 75, 78–81, 83, 104, 190, 199
Mark, Sid, 139
"Mark of Jazz" (PBS-TV), 139
Marquez, Sal, 131
Marsala, Joe, 33–38, 43, 44, 60, 111, 189
Marsala, Marty, 37
Martin, Freddy, 116, 201
Martin, Lowell, 68

Martin, Tony, 74
Marty's (New York City club), 91, 207
Marty's Bum Steer (New York City restaurant), 140
Masters, Charlie, 27
May, Billy, 43
MCA (agents), 97, 108
Meadowbrook (N.J. club), 67, 69, 88, 92, 98, 147
Mello-Larks, 200
"Melody and Madness" (CBS radio), 45, 49, 50
Menza, Don, 137
Mercer, Johnny, 196
Mercury recordings, 94, 117
"The Merv Griffin Show" (TV program), 148, 201
Metronome All-Stars, 66, 94
Michaels, Lloyd, 141
Michaud, Arthur, 84
Michigan State University, 151
"Midnight Cowboy," 131–32
"The Mike Douglas Show" (TV show), 130, 139
Miles, Butch, 187–88
Milk, Harvey, 150–51
Miller, Glenn, 69, 78, 186
Mills, Marty, 148–49
Milwaukee Symphony Orchestra, 144
Mince, Johnny, 53
"Mr. Drums" (video cassette), 201
Mister Kelly's (Chicago club), 139–40
Mok, Michael, 49–50
Mondello, Toots, 66
Monte, Pee Wee, 114
Mooney, Harold, 117
"Moonglow," 50n
Moore, Constance, 197
Morehouse, Chauncey, 191
Morello, Joe, 180
Morgenstern, Dan, 120
Morrow, Buddy, 164
Mosconi, George, 150–51
Most, Sam, 121
Movies of Buddy Rich: *Broadway Melody of 1940,* 46–47; "Buddy Traps in Sound Effects," 26, 27, 28–29, 196; *Dancing Co-ed,*

Movies of Buddy Rich (*Cont.*)
45–46, 49, 65, 190, 197; with the Dorsey band, 64, 65, 69, 71–72, 75, 76, 78, 86, 87–88, 197–98, 199, 200; drums used in, 190; *Du Barry Was a Lady,* 76, 79, 199; *Earl Carroll's Sketchbook,* 200; and the Freddy Martin orchestra, 116, 201; *Girl Crazy,* 78, 199; "Harry James and His Music Makers" (short), 200; *How's About It?* 78, 199, 200; with the James band, 200, 201; *Las Vegas Nights,* 64, 65, 69, 197–98, 200; and the Marine enlistment, 75; and moonlighting from Dorsey band, 199; *Phantom Lady,* 201; *Presenting Lily Mars,* 78, 199; Rich bands in the, 26, 27, 28–29, 78, 196, 200; with the Shaw band, 45–47, 196–97; *Ship Ahoy,* 71–72, 198; "Symphony in Swing" (short), 196–97; *Thrill of a Romance,* 86, 87–88, 200; "Thrills of Music" (short), 200
Mulligan, Gerry, 201
Mullins, Bitsy, 94
Mundy, Jimmy, 66
"The Muppet Show" (TV show), 149–50
Musso, Vido, 89, 191
"My Heart Stood Still," 40

Napoleon, Marty, 106
Nase, Sam, 164, 167, 168–69, 173, 176
Nate 'N' Al's (Hollywood deli), 148–49
NBC Impromptu Ensemble, 117
NBC Orchestra, 117
Nelson, Oliver, 121
Newport Jazz Festival, 120–21, 122, 129, 133
Newsom, Tommy, 144
"Nightmare," 44
Nistico, Sal, 138
Nola studios, 91
Norgran recordings, 115–16
"Norwegian Wood," 128
"Not So Quiet, Please," 72, 98, 200
Novak, Larry, 144

O'Curran, Betty Jo, 103, 109–10
Oh, Say Can You Sing (WPA show), 31
"Old Man River," 101
Oles, Louis, 104
Oliver, Sy, 43, 52, 53, 59, 61, 66–67, 69, 72

"One Foot in the Groove," 44
"The One I Love," 58
"One Night Stand" (Shaw recording), 44
"One Night Stand" (TV special), 137, 201
"One O'Clock Jump," 66
"Only Forever," 59
"Oop Bob Sh'Bam," 94
Osborne, Donny, Jr., 142, 150, 151, 187, 192
Osborne, Donny, Sr., 187, 191–92
Osmond family, 135–36
Osterman, Jackie, 30
"Our Love Affair," 59

Pacific Jazz recordings, 129
Page, Walter, 185
Palace (Cleveland, Ohio, theater), 146–47
Palladium (Hollywood): and the Dorsey band, 64–66, 69, 71–72, 75, 76–78; and the Dorsey TV special, 165–66, 177; and the James band, 112, 113, 114; Rich as a marine plays at the, 79; Rich's bands at the, 92, 93, 100, 103; and the Spivak band, 69, 83–84
Palladium (London), 130
"Palladium Party," 114
Palmieri, Remo, 90
Palomar (Los Angeles ballroom), 42, 45, 46, 66
Panther Room (Chicago), 94
Paramount (New York City theater), 56, 60, 67, 75, 83, 97–98, 101–2, 106, 135, 145
Parker, Charlie, 92, 94, 104
Park West (Chicago, Ill., club), 149
Pastor, Tony, 39, 43, 45, 47, 48, 51, 196–97
Pateakos, John, 82
Paul Masson winery, 160
Payne, Sonny, 187
Peck, Steve, 148, 150, 161, 187–88
Perlow, Steve, 121
Peterson, Chuck, 54, 64, 72, 75
Peterson, Oscar, 95, 114, 134
Petrillo, Jimmy, 76
Pettiford, Oscar, 100
Phantom Lady (movie), 201
Phillips, Flip, 95, 111
Pied Pipers, 53, 58, 78, 197
Pin Wheel Revel (broadway show), 18–19

Plantation Club (Los Angeles), 86, 87
Plugged Nickel (Chicago club), 192
"Poor Little Rich Bud," 93
Porcino, Al, 130, 131
Porter, Cole, 43
Potter, Larry, 116
Powell, Bud, 104, 204
Powell, Eleanor, 46–47, 72, 198
Powell, Jack, 27
Power, Tyrone, 65
Presenting Lily Mars (movie), 78, 199
Privin, Bernie, 45
Purtill, Maurice, 78, 186, 189, 199

"Quiet Please," 59

Radio appearances, 38, 45, 66, 69, 72, 80, 120, 144
Raeburn, Boyd, 43, 92
Raskin, Milt, 75
"Rattle and Roll," 90, 91
Raye, Martha, 69, 170
RCA recordings: and the Berigan band, 39; and the Dorsey (Tommy) band, 58–59, 66, 68, 72; of Rich's bands, 136, 137; and the Shaw band, 43, 50n. *See also* Bluebird records
Recordings of Buddy Rich: with the Andrews Sisters, 36; with Bregman, 117; with Brown (Ray), 104; with Cole (Nat King), 88–89; with Condon, 104; with Davis (Sammy), 122; with De Franco, 115; with the Dorsey (Tommy) band, 58–59, 66–67, 68, 69, 72; with Edison, 115, 117; with Eldridge, 115; and finances, 90; with Fitzgerald, 90; with Gibeling, 117; with Gillespie, 115; with Goodman, 90, 91; with Hampton, 115, 116; with James, 114; with Jazz at the Philharmonic, 110, 114, 120; with Krupa, 107, 110, 117; with Kyle, 94; with the *Metronome* All-Stars, 66, 94; with Mooney, 117; and moonlighting from Dorsey's band, 88–90; with the NBC Impromptu Ensemble, 117; with the NBC Orchestra, 117; with Parker (Charlie), 104; with Powell (Bud), 104; of Rich's bands, 94, 104, 117, 120, 129, 131, 132, 133, 139, 191, 201; with Roach, 117; with the Shaw band, 44, 48, 114, 185–86; as a singer, 115–16; with Tatum, 116; with Tormé, 98, 147, 154; with Young (Lester), 104, 117
Reddie, Bill, 124–25, 130
Regal (Chicago theater), 98
Regan, Phil, 197
Reid, Dottie, 92
Religion, Rich's beliefs about, 219
Renaissance ballroom (Harlem), 99
Reprise recordings, 122
Resnick, Joan, 168, 171
Reynolds, Tommy, 43
Rich, Bess (mother): and the Australian tour, 20–21; death of, 100, 146; and Lana Turner's visit, 74; marriage of, 4; pregnancies of, 4–5, 6, 20; Rich's relationship with, 13–14, 23, 36, 56–57, 67, 100, 146; Robert's relationship with, 13–14, 23, 24, 67, 100; in vaudeville, 4–6, 8–18
Rich, Buddy (Bernard): birthdays of, 104, 131, 148–49, 164; birth of, 6; childhood of, 7, 9, 22–25; as a dancer, 26, 200; death of, 176–77; debut of, 10–11; education of, 22, 24, 85; as an emcee, 29, 133–34; endorsements by, 190, 192; and fans, 57–58, 96, 119, 139, 213; funeral of, 178–79; hairpieces of, 163–64, 210; as an innovator, 177; and karate, 203; and the ladies, 37, 57, 66, 69, 73–75, 103; logo of, 190; marriages of, 89, 112, 113–14; memorial services for, 179–80; mood swings of, 135–36, 137, 150–51; as "Pal," 10–14; passions of, 202–4; philosophical moods of, 149, 152–54, 218–19; as a prankster, 57–58, 143, 148–49, 154–55, 204–8, 210; self-image of, 29, 30; as a singer, 26, 85, 92, 94, 115–16, 118–20, 133–34, 200; as a stooge, 30; as "Traps," 14–30, 188, 189; in vaudeville, 10–31
Rich, Buddy (Bernard)—finances of: and the clubs, 138, 139, 140; and the Dorsey band, 61, 115; and endorsements, 192; as a family breadwinner, 11, 12–13, 16, 20, 24–25, 61; and his bands, 91–92, 95, 97, 102; and houses, 136; with the James band, 129; and marriage, 112; in the 1950s, 116; in the 1940s, 84–85; in the 1970s, 138; in the

Rich, Buddy (Bernard) (*Cont.*)
1930s, 30, 38; and profligacy, 84–85, 105–6, 129, 132, 134; and recordings, 90; as a singer, 116; and tax problems, 105, 129–30, 133, 134, 144

Rich, Buddy (Bernard)—health of: and back problems, 136–37, 150; and the brain tumor, 166–77; and the broken arm, 97–98; in childhood, 22; and heart problems, 117–18, 156–58; and his grandson, 211

Rich, Cathy (daughter): birth of, 115; and memories of Rich, 208–12; in New York, 139; and Rich as a father, 115, 130, 145, 208–12; and the Rich orchestra, 181; and Rich's birthdays, 164; and Rich's brain tumor, 168, 169, 170, 174, 211–12; and Rich's funeral, 179; and Rich's heart problems, 156; and Rich's memorial services, 179; as a singer, 128, 210; song about, 165; and the theatrical tribute to Rich, 180; and Tormé, 161, 165, 205; TV appearances of, 148

Rich, Elaine (sister-in-law), 179, 181

Rich, Josephine (sister): birth of, 5; childhood of, 5–6, 8, 9, 15, 23, 24, 25; current activities of, 181; and family relations, 25; and Lana Turner's visit, 73–74; and Rich's childhood, 22–23; and Rich's finances, 105; and Rich's funeral, 178; and Rich's health problems, 156; Rich's relationship with, 56–57, 67, 130, 168, 170; in vaudeville, 5–6, 8

Rich, Josh (nephew), 144, 179

Rich, Lisa (niece), 179

Rich, Louise (step-mother), 129, 146

Rich, Marie Allison (wife): and cars, 202; current activities of, 181; and Krupa, 107–10, 112; marriage of, 110–14; meets Rich, 107–9; and New York City, 136, 139; and Rich's birthdays, 164; and Rich's brain tumor, 167–76; and Rich's desire to quit drumming, 118–20; and Rich's funeral, 178, 179; and Rich's health problems, 118, 156; and Rich's memorial services, 179; and Rich's pranks, 207, 208; Rich's relationship with, 129, 130, 145, 210; and the

tax problems, 130, 132; and Tormé, 161–62, 173, 174, 176

Rich, Marjorie (sister): birth of, 4; childhood of, 6, 8, 15, 20, 23, 25; current activities of, 181; as a dancer, 8–9, 24, 32, 52; introduces Rich to Betty Jo, 103; and Lana Turner's visit, 73, 74; marriage of, 9; and Rich joins the Dorsey band, 52; and Rich's apologies, 162; and Rich's childhood, 22; and Rich's finances, 105; and Rich's funeral, 178; and Rich's health problems, 156; and Rich's relationship with his father, 146; Rich's relationship with, 56–57, 67, 130, 168, 170; in vaudeville, 9

Rich, Martin "Mickey" (brother): Bess's relationship with, 23; birth of, 20; and cancer, 168, 170, 179; childhood of, 20, 22, 23, 24; death of, 181; and Lana Turner's visit, 74; as a musician, 67, 93–94; as a producer/writer, 103; and Rich's broken arm, 97; and Rich's finances, 105; and Rich's funeral, 179; and Rich's health problems, 156; Rich's relationship with, 56–57, 67, 93–94, 130; and Tormé, 102

Rich, Robert (father): and the Australian tour, 20–21; Bess's relationship with, 13–14, 23, 24, 67, 100; and the child labor laws, 17, 20; "civilian" jobs of, 4, 6, 7; death of, 146; as a father, 22, 23; and finances, 105–6; marriages of, 4, 129; as a prankster, 25, 204, 207; in vaudeville, 3–6, 9, 10–18, 20–21, 23, 25

Rich, Robert—Rich's relationship with: and Buddy as a child/young man, 13–14, 23, 24–26, 29, 31, 32, 37; and Buddy leaving vaudeville, 36, 40; and Buddy with the Dorsey band, 56–57, 64, 67; in Florida, 129, 130; and his father's death, 146; and Rich's finances, 105; and Robert as Buddy's manager, 27–28, 60

"Rich at the Top" (TV special), 137

"Rich-ual Dance," 93

Ritchie, Carl, 9, 32, 52, 67, 94, 134

Ritchie, Marjorie. *See* Rich, Marjorie

Roach, Max, 93, 117, 119, 135, 180, 187

Robinson, Les, 47

Rock and roll, 131, 141, 187, 191

Rodney, Red, 94
Rogers Drums, 191
Rollini, Adrian, 36
Rooney, Mickey, 64–65, 78, 199
Rosengarden, Bobby, 124
Ross, Annie, 164
Ross, Marty, 140, 142, 206, 207
Russell, Curly, 111
Russell, Nipsey, 141
Russin, Babe, 37

Sahara Hotel (Las Vegas), 124
Sands Hotel (Las Vegas), 122
"Saturday Night Swing Session" (CBS radio), 38
Savitt (Jan) band, 57
Savoy ballroom (Harlem), 46, 64
Schutz, Buddy, 186
Schwartz, Norman, 147
Scott, Ronnie, 131, 135, 158
Sears, Al, 79, 90
Sentimentalists (Dorsey band), 59
"Sentimental Swing: The Music of Tommy Dorsey" (TV special), 164–66, 201
"Serenade to a Savage," 72
"Serenade to the Spot," 69
Severinsen, Doc, 122–23, 153
Seymour, Maurice, 189
Shapiro, Artie, 29, 33–35
Shaughnessy, Ed, 124, 168, 178–79, 187, 213–14
Shavers, Charlie, 88–89, 90, 94
Shaw, Artie: health of, 45; interview of, 49–50; and Lana Turner, 65; leadership abilities of, 39; marriage of, 70; and Rich's funeral, 178; Rich's relationship with, 41; and World War II, 79, 87
Shaw (Artie) band: disbanding of the, 47–50, 51; and the Gramercy Five, 50n; in the movies, 45–47, 196–97; popularity of the, 43–44, 47, 49; on radio, 45; recordings of the, 43, 44, 46, 49, 50n, 114, 185–86; Rich plays with the, 40–50, 111, 114, 115, 190, 193, 194, 195; Shaw reforms the, 50n; size of the, 53; strings in the, 70
Shearer, Norma, 155
Shearing, George, 160

Ship Ahoy (movie), 71–72, 198
Sims, Zoot, 105
Sinatra, Frank: arrangements for, 70; arrest of, 67–68; backs Rich's band, 91–92, 95; and the Dorsey (Tommy) band, 52–68, 70, 75, 197, 198; Dorsey's relationship with, 53, 57, 63–64, 67, 91–92; and fans, 57–58, 59; fight between Rich and, 62–63; and the James band, 52; and jazz polls, 94; movies of, 85, 197, 198; recordings of, 52, 58–59, 122; Rich's band backs, 106, 131; and Rich's brain tumor, 168, 170, 171; and Rich's funeral, 178, 179; Rich's relationship with, 57, 58, 59–60, 61–64, 75, 91, 92, 202, 204; as Rich's roommate, 53–54, 56; and the theatrical tribute to Rich, 180; TV appearances of, 201
"Sing, Sing, Sing," 89, 191
Singleton, Zutty, 186
Skelton, Red, 72, 76
"Sleepy Lagoon," 52, 72–73
Slingerland Drums, 37, 96–97, 100–101, 180–81, 187, 189–93, 195
Smiley, Allen, 86
Smilin' Through (movie), 155, 159–61, 163
Smith, Tick, 49
Smith, Willie, 94, 95
Smithsonian Institution, 180–81
"Some Other Time," 85
"Something's Coming," 125
"The Song Is You," 75
"Song of India," 51, 197
South Africa, 131
Spivak, Charlie, 79, 83, 90, 177
"Spotlight Bands" (radio program), 69, 72
Springfield, Dusty, 126–27
Stafford, Jo, 53, 55, 56, 62, 64
"Star Dust," 50n
"Stars and Stripes Forever," 14, 19, 20, 26, 27, 196
Stevens, Leith, 38
Stoller, Alvin, 90, 186, 213
Stordahl, Axel, 58, 70
Strand (New York City theater), 26, 44
Stratemann, Klaus, 201
Sunset recordings, 88
"Surprise Party," 94

Sutherlin, Jean, 89, 103
"Swanee River," 59, 66–67
"Swing High," 59, 67
"Swingtime Up in Harlem," 69
"Symphony in Swing" (movie short), 196–97

"Table d'Hote," 196
"Take It and Git," 199
Talk of the Town (London club), 131, 145
Tate, Buddy, 87
Tatum, Art, 116, 177
Terrace Room (Newark club), 92
Theilmans, Toots, 154
"This Love of Mine," 57
"Three Day Sucker," 141
Thrill of a Romance (movie), 86, 87–88, 200
"Thrills of Music" (movie short), 200
Thunderbird (Las Vegas hotel), 120
Tivoli (Chicago theater), 17
Tivoli (Sydney, Australia, theater), 20–21
Tizol, Juan, 201
"Today" (TV show), 139
"Together Again for the First Time," 98, 147, 154
"Tommy" (rock opera), 141
"The Tonight Show" (TV program), 122–23, 133, 144, 153, 201, 203
Top of the Plaza (Rochester, N.Y., hotel), 137
Tormé, Ali Severson, 160, 172
Tormé, Daisy, 160, 176
Tormé, Mel: and cars, 98, 202–3; and Cathy Rich, 161, 165, 205; divorce of, 108, 145, 146, 147; fans of, 101; finances of, 147; and Goodman, 91; and Krupa, 106–7, 137; in London, 145; and Marie Rich, 161–62, 173, 174, 176; marriages of, 101, 108; and Mickey Rich, 102; and the Paul Masson winery appearance, 160; and Rich's memorial service, 179; and the theatrical tribute to Rich, 180
Tormé, Mel—Rich's relationship with: and birthdays, 143, 164; and the book, 174–76; and the broken friendship, 160–63; and cars, 98, 202–3; and the Dorsey TV special, 177; and the Down Beat interview, 175, 193; and drugs, 135; and drumming, 85–86, 101–2, 153–54; and the first meeting

between them, 83–84; friction in the, 101–2; and gifts, 143, 148–49, 159–61, 163, 176; and kidding, 46, 114–15, 142–43; and performances together, 101–2, 135, 137, 141–43, 145, 146–47, 148–49, 150–51, 154–55, 161, 164–66, 205–7; and pranks, 148–49, 154–55, 204–8; and Rich's back/heart problems, 150, 157–58; and Rich's brain tumor, 171–72, 173; and Rich's philosophical moods, 149, 152–54, 218–19; and Robert Rich's death, 146; and the Smilin' Through movie, 155, 159–61, 163; and the song about Cathy, 165; and tax problems, 129–30; and telephone calls, 144–45, 163–64; and "Together Again for the First Time," 98, 147, 154; and Tormé's divorce, 146, 147
"The Touch of Your Hand," 85
Tough, Dave, 186, 189
Toxton, Candy, 108
"Trade Winds," 59
"Traffic Jam," 46, 197
Treitman, Arnold, 118
"The Trombone Man Is the Best Man in the Band," 198
"Trumpet Blues," 198
Tucker, Orrin, 43
Tunnell, George, 57
Turner, Hugh, 201
Turner, Lana, 45, 46, 65, 69, 70, 71, 73–75, 76, 77–78, 197
TV appearances: in England, 131, 149–50; in 1949, 103–4; in the 1950s, 120; in the 1960s, 122–23, 128–29, 130–31; in the 1970s, 132, 133, 137, 139, 144, 148; in the 1980s, 153. See also name of specific show

UFOs, Rich's beliefs about, 204
Union, musicians', 76, 97

Vane, Danny, 75
Van Heusen, Jimmie, 85
Ventura, Charlie, 106
Verrell, Ronnie, 150
Verve recordings, 107
Viola, Al, 178
Vitaphone studios, 26, 27, 28–29, 196
Vox drums, 191

Wald, Jerry, 43
Waldorf (New York City hotel), 145
Warrington, Tom, 178
Webb, Chick, 29, 46, 49, 185, 212
Weed, Buddy, 90
Weeks, Jean, 106
Wein, George, 133, 180
Weiss, Sid, 47–48, 54, 55
Weitman, Bob, 145
"Well, Git It!" 72, 75, 76, 199
Wells, Dickie, 99
Werth, Paul, 171, 172–73
Westbury, N.Y., 181
Weston, Paul, 55
"West Side Story," 124–26, 127, 130, 131,
    144, 146, 150
Wettling, George, 38
Wheeler, Bert, 197
"Whispering," 59
White, Dan, 150–51
"Wide World of Sports" (ABC-TV), 203
William Morris agency, 97
Williams, Andy, 135

Williams, Cootie, 66
Williams, Esther, 86, 200
Wilson, Sam, 3–4, 5, 7–8
Wiltern (Los Angeles), 181
Winter Garden (New York City theater), 9,
    19
"Without a Song," 69
Woolrich, Cornell, 201
World Pacific recordings, 131
World's Fair (New Orleans), 161, 165
World War II, 71, 75–81, 86–87
Wright, Edythe, 51

Yeager, Bob, 157, 158
"Yes, Indeed!" 69
"You Made Me Love You," 52
Young, Lester, 43, 46, 86, 90, 94, 104, 106,
    117
Young, Snooky, 164
Young, Trummy, 94, 95

Zildjian, Armand, 1331